KU-166-219

WINNER SELLS ALL

AMAZON, WALMART, AND THE BATTLE FOR OUR WALLETS

WINNER SELLS ALL

JASON DEL REY

HARPER
BUSINESS

An Imprint of HarperCollinsPublishers

WINNER SELLS ALL. Copyright © 2023 by Jason Del Rey. All rights reserved. Printed in the United States of America. No part of this book may be used or reproduced in any manner whatsoever without written permission except in the case of brief quotations embodied in critical articles and reviews. For information, address HarperCollins Publishers, 195 Broadway, New York, NY 10007.

HarperCollins books may be purchased for educational, business, or sales promotional use. For information, please email the Special Markets Department at SPsales@harpercollins.com.

FIRST EDITION

Library of Congress Cataloging-in-Publication Data has been applied for.

ISBN 978-0-06-307632-7

23 24 25 26 27 LBC 5 4 3 2 1

For my parents, Patricia and Bernard,
who stressed curiosity, compassion, and preparation while raising me

and for my wife, Tyrene,
who inspired me to become a better man while saving me

"There is only one boss: the customer. And he can fire everybody in the company, from the chairman on down, simply by spending his money somewhere else."

—SAM WALTON

CONTENTS

WINNER SELLS ALL

PROLOGUE

The first time I met Jeff Bezos, I asked him what he was wearing.

It was the spring of 2016, and I had been hoping to sit down with the then-CEO of Amazon before he appeared onstage at an annual tech event hosted by my employer at a California cliffside resort. At the time, I had been reporting on Amazon for three years but still hadn't met Bezos other than a passing hello as he was whisked out the door at a different conference two years earlier. As disappointing as that was, it was not all that surprising. As Bezos's wealth and fame ballooned, his PR team shielded him from the journalists who knew his company best. I can't say I totally blamed them: the Amazon story was splintering away from a pure, feel-good tale of great American ingenuity into a narrative with more complicated offshoots, and he or his advisers seemed to have determined that avoiding the toughest conversations was the smart move.

So, when I was told by Amazon's PR department that a meeting wasn't going to happen, I decided to make my own meeting by waiting for Bezos backstage. I wasn't planning to ambush him; I was simply looking to strike up a conversation that might create an opening for more substantive discussions down the line. As the event approached, I strategized about what my opening line should be; I knew it would only be a matter of time before his security team or his PR handlers made my life difficult. Then I got some inspiration: *Fortune* magazine had recently ranked Bezos No. 1 on their 2016 list of the fifty "World's Greatest Leaders" and, in the accompanying profile, the famous entrepreneur mentioned one of the new Amazon initiatives in which he was most interested: the company's foray into private-label clothing—basically, clothing lines that Amazon would source, brand, and sell itself. Not necessarily the sexiest of product categories, but one that my nerdy retail brain was also interested in, so I decided to latch on.

With that in mind, I thought I might succeed both at showing Bezos that I was paying close attention and at making him laugh if I opened with something like: "Hey, Jeff. I'm Jason Del Rey from Recode. I recently read that you are spending a lot of time on Amazon's private-label business. Are you wearing any Amazon brands today?"

On the day of the event, Bezos stood alone backstage, watching the onstage interview that preceded his from a monitor. He was dressed in a dark blazer, dark denim jeans, and light-colored button-up, along with brown leather dress shoes. I walked over and shook his hand as I introduced myself, and then delivered some version of the lines I had planned out in my head. After digesting my question for a moment, one of the world's richest men shot back with two questions of his own.

"Did you just ask me what I was wearing?" he deadpanned. "Am I on a red carpet?"

I waited for his mouth to crack into a smile or for him to unleash his trademark booming howl. Neither happened. Instead, one of his PR handlers must have sensed his unhappiness from afar and raced over to intervene.

"Did you just ask Jeff Bezos what he is wearing?" the spokesperson shrieked as Bezos retreated, I assumed, for good. I tried to explain the context, but it didn't seem to register. Much to my surprise, though, Bezos returned a short while later, after helping himself to a nonalcoholic drink.

"What are *you* wearing?" he volleyed back. I explained, awkwardly, that my outfit was selected by a stylist working for a service called Trunk Club, an independent startup that had sold to Nordstrom in 2014 for $350 million. I didn't mention that my sister had gifted me the service (in part because she knew I was a terrible decision-maker and in part because I needed to step up my fashion game in advance of hosting a new conference of my own). What I did reveal to Bezos was that the service required that you trust the advice of a random human to pick out your clothes—one undoubtedly with some type of fashion sense, but perhaps not exactly *your* fashion sense.

Aha, Bezos said, nodding along. I wondered what the person who had reinvented bookselling, then blown up the entire retail landscape through digital commerce, thought of a rather old-school approach. Leave it all to *humans?* For innovators like Bezos, wouldn't the ideal service use technology to outsmart humans? Bezos explained that his preference would actually be a combination of both: computers to provide a selection of algorithmically generated clothing options, which a human stylist would then filter to make the best, final choices. At the time, another startup, called Stitch Fix, was offering a version of that service. But sure enough, in 2019, Bezos's idea would manifest itself when Amazon unveiled a rival service of its own.

Bezos then excused himself to take the stage, but his words lingered. It was just one of many examples where Bezos had crafted a vision of Amazon's future that seemed outlandish—Amazon, a fashion stylist?—only to become a service years later that at least some found appealing. Not all of the crazy ideas would pan out; but many did, and in industry-shattering ways. He and his deputies had done it with bookselling; then cloud computing with Amazon Web Services; video streaming with Prime Video; voice assistants with Alexa; grocery delivery with Amazon Fresh; and now he was trying it with fashion, too—no matter the critics or the risk of failure. His penchant for cooking up wild ideas, but then bolting them down with technology and operational rigor, had helped transform his company into a global powerhouse, even if the fashionistas or incumbents in other industries he infiltrated turned up their noses—at least initially. Walmart chief among them.

My discussion with Bezos, though, also reinforced a few other things I had learned about the way he and his company were evolving. On one hand, the company's avoidance of an initial meeting with me, plus the terror that appeared to overcome the PR rep when they realized I was speaking to Bezos without preapproved permission, confirmed that Amazon didn't want to have tough conversations—at least not with informed outsiders who understood both the good and bad of the company's business and labor practices. It was, as retail and PR industry veterans had long told me, a similar approach that another high-flying industry titan had once taken: Walmart.

Of course, before Amazon came along, Walmart was the big bad bully of retail and American capitalism, with a reputation for squeezing suppliers until they moved operations to cheaper labor overseas, paying its workers next to nothing, and decimating mom-and-pop shops while plundering their local communities for tax breaks. While Walmart was a savior to tens of millions of Americans who sought its bargain-bottom deals, others viewed it as Public Enemy No. 1. But after decades of ignoring or dismissing top criticisms—founder Sam Walton himself said in his 1992 memoir, "I don't want to be too critical of small-town merchants, but the truth is that a lot of these folks just weren't doing a very good job of taking care of their customers"—the company's third CEO, Lee Scott, chose a different path in the mid-2000s. He sought out and listened to critics, whether outside groups or reporters, and even agreed with some of them.

"Over the last couple of years I've been spending much of the time talking about all the negative publicity we've been getting, not from the standpoint that we hate the press, but by asking our people what we are doing that allows people to perpetuate these kinds of negative discussions about Walmart," Scott said in 2005.[1] "We can't just fall back on the idea that we should have some leeway because we don't mean to do any harm. We're going to be judged on how we react to racism, or sexism, or these other issues when we find them going on, and I tell everyone we have to react more dramatically and in a less forgiving, harsher way to behaviors that don't measure up."

Self-serving or not, there seemed to be a conscience growing inside Walmart that was mostly invisible to outsiders in the first few decades of the company's rapid growth. Yet in the years that followed, as similar waves of scrutiny crashed ashore in Amazon's backyard, the tech giant did not seem to have learned from Walmart's approach. Amazon had in many ways become Walmart 2.0, for better or worse. One could argue that the company's immense selection and low prices were at least as devastating to competition as Walmart was. Plus, Amazon added a third ingredient to its cocktail of innovation and competitive destruction: one-click shopping coupled with speedy delivery. But the company's famed "customer obsession" was not accompanied by the same level of employee obsession, which meant a grueling pace and meager wages for workers. That, in turn, transformed Amazon into a natural target for unions, labor activists, and concerned lawmakers as well.

"There is just blanket dismissal of any criticism being real," US congresswoman Pramila Jayapal, whose district includes Amazon's hometown of Seattle, once told me, referring to Amazon's usual response to critics. "There isn't really the opportunity to say, 'Here are things I'm hearing, things being reported and what is the response?' The response is almost always, 'That is ridiculous, this is a conspiracy, and someone is out to get us.'"

*   *   *

But Bezos's comments to me about a better solution to an old-school retail problem also reminded me that he and his company did not totally disregard the old ways of doing business. He wanted to take those practices, turn them perhaps 90 or 180 degrees, and infuse them with technology if the company believed the result would be cheaper, smarter, or otherwise better. Bezos and company didn't despise traditional retailing; they thought it could be a whole lot more convenient for the people who they believed should matter most: customers.

Again I was reminded of Sam Walton and the retail goliath he built from Walmart's headquarters in Bentonville, Arkansas, and out across small-town America. Walton and company didn't upend the retail industry in the 1980s and '90s by demolishing it and inventing something altogether new; instead, they reinvented it. Walton's memoir is full of odes to the inventions and tactics from competitors he happily borrowed from: cash registers up front from Ben Franklin stores and loss leaders or "image" items from early discounters like Gibson's. Checking out the competition was one way Walmart "tried hard to make up for our lack of experience and sophistication," Walton wrote. (A look at Amazon's famed "Leadership Principles" shows Jeff Bezos's company also borrowed ideas from the titan of physical retail. At least two of Amazon's original fourteen corporate tenets were inspired by Walton's Walmart culture: Bias for Action, and Frugality.)

But despite Walmart's onetime appreciation for competition, the go-go Supercenter-building sprees of the 1990s and 2000s opened up blind spots. The top-down centralized operating structure that allowed for the precision and ruthless execution of the Supercenter rollout seemed to lessen the appreciation for competition—at least in a new digital world. There was no time for it. Walmart leaders were consumed by the massive revenue and profits associated with its Supercenters, and mostly ignorant to the threat and promise of the internet.

In a way, Sam Walton feared a future like the one Walmart was barreling toward. He wrote of the danger of morphing into a "centrally driven chain, where everything is decided on high and passed down to the stores."

"[I]n a system like that," Walton wrote, "there's absolutely no room for creativity, no place for the maverick merchant . . . no call for the entrepreneur or the promoter. Man, I'd hate to work at a place like that, and I worry every single day about Walmart becoming that way."

By 2014, when a forty-seven-year-old company lifer named Doug McMillon became Walmart's fifth CEO, Walton's fears had largely come true. So McMillon would make a giant bet on a new generation of entrepreneur and promoter to help rescue the traditional retail titan from an Amazonian attack.

*   *   *

On the morning of March 4, 2022, I found myself seated at a blue plastic picnic table outside an indistinctive squat brick building in the northwest corner of Arkansas. This was the home of Walmart, the greatest disruptor that the United States retail industry had ever seen—until a certain upstart two thousand miles to the northwest began carving off a little bit of customer spending here, and a little bit over there, until no responsible competitor could ignore it any longer.

On this day, I would be visiting with the man charged with holding onto integral pieces of Walmart's past while choosing wisely where to adopt from those leading into the future. Doug McMillon was handsomely compensated for this job—north of $20 million annually in cash and stock. But his task was not easy. While Jeff Bezos and the rest of his company had spent the 1990s and early 2000s bending the retail industry to their will, Walmart had long treated online commerce as a cute side project, establishing a separate headquarters in Silicon Valley, where it was easy for Walmart's leadership team to sometimes forget that it even existed.

It's hard to reject your own DNA. And Walmart's DNA was built around in-store sales and heavy profits—two things that Amazon rejected for much of its history. While Walmart trained Wall Street to regularly expect profits, Bezos preached the opposite message. We are investing in growth *instead of* profits, he told Wall Street, but someday when we have snapped up enough market share, we promise we'll have tons of excess cash to show for it. That was Amazon's long game and Wall Street investors gave the company a very long leash. Amazon was also able to exploit a tax advantage over its brick-and-mortar rivals for the first decade and a half of its existence that only helped. Amazon was a nimble, fast-moving giant, while Walmart's profit-heavy success, and expectations from investors demanding more of it, gave the traditional retail titan less flexibility.

But McMillon was determined to awaken Walmart from its digital slumber and acknowledge the existential threat that Amazon posed. Along the way, he had to drag many Walmart lifers toward a new future, which could be an uncomfortable one. The symbols of this attempted transformation were evident beyond Walmart's walls and all over Bentonville on my visit. On the day before my meeting with McMillon, I met a top Walmart official for a patio lunch at BlakeSt., a members-only club housed in a renovated 1887 farmhouse developed by one of Sam Walton's grandsons. In the background, a member did laps in the temperature-controlled outdoor pool. Someone called it Bentonville's version of Soho House.

From BlakeSt., or really any downtown Bentonville location, construction cranes were a common sight, reminding me of a scaled-down version of the controversial boom in Seattle that some longtime city residents have blamed Amazon and its ascent for. As my gaze shifted up and out the window during one Lyft ride across town, the driver put it best: "More buildings, more homes, more everything."

One major component of the "more everything" boom was a brand-new Walmart campus beginning to take form. It was around 350 acres in total, with a long menu of amenities aimed at attracting a new type of professional that McMillon and company desired to continue to modernize the company and defend against the Amazon attack. Among the new perks was one that caused employees to do a double take, and its CEO thus needing to mention twice.

"You'll see improved parking, meal services, fitness, and natural light—yes, natural light," McMillon wrote in announcing the opulent new campus in 2017. The Walmart "home office," on the other hand, originally opened in 1971 and was once best known for its bare-bones aesthetic and, as McMillon's note hinted, a dearth of windows. But how would Walmart's new home reflect on traits the company had long been proud of, company long-timers wondered?

"To what extent does that now mean that you don't own frugality— that suppliers aren't going to walk in and say, 'Hey, these guys aren't messing around?'" Marcus Osborne, a former longtime executive in the company's health care division, said of the new office plans. "To what extent does it sort of take the focus off the customer?"

"When you're sitting in the old home office," he continued, "all you had were these nasty cubes, but you saw merchandise everywhere, and it was just—you were surrounded by this stuff. And it forced you to—we were constantly reflecting on customers. I think that's where this is going to be a challenge. And I see it for a lot of companies, but I think it's going to be the hardest for somebody like Walmart, because of its history and legacy."

Yet some kind of Walmart transformation was necessary and long overdue. Amazon made sure of that. It first attacked Walmart in general merchandise—from books to electronics. Then it went after Walmart's core grocery business, both in the digital world and later the physical world. Along the way, the tech giant carried out a yearslong offensive to convince Walmart's most valuable customers to defect to Amazon Prime. Not all efforts were successful, but the pace was unrelenting. For the first time since the launch of the Supercenter, Walmart was on its back feet. Walmart, "Everyday Low Price" stalwart, destroyer of any and all competition, was finally an underdog.

For many years, Walmart leaders didn't even acknowledge this, in part because Sam Walton's and Jeff Bezos's companies operated mostly in separate spheres—one a massive brick-and-mortar retailer, the other an online giant. But in 2016, Walmart aggressively moved into the world of e-commerce, while Amazon would soon make big bets on physical retail. The resulting rivalry was a no-holds-barred power struggle for dominance as Amazon's ambition only grew and Walmart's homegrown CEO attempted a business reinvention for the ages.

Along the way, retail experienced an unprecedented shift accelerated by the Covid pandemic. Customers moved more of their purchases online and began expecting more convenience from physical retailers, while mom-and-pop stores and once-prominent chains alike were being wiped out or forced to do business with industry giants. Amazon and Walmart reaped the rewards, with the two accounting for nearly $1 out of every $2 spent online in the US. But as the two megacorporations have consolidated retail power, troubling consequences have also emerged—for consumers and small merchants facing fewer buying and selling options, and millions of workers paid meager wages for demanding and sometimes dangerous work.

For the last ten years, I've been covering this battle between Amazon, Walmart, and other upstarts that have tried to contend with these behemoths of global retailing. I've done it in hundreds of written articles for Recode; a hit documentary podcast called *Land of the Giants*; and my own annual confab for industry heavyweights, called Code Commerce. Through that work, I've spoken with thousands of people who have insights into how and why these two goliaths operate the way they do, up and down the power spectrum; from $15-an-hour employees struggling through their first week on the warehouse floor to small-town merchants who depend on the platforms for their livelihood, to executives making decisions that impact hundreds of millions of people around the globe. That credibility helped me persuade both Amazon and Walmart to agree to interviews with many of their top decision-makers between 2021 and 2022. But this is not a book of access; history is written from many sides, and their side of the story provides just one point of view. As a result, I also spoke with other current and former executives, employees, and industry insiders—more than 150 in total—to provide a holistic view of the events in the hundreds of pages that follow.

The result is the story of the defining business clash of this generation—a battle waged for our loyalty and wallets, with hundreds of billions of dollars at stake and millions of jobs on the line. It's the story of two industry titans dueling to become the go-to provider of any product you could imagine for hundreds of millions of people worldwide. It's the story of legacy-defining multibillion-dollar bets to try to win—at all costs.

But this is also a tale of ego and revenge, with legendary executives and ambitious entrepreneurs battling to invent the future—sometimes between rival companies and sometimes within the same company walls. As both companies continue to expand their respective empires into new susceptible industries, my hope is that this account will serve for decades to come as the key to understanding how Amazon and Walmart are changing the way we shop, live, and work—for better or worse.

WHAT IF?

On a late summer day in 1998, Robert Davis marched down Walmart's Executive Row to the office of CEO David Glass and attempted to alter the arc of business history with a single bet.

Davis was a Mississippi native and self-proclaimed introvert with a dream of one day retiring to a log cabin in the woods. He was also a marketer by education, a technologist by choice, and a software engineer by trade. At the time, he had spent a few years overseeing a skunkworks team that was intent on making sure that Walmart would embrace the opportunity of selling through a new, emerging channel called the World Wide Web. It might be hard to remember now, but back in 1998, Amazon was just starting to dabble with selling merchandise other than books. Walmart, on the other hand, had access to just about every category of product imaginable, and the resources, pricing, and logistics prowess to blow their tiny rival away.

Jeff Bezos seemed to recognize this, because a year earlier, the Amazon founder and CEO had started poaching Walmart bigwigs away from Bentonville. First it was Rick Dalzell, a Walmart IT leader who oversaw the retailer's innovative data-warehousing initiatives and whom Bezos recruited to be Amazon's first chief information officer. Dalzell was a burly West Point graduate and Army veteran who loved solving hard problems almost as much he did fly-fishing and Army football. Dalzell did not believe Walmart was taking e-commerce seriously enough and was enchanted by the vision he and Bezos shared for how the web could enable building a personalized store for each and every customer.

A year after joining Amazon, Dalzell phoned his former Walmart colleague Davis to offer him an Amazon job of his own. Davis informed Dalzell that he was unlikely to follow him to the hot internet darling; he had been at Walmart for a dozen years by then and could envision working for the retail behemoth for the rest of his career.

"I drank the Kool-Aid and was very devoted to Walmart," Davis told me in late 2021, in what he said was his first and only interview on the subject.

At the time, Davis and his wife had just bought a new house on three acres of land out in the Arkansas countryside. "It was perfect," he said. He also knew that the Amazon offer amounted to a 25 percent pay cut in cash compensation, because the tech startup loads up its job offers with stock. Still, he was intrigued by one thing that the Seattle-based online bookseller offered that he wasn't convinced Walmart leaders did: a steadfast belief that the future of the retail industry was going to happen on the internet.

At Walmart, Davis had become frustrated by what he saw as a lack of commitment to e-commerce. Yes, management had granted him and a small group of peers the freedom to experiment with internet retailing by selling gift baskets online during the 1995 holiday season for the company's Sam's Club division. Yes, a year later, they were given the green light to launch Walmart's first online storefront. But to really take advantage of the opportunity being presented, Davis believed deep in his gut that he and his peers needed more support from the company's powerful merchandising and warehouse divisions. He also wanted the CEO to declare to the rest of the company that internet retailing at Walmart was more than just a test.

He needed the logistics division to know that when he requested that they slap a Walmart.com sticker on all those Walmart trucks that crisscross the country every day, the request had backing from the top and "No" wasn't going to be an acceptable response. He needed the warehouse division to know that if he asked that they start prioritizing online order shipments alongside pallet shipments headed to stores, the CEO was on board with his request. And he needed the IT division to know that when the internet marketing leader asked them to prioritize an email solution to communicate with Walmart.com's earliest customers, they wouldn't tell him it would take a few years to get to it.

"What I wanted David to do was convene the troops and say, 'We gotta figure this out,'" Davis recalled.

Seated across from Glass, Davis made the most powerful case you could at Walmart: he "bet his badge" on the idea. In doing so, Davis was agreeing that if Glass backed him with a bigger e-commerce commitment, but then the plan failed, Davis would pack up his bags and hit the road for good.

"David said, 'No, I won't take that bet,'" Davis told me.

The denial from Glass, who died in 2020 at the age of eighty-four, was somewhat ironic. Before succeeding Sam Walton as CEO, Glass was one of the Walmart executives most responsible for convincing the founder to embrace certain kinds of technology. The year before Walton handed over the chief executive title to his trusted lieutenant, Walmart finished rolling out the largest satellite communications system in the US, connecting its stores, warehouses, and home office. Earlier, Glass was the brains behind heavy investments in automating certain tasks inside warehouses via conveyor belts and barcode scanners. And the creation of Walmart's once industry-leading Retail Link system, which provided suppliers with daily store-level sales data for their products, happened on Glass's watch as CEO.

"[O]ne of the main reasons we've been able to roll this company out nationally was all the pressure put on me by guys like David Glass . . . to invest so heavily in technology," Walton wrote in his 1992 memoir. "[O]ur fellows were just absolutely convinced that computers were essential to managing growth and keeping down our cost structure. Today, of course, they've been proven so right that they look like geniuses."

But up until the late 1990s, those massive technology investments were mostly geared, in one way or another, toward improving Walmart's core business of selling obscene amounts of merchandise at dirt-cheap prices out of physical stores. An online store, on the other hand, felt like something altogether different, and one with limited potential. While Glass could get behind some types of innovation, he was also the type of executive who had his assistant print out his emails rather than accessing them himself. Personal computers were not exactly his thing.

When Glass informed Davis that he wouldn't accept his bet to double down on Walmart's e-commerce efforts, the CEO predicted that Walmart's online store would never register more sales than the largest single Sam's Club brick-and-mortar location, Davis recalled. That may sound absurd now, but sales data at the time backed it up. In 1997, Amazon posted revenue of just $148 million, while Walmart celebrated its first $100 *billion* sales year. Walmart stores were firing on all cylinders. Who could blame Glass?

Davis did. And he decided it was time to go.

"I'll take it to my grave how big of a mistake it was and how impactful it would have been to retail if we had done what I was advocating," Davis told me.

Amazon Calling

Davis, who had envisioned growing old in Bentonville, soon gave his notice, packed up the dream house he once thought would be his forever home, and set out on a two-thousand-mile road trip in his pickup truck from northwest Arkansas to the Pacific Northwest. Somewhere around Montana, or maybe it was the Dakotas, a news flash blared out of his car radio. Walmart, the radio voice said, had filed suit against Amazon for allegedly stealing trade secrets through the hiring of former Walmart employees.

Davis was stunned. He pulled off the highway at the next exit and found a pay phone to call his old Walmart buddy Dalzell, who was slated to become his new Amazon colleague.

"Should I keep driving, or should I turn around?" Davis asked.

"Come on," Davis recalled Dalzell telling him, "but instead of orientation, the first thing you're going to do is meet with the lawyers."

When Dalzell had made the same leap to Amazon a year earlier, his bosses at Walmart thought his move was bold, but a bit nutty; there was no possible way that this niche internet business, a money-sucking one at that, had any future that could rival that of the king of brick-and-mortar retail.

But they seemed to get over it just fine. After Dalzell spoke at an industry conference with the goal of attracting new recruits to Amazon, Lee Scott—a top Walmart executive who rose from living in a small trailer with his family while paying his way through college to eventually succeed David Glass as Walmart's third-ever CEO—mailed Dalzell a cutout photo from the event along with a friendly message. "It said something like, 'You guys are looking good,'" Dalzell told me more than two decades later. "It was a positive note. It wasn't snarky or anything. It was a very nice note."

But by late 1998, less than a year and a half after Bezos had poached Dalzell from Bentonville, the good feelings were gone. It wasn't just that Amazon had stolen one of Walmart's brightest technical minds in Dalzell, but that it didn't stop there. Bezos also lured Jimmy Wright, a hard-charging Walmart logistics executive, to drastically expand Amazon's warehouse footprint. Drugstore.com, a dot-com darling of which Amazon owned nearly half, began going after Walmart talent as well.

Then there was Davis, the architect of Walmart's earliest e-commerce tests. All these years later, he still wondered if his hire was more calculated than it may have first seemed. He was essentially the only software engineer responsible for Walmart's first online retail website. And when he left Bentonville in 1998, he took the virtual keys with him.

Sure, he had been happy with the move to Amazon and thankful that Dalzell brought him on board—for thirteen years at Amazon, he was surrounded by people as passionate about the future of e-commerce as he was. The job also gave him the financial security to retire to his log cabin out on eleven acres of land at the age of fifty-five. But some things just didn't add up; chief among them was the fact that Dalzell hired Davis to oversee key technology areas for Amazon that weren't actually within his expertise.

"It very well could be that Rick didn't so much want me at Amazon as he wanted me out of Walmart," Davis told me. "I don't know. I've never asked Rick that and I wouldn't expect him to tell me. But I've wondered that forever. If Amazon wanted to stop Walmart, I was the guy and there was nobody to back me up."

While it seemed obvious that Davis's departure from Walmart would slow down the retailer's online efforts, that was never the goal, Dalzell later told me. Davis was wicked smart and bold, with a thirst for solving hard technological problems. Before his work in e-commerce, he also played a critical role in modernizing Walmart's point-of-sale systems, the computerized checkout stations that replaced old-school cash registers.

"Robert was in my opinion the top point-of-sale guy in the world," Dalzell told me. "I knew that payments was a critical long-term component of how we would serve our customers at Amazon and I could picture nobody better than him to solve those problems."

Dalzell said that Davis's payments expertise and advice were especially crucial to Amazon's efforts to fine-tune its revolutionary 1-Click payments system, which allowed customers to place orders without having to reenter their payment card information again and again.

"You can reassure him for me," Dalzell said, "he was just a star and we were after stars."

No matter the reasoning behind Davis's appeal, his arrival at Amazon coincided with Walmart's lawsuit against Amazon, Dalzell, and Drugstore.com. The suit hung over the Walmart contingent at Amazon for the better part of the next six months, until a settlement was reached in April 1999 without any money changing hands.[1] Dalzell, ever the diplomat, maintains that he doesn't take the suit personally.

"I have nothing but respect and praise for both companies," he told me.

The legal maneuver was a "tool," he said, and one that Amazon too has employed over the years. But at the time, it was hard for him and his wife to remove the emotion from the situation, especially when company lawyers were removing mementos from his home as part of discovery, the pretrial process where evidence is gathered and disclosed between parties. The Sam M. Walton Award of Excellence was the memento that got to him the most.

"That felt a little like a personal affront," he said. "But," he added, "it wasted a lot of their money and time."

At Amazon, Dalzell got to work as Bezos's tech consigliere and oversaw many critical technology initiatives that made Amazon more efficient, its website more resilient, while cutting dollars wherever he could. In 2000, for example, Amazon was burning cash at a breakneck pace, and the capital markets dried up for dot-com companies. The company was facing what appeared to some as an existential crisis, exacerbated by a credit analyst's regular research notes predicting that the e-commerce darling might run out of cash.[2]

In a crucial meeting of top Amazon executives during this time, Amazon's chief financial officer, Warren Jenson, who once dressed up as "excess inventory" for the company's annual Halloween costume party, outlined a whiteboard calculation of Amazon's financials and what the company would need to do to eke out an annual profit. The numbers were ugly, and Jenson recalled Dalzell telling the room that the profit goal was implausible.

"If we can't do it," Jenson replied at the time, "we should save our shareholders a lot of money and pack it in."

Two weeks later, Dalzell came bounding down Amazon's office hallway inside Seattle's old Pacific Medical Center tower, Jenson said.

"I got it!" Dalzell crowed.

One of Amazon's largest technology expenses was data servers, then supplied by Sun Microsystems—the leading source, but an expensive one. Dalzell decided to rip them out, replacing them with Hewlett-Packard hardware and Linux open-source software. It was risky, it was bold, but it paid off. "For every $1 spent on the new hardware, he saved $10 in license fees, maintenance, and expected hardware upgrades," *Business 2.0* magazine reported. The decision helped Amazon dramatically cut its capital expenditures, while the tech upstart's R&D spending kept growing but shrank as a percentage of the company's revenue.[3] Without the move, it's possible Amazon would have been toast before its tenth birthday.

"Rick was the unsung hero of that era," Jenson recalled.

The Walmart veteran saved the day for the potential Walmart killer, though Dalzell downplayed Jenson's characterization, spreading out the credit.

"In a startup environment, almost everybody is an unsung hero."

But Dalzell's influence was profound even beyond the server solution. His technology teams spent years building e-commerce software tools at Amazon that would evolve into technology platforms now responsible for around $100 billion of Amazon revenue, through Amazon's Web Services division and its ads business.

"The thing I'm most proud of . . . was we set the company up in a way to move fast, and to . . . have it working towards being the most customer-centric company in the world, a goal that I actually could personally buy into," Dalzell told me.

One of the keys to moving fast at Amazon was the creation of so-called two-pizza teams, which were composed of ten employees or fewer, with different skill sets and different roles, but who were all aligned on one project and could work autonomously as a group without much involvement from other teams. Dalzell first experienced a flavor of this at Walmart, where an IT leader named Bobby Martin created "strategy" teams, which matched IT employees with a business division for both goal-setting and performance evaluation. At Amazon, Dalzell shared these Walmart insights with Bezos, who took the idea to the next level; he granted the two-pizza teams great independence that allowed them to sidestep the halting bureaucracy of inter-department communication.

Still, for Dalzell, like Davis, the move out of Bentonville was a painful one. He had only agreed to join after a monthslong courtship by Bezos, and a tortuous decision-making process that ended when his wife, Kathryn, convinced him to be real with himself and bet on his gut instead of corporate loyalty.[4] He wasn't planning to leave when Bezos came calling, but his departure, along with that of Davis and the others, did seem to light a digital fire under the collective pants of Walmart leadership.

"The only thing that gets you aligned," Dalzell told me, "is when a new competitor like an Amazon . . . pop[s] up and you realize, 'Holy smokes, this thing is legitimately for real.'"

Walmart Online

That, it seems, is how Walmart's thinking played out. In the late 1990s, a young Walmart executive who had married into the Walton family—Greg Penner—made his opinion clear: Walmart needed to set up its e-commerce operation as a separate company from the one in Bentonville.

Penner believed that Walmart leaders back in the home office wouldn't be the ones best equipped to confront this new digital reality. Penner, the son-in-law of Walmart chairman S. Robson Walton, known as Rob, had suggested Walmart partner with a Silicon Valley venture capital fund on the new scheme. The choice was Accel Partners. Penner brought an outsider's perspective to Walmart, both in personal and professional ways. He was from California, the son of two sex therapists, and had studied with his future wife, Carrie Walton, at prestigious universities on the coasts: first at Georgetown University, in Washington, DC, where the couple met, and later at Stanford's Graduate School of Business, in Northern California. Before joining Walmart, Penner worked as a financial analyst for Goldman Sachs and as a partner at a venture capital firm.

Penner's e-commerce push was backed up by the management consulting firm McKinsey & Company, which had outlined what the opportunity for Walmart.com looked like, and it was big: up to $500 million in sales. In March 2000, the Walmart.com joint venture hired the CEO of Gap's Banana Republic, Jeanne Jackson, who also ran Gap's internet division, to run the spin-off company with plans to relaunch the floundering site in October, before the holiday shopping season. The initial projection for Walmart.com fourth-quarter sales that year was $150 million; by the fall, Jackson slashed that projection to $75 million. In the end, Walmart.com finished the period with just $28 million in sales.

"The web traffic projections were right, but the conversions were wrong," John Fleming, a former Target executive who was Walmart .com's first chief merchant, told me.

Walmart.com had predicted that around 5 of every 100 website visitors would end up making a purchase. Instead the ratio was closer to 1 out of every 100. On a large scale, that differential adds up to a massive problem.

Years later, Walmart's corporate website would herald the year 2000 as the launch of Walmart Online, since that was when the company began investing in e-commerce in a significant and more strategic way. Any mention of the 1996 launch of Walmart's actual first shopping site, on the other hand, when Davis and a small group of peers first put Walmart on the digital map, is buried deep within the website of the Walmart Museum. Brian Hess, the internet marketing leader for Walmart's first shopping site in the mid-1990s, considered the timeline a snub and "a knife in the heart."

"I felt like we were being innovative," he told me. "I felt like we were helping Walmart learn about a new way to do retail.

"And then for them to say that we didn't really start it then—that it was four years later," he added, looking perplexed, "I'm like, well, then what were we doing exactly?"

The new Walmart Online joint venture survived the holiday season in 2000, but the fallout was significant. Walmart.com had purchased more than $100 million in inventory, but most of it had to be liquidated at a loss. Luckily, the e-commerce executives were able to utilize Walmart stores to sell the inventory; if this had been an independent e-commerce startup, the miscalculation would have been a death knell.

Even still, layoffs ensued. By mid-2001, less than a year after the Walmart.com relaunch, Walmart decided to buy out Accel Partners' ownership stake in the venture and fold the spin-off operation back into the parent company. Jackson, the former Banana Republic and Gap executive, lasted less than two years in the top role before leaving amid the restructuring.[5]

Walmart executives had expected that the website would attract different customers than Walmart stores did, "but that didn't happen at all," Fleming, who took over for Jackson as Walmart.com CEO, told me. The vast majority of people who were making purchases on the website were the same people who were making purchases in Walmart stores.

"It became clear . . . it needs to all work together, and it's never going to get support from Bentonville as a separate company," Fleming said.

Years later, Penner, who would go on to succeed his father-in-law, Rob Walton, as Walmart's chairman in 2015, told attendees at a conference what he learned from the experience.

"We found that didn't work because we weren't leveraging all the assets that we had at the core company," he said.

Publicly, Walmart's then-CEO, Lee Scott, said the site would still offer delivery to customers' homes, but would also focus on highlighting the goods that customers could purchase at their nearest Supercenter. Internally, Walmart was facing the innovator's dilemma: online sales could siphon sales from the cash machine that was its Supercenter stores. As a result, it seemed, Scott was going to kick the dilemma down the road and make the website do more heavy lifting in the name of increased store sales, rather than vice versa.

"Eighteen months ago, I would have told you that the No. 1 opportunity was buying over the Internet and delivering direct to customers' homes," Scott said at the time.[6] Now Scott was implying the internet should instead be utilized to boost in-store sales.

Still, over the next four years, Walmart.com grew at a 50 percent or higher clip, eclipsing $1 billion in sales in 2005.[7] Even more important to Walmart executives in Bentonville, though, was that the web operation was getting closer to breaking even, while Amazon continued to burn cash to fuel growth.

"Everybody was thrilled and that was a mistake," Fleming, the former Walmart.com CEO, said of leaders celebrating progress toward profitability more than revenue growth. "Because during that same time frame, Amazon invested, say, $4 billion, and we invested a couple hundred million."

Meanwhile, Amazon's revenue was around eight times as much as Walmart.com's. Fleming would end up getting promoted to chief merchandising officer for all of Walmart, and relocate to Bentonville, where digital sales were still mostly an afterthought.

On the path to the first billion, Walmart did roll out some digital experiments that utilized the advantage the retailer held with its massive store footprint. One of them was a photo-printing business that guaranteed prints would be ready at a local store within one hour of a customer placing an order online. Each day, thousands of online customers used the new service.

"Probably the biggest impact we had from a consumer perspective was uploading your photos online, and then choosing to make prints and pick them up in a store," Fleming said.

Walmart also experimented with bringing the website to existing customers by putting kiosks in Supercenters to advertise the broader product selection on Walmart.com. The experiment was a dud.

During this time, one Walmart.com executive encouraged his fellow digital leaders to begin listening to Amazon's earnings calls with Wall Street analysts to educate themselves about the insurgent competitor. What the executives heard on one call, about how much Amazon was spending on logistics and site improvements, flabbergasted them.

"We're like, Wow, two and a half billion dollars that they're going to invest in one quarter," one of the former executives said, "and we're getting jammed up about like losing $20 million this year."

Part of the issue was internal competing interests at the time, where Walmart.com's leader would hear "invest, invest, invest" from one side of the organization and "why are you losing money?" from the other.

"It felt like it was a no-win situation trying to figure out how to grow Walmart.com in those times," the former executive told me. That push-and-pull, between growth and profits, and e-commerce leadership and store leadership, would rear its head over and over again in the years to come.

At the time, Walmart also followed a young high-flying tech company called Netflix into the online DVD rental business. The Bentonville giant attracted more than 300,000 subscribers to its own service. But, in a sign of things to come, Walmart executives balked at a price tag that easily extended into the tens of millions of dollars—at least double the annual budget for all of Walmart.com—that would be necessary to build a scalable digital platform and warehousing and fulfillment system tailored specifically to DVD subscriptions. As a result, e-commerce executives cut marketing intended to attract new subscribers, and watched as existing subscribers fled the service. Walmart needed a way to exit the business "gracefully," a former executive told me. Eventually, just two years after launching its DVD rental service, Walmart cut a small deal to essentially sell its subscriber base to Netflix.

During these early years, cultural differences between the brick-and-mortar and online teams began to show. For about a decade, starting in 2000, Walmart's e-commerce operation was headquartered out of a building on San Francisco Bay in Brisbane, California, dubbed the Luke Skywalker building due to its futuristic and dramatic frame, and how it differed from a nearby imposing all-black building dubbed Darth Vader. While the HVAC system in the headquarters rarely worked properly, and the structure seemed to be on the verge of collapse during big storms, the office sported floor-to-ceiling windows throughout, with preposterous views of the water. To some, this was a perk; who doesn't love nice views? Except that Walmart's "home office" back in Bentonville was known for its bare-bones aesthetic, including limited windows. Sunlight, apparently, was a distraction.

So when the Bentonville store buyers took their pilgrimage to Silicon Valley every so often—and saw all that glass—they seemed unnerved.

"It's like they were walking into a porn shop," a Walmart.com executive said. "It's like they were committing a sin."

It was an early, if mild, sign of more potent conflicts to come.

Price Wars

As Walmart was starting to navigate the digital terrain of retail in the early 2000s, Amazon was going through its own growing pains. And inside Jeff Bezos's company, executives looked to Walmart for inspiration.

Greg Greeley, who joined Amazon from Sun Microsystems in 1999 and would end up running Amazon Prime during his nineteen-year career at the company, knew Amazon could glean insights from the Walmart story.

"I was encouraging everyone to read Sam Walton's book, *Made in America*," Greeley, a self-professed retail industry history buff, told me. "The things in there about leadership and ownership just bounce out."

Jeff Wilke, who also joined Amazon in 1999 and would ascend to CEO of Amazon's global consumer business, acknowledged another Walmart stalwart that the tech startup's leaders eventually embraced: everyday low prices. Walmart spent a relatively low percentage of its sales on advertising or discounts. Instead it used the money a normal retailer would pour into advertising to keep prices low on a daily basis. As one of Walmart's CEOs, Lee Scott, would later tell Jeff Bezos, "Our marketing strategy is our pricing strategy."[8]

"Walmart has a reputation for low prices, and that's something that's been a part of the Amazon offering for a long time," Wilke told me in early 2021, a few days before he retired from Amazon. "In order to achieve low prices, you have to be efficient and there are a number of retailers who have become quite efficient and are inspiring in that way."

But Amazon's attention to pricing took what some saw as an anti-customer twist in the early years. In 2000, some eagle-eyed consumers noticed that different customers were being charged different prices for the same DVDs, seemingly based on factors such as which web browser or internet service provider they were using. After customers compared notes on an online forum and the press covered the news,[9] Amazon denied that the price differences related to customer demographics, but the test, whatever the motivation, risked customer trust. And that was a no-no.

"What we did was a random price test, and even that was a mistake because it created uncertainty for customers rather than simplifying their lives," Bezos said in a press release following the snafu.

The next year, after a formative meeting with Costco cofounder Jim Sinegal, Bezos made his view on pricing clear at an internal executive meeting.[10] "Like Walmart and Costco," Bezos said, "Amazon should have everyday low prices." Later that year, Bezos announced this change to the world on an earnings call.[11]

"There are two kinds of retailers," Bezos said. "There are those folks who work to figure how to charge more, and companies that work to figure how to charge less, and we are going to be the second."

This view, and the price-matching policies it engendered, weren't without their setbacks. In the early 2000s, Amazon would research product promotions of brick-and-mortar rivals by picking up their weekend circular and then deciding to match or beat their price. But there was some nuance that was lost in this process. While a rival like Walmart or Best Buy got funding from the manufacturer of the merchandise to run the promotion, and would limit the sales event to just one day, Amazon was absorbing the discount itself and would sometimes extend the length of a promotion for many days.

"We would lose our shirts on that," former Amazon executive David Glick told me.

But around 2004 or 2005, there was a change.

"We quit thinking about 'How do we optimize pricing?'" Greeley told me, "and [switched to] 'How to just make sure that the customer doesn't feel like they're being punished for shopping on Amazon—that you're not paying for the convenience with higher prices.'"

In a new division, the company eventually set up a specialized pricing team that created what was called the competitive monitoring tool. At its core, it was an automated computer system that fanned out across the internet, gobbled up the product prices on competitors' sites, including Walmart, and fed them back into the Amazon machine. With this information, Amazon's pricing system could decide when to match Walmart's pricing and when to get even more aggressive and beat it.

"Jeff wanted to be sharp with respect to pricing," Glick told me. "And Walmart let us beat them on price for a long time. We were matching them or beating them, and they weren't matching us."

Walmart's website was just "an open door," according to another former executive. Internally, Bezos called it a "gift."

"They were the inventors of winning on price—killing all the local retailers on price," Glick said. "So, we were all sort of surprised they would let us beat them on price."

One Walmart.com executive from the era said that while the Walmart Online group sought to match Amazon prices aggressively, Walmart's store leaders would rain hell down on their digital counterparts if that meant offering lower prices online than in Walmart stores. Walmart store leaders didn't mind the digital operation, unless, of course, it was cannibalizing sales that could have, or should have, been taking place inside Walmart's more profitable stores.

In fact, a 2002 *Wall Street Journal* article marveled at the similarities in pricing strategies between Walmart and its younger rival.[12]

"Discount retailers such as Wal-Mart Stores Inc. continually lower prices by squeezing inefficiencies from their operations, sacrificing fat profit margins on products in favor of selling in high volumes. By adopting this [same] strategy, Amazon appears finally to be doing what industry officials have long said the Internet would allow retailers to do—drive down prices aggressively for consumers."

In 2005, Amazon took another step in outmaneuvering the competition on price. Led by a vice president named Suresh Kumar, who would one day become Walmart's chief technology officer, Amazon's retail systems division created a computer tool that could automatically calculate the contribution profit of every item sold on the website. While competitors might look at the gross profit of a piece of merchandise, Amazon dug deeper. Take, for example, a $10 toy with a 40 percent gross margin, meaning that a retailer in theory could make $4 after accounting for buying the toy at a wholesale price. But the 40 percent margin meant nothing if that toy had to be packed in some unique box that cost more than a regular box, or if the cost of picking it off a shelf and shipping it was $5 alone.

"It was revolutionary when we launched it," Glick told me.

Over time, Walmart began stepping up its online pricing game, at times giving Amazon a run for its money. In 2005, for example, Amazon executives were preparing for the launch of the sixth book in the Harry Potter series, *Harry Potter and the Half-Blood Prince*, with the company promising release-day delivery to more than 1.5 million customers—on a Saturday.

But shortly after Amazon shipped those orders, Walmart.com dropped its own price on the book. Greeley, then the vice president for Amazon's physical media categories including books, had a decision to make: refund nearly $1 or more to each of the 1.5 million preorder customers, or stand pat with what was already a 40 percent discount off the retail price. It was late at night and Greeley didn't think there was time to check with either Bezos or Amazon's chief financial officer. He decided to go ahead with the refunds. Bezos would later say he agreed with the decision.

While it was the right thing to do for customers, Greeley thought, there seemed to be another major factor at play.

"It felt like it was all about Walmart," another Amazon employee familiar with those discussions told me.

The focus on matching Walmart on price also created some issues, like when Amazon's pricing tool would repeatedly lower the price on an item to match its competitor, leading to what insiders dubbed a death spiral. Amazon created a specialized team to try to determine how and when to decide that its pricing tool should pull back and no longer match Walmart's lowest price on a given item, but instead match the next-lowest price from a competitor. The initiative was called Project Nessie. In the end, the program was scrapped when it was determined that the tool did not lead to more profitable outcomes, according to Amazon spokesperson Jordan Deagle.

Still, while Amazon's pricing spy system helped it go toe-to-toe with Walmart on pricing for online orders, it was much more difficult to track—and compete against—Walmart's in-store prices. Remember, for much of Walmart's history, the Bentonville giant not only sold goods at lower prices in stores than on its website, but those in-store prices changed between individual locations as well, depending on factors including where stores were located. Amazon, however, didn't just aspire to have the best prices on the internet; Jeff Bezos wanted to show shoppers the best prices anywhere.

In the early 2000s, Amazon was gearing up to start selling health and personal care items and executives wanted to make sure their per-unit prices matched or bested bigger rivals like Walmart and Target, no matter the short-term financial ramifications.

"We had the mandate that we were not going to be undercut by anybody," said Meredith Han, a product manager on the team.

To track in-store prices of the larger retail mainstays, Amazon hired a temp worker to visit stores and jot down the prices of competitive products. Perhaps it was the clipboard she carried, but it didn't take long for her to get booted out of a Walmart store. The next approach was less conspicuous, with employees purchasing key products from rival stores, solely to vacuum up pricing information. Han was in her twenties and not yet a mother, but found herself filling her cart with various diaper brands and pack sizes. She'd return to headquarters and dump her haul into the cubicle of the temp employee, who would then input the per-unit prices into Amazon's computer system.

"It was very crude, but it was effective at getting up and going," she said.

Years later, in the lead-up to the 2010 holiday season, Amazon revealed what it thought was a better solution: an app for iPhones called Price Check. Shoppers could open the app in a store and scan a barcode on a piece of merchandise and instantly see the cost of the same item on Amazon.com. For Amazon, it wasn't just a data play to learn how its prices compared to competitors in physical retail; it was also a very tangible way to urge shoppers to move some of their in-store spending online.

In December 2011, Amazon took this tactic to the next level: it offered shoppers who used the Price Check app a 5 percent discount—of up to $5—on three different items.[13] Inside Amazon, executives viewed the app as a tactic for gathering intelligence on merchandise prices inside big-box stores like Walmart or Best Buy. But in light of the holiday promotion, small businesses and politicians viewed it much more harshly. It didn't matter that the promotion intentionally excluded bookstores, a category of independent retailer that Amazon had already proven it had the power to decimate.

"Amazon's promotion—paying consumers to visit small businesses and leave empty-handed—is an attack on Main Street businesses that employ workers in our communities," Senator Olympia Snowe, the top Republican on the US Senate Committee on Small Business and

Entrepreneurship, said in a statement at the time.[14] "Small businesses are fighting every day to compete with giant retailers, such as Amazon, and incentivizing consumers to spy on local shops is a bridge too far."

Inside Amazon's headquarters, Bezos fumed.

"I told you this was going to happen!" Bezos lambasted his staff, according to a former executive who witnessed one tirade.

One of Amazon's Leadership Principles states, "Leaders . . . think differently and look around corners for ways to serve customers." But in this case, Bezos believed Amazon leaders failed to look around corners and see how Amazon's intentions might be perceived, or even twisted.

"Jeff thought it was ham-fisted execution because we weren't out there saying this is basically focused on big-box stores," Craig Berman, Amazon's head of communications during the time, told me. "He didn't like that small businesses got dragged into it. That was not the goal at all. And he felt like if [customers] knew we were going after Walmart, Target, or Costco, no one would care. That's a big company going after a big company. But don't go after the small guys, because you'll get your ass kicked—and he was right."

Tax Advantage

Behind the scenes, a coalition known as the Alliance for Main Street Fairness was helping to push the narrative that the Amazon promotion was an attack on small business.[15] Walmart and other big-box retailers were behind it, though they had originally started working together to pressure state governments to begin requiring Amazon to charge online shoppers sales tax.[16] Because Amazon wasn't required to collect sales tax from its customers in most states if it didn't have a physical presence there, the company enjoyed an unfair pricing advantage over its brick-and-mortar rivals, who were required to collect tax on top of a product's retail price, the argument went.

"The rules today don't allow brick-and-mortar retailers to compete evenly with online retailers, and that needs to be addressed," Raul

Vazquez, Walmart's executive vice president of global e-commerce, said at the time.

Of course, the idea that Walmart of all corporations was funding a coalition ostensibly supporting Main Street small businesses was comical to anyone with an unbiased view. Long Public Enemy No. 1 of mom-and-pop retail shops, Walmart had successfully developed and burnished a reputation for single-handedly eviscerating independent stores upon entry into new communities.

Nonetheless, Amazon's tax advantage was crucial to its early success and the company went to great lengths to keep it that way. Executives produced color-coded maps for new employees to show them which states were safe to travel to on work trips, and which needed approval because of "strict laws about what employee actions would force a company to collect taxes there, or with aggressive tax offices."[17]

The sales tax factor played a crucial role in where Amazon located its warehouses for the first fifteen years or so of its existence. If Amazon had a warehouse in a state, it might need to collect sales tax there. So, Amazon officials sought out warehouse properties in states with relatively small populations, and where Amazon didn't have a lot of customers. One of the company's first five warehouses, for example, was located in the small Midwest town of Coffeyville, Kansas.

As the country struggled to recover from the Great Recession and seek out new revenue sources, several states went after Amazon on the tax issue. In 2012, Amazon settled tax disputes in large states like Texas, Pennsylvania, and California, agreeing to start collecting sales tax at a future date. But whether rivals like Walmart knew it or not, the agreement wouldn't slow Amazon's growth; in some big ways, it helped Amazon ramp things up.

During his decade at the company, a top Amazon tax official kept a notebook packed with every major project or innovation that was held up by tax concerns. Bezos would sometimes ask to see it and geek out in anticipation of what was to come. By the early 2010s, the list had surpassed eighty projects.

"It was clear to me that if you really removed those [tax] constraints, there was a huge amount of ideas that could be unleashed," someone familiar with the list told me.

Having agreed to start collecting sales tax in key states, Amazon set out on a massive warehouse buildout across the country in the years that followed. In 2016 alone, Amazon opened twenty-six new warehouses, or an average of one every other week—a pace that would have seemed unfathomable early in the company's history. (Within a couple of years, that rate of buildout would seem conservative.) The expansion not only helped reduce shipping costs on individual orders but also sped up delivery times for Amazon Prime members, the company's most prized customers. In the process, the advantage of immediacy that Walmart stores had over Amazon began to shrink.

"Everyone was screaming about Amazon expanding too fast, doing too much, and not paying sales tax, and they just didn't see that was the barrier," Berman, the former head of communications, said. "That was the thing that was holding Amazon in check. The single biggest advantage that physical retail had at the time completely went away and was gone as soon as Amazon started expanding the warehouses."

Walmart did in fact have a way to combat Amazon's warehouse expansion even before it happened. But the company would have to do something it had not consistently been able to do well enough for much of its online history: get store leaders and e-commerce leaders to work together. Even from its earliest days in e-commerce, when Robert Davis built Walmart's first website in the mid-1990s, Walmart shipped some of the merchandise from stores. Walmart's 1997 annual report mentioned a store manager who shipped orders for "Wal-Mart Online, our World Wide Web site" out of Store 96 in Harrisonville, Missouri. An image accompanying the report featured the manager standing in front of a computer in a small stockroom with shelves stacked with boxed merchandise and plastic containers. The caption read: *Ann Burchett: Personal shopper in cyberspace.*

But during the early 2000s, Walmart had only modest success in leveraging its physical stores to fulfill digital orders. By around 2005, Amazon leaders believed they had matched or beaten Walmart on both product prices and on merchandise selection, but still potentially trailed Walmart in convenience because of Walmart's sprawling network of stores and how those physical outposts could be used as pickup locations or delivery points for speedy online orders. But over time, Amazon executives watched in disbelief as Walmart seemingly failed to focus on one of its key advantages.

"All they had to do was exploit that," said Bill Carr, a longtime Amazon executive.

Inside Walmart, the advantage did not seem that easy to capitalize on. To combat free-shipping offers from other retailers, including Amazon, Walmart leaders did start testing a service called Site to Store around 2002, and then rolled it out to more than three thousand Walmart locations between 2004 and 2007. The service allowed Walmart.com customers to place an order online and have it shipped to a nearby store, where they could later pick it up for free.

"There was a time when the online and offline businesses were viewed as being different," Walmart.com chief executive Raul Vazquez said in 2009. "Now we are realizing that we actually have a physical advantage thanks to our thousands of stores, and we can use it to become No. 1 online."[18]

Those same executives who rolled out Site to Store also experimented with a service, called Buy Online, Pickup in Store (BOPIS), that would eventually become mainstream across the industry years later, with its real shining moment coming during the Covid-19 pandemic. Walmart's BOPIS program was meant to provide online customers with orders that could be picked up faster than deliveries from Amazon and other e-commerce rivals would arrive at online shoppers' homes.

But the merchandise was coming from the shelves of a Walmart store, rather than those in a neatly stocked warehouse, and it was difficult to keep track of a store's inventory in real time to promise online customers that the item they ordered would still be there when they arrived. Successful, busy Supercenters also didn't want to spend money to add staffing to effectively support the program. That meant that Walmart stores that could support the experiment were those that were not very busy, which ultimately meant that there was not much customer demand in the region, either in the store or online.

"You only got access to those stores when they were inefficient, because they probably never should have been built," a former executive told me.

By the time Walmart publicized a BOPIS service in a meaningful way, it was already 2013. Even then, the difference in commitment from the stores division and e-commerce division manifested itself in a poor customer experience. Pickup points were often placed in the back of a giant Supercenter, and finding directions—from either a sign or a store associate—could be a challenge. Orders were often lost. Store visits for orders that were already placed online stretched for as long as thirty minutes. Super convenient these visits were not.

"The friction in the beginning was because stores wanted to share credit for revenue," a former Walmart e-commerce manager told me. "We ended up sharing half credit but still their heart wasn't there."

When Walmart's fourth CEO, Mike Duke, recruited a new chief technology officer for the company's e-commerce division in 2011, he said he was "in it to win it" in e-commerce and would "double down, or even triple down" on investments. To some insiders, though, it already felt far too late.

"We weren't aggressive enough in demanding resources or painting Amazon as an existential threat," a former Walmart.com leader told me. "As a result, we lost a lot of [market] share."

To make matters worse, there were other, younger e-commerce players also playing to win. In the late 2000s, a new threat to both Amazon and Walmart emerged. It was an e-commerce startup called Quidsi, based in New Jersey, of all places, that was offering fast delivery of low-priced diapers to the homes of young city moms who shopped on Diapers.com.

Inside Amazon's consumer packaged goods division, this competitor's growth was a "head-turning thing," according to a manager from the time. By early 2009, Amazon executives had already directed staff to make sure that internal systems were price-matching Diapers.com on every product they sold.

"[T]hey may be giving us a run for our money," Amazon executive Doug Herrington wrote in an email to colleagues.[19]

When a vendor notified an Amazon manager that the startup

planned to launch another site, called Soap.com, to offer a broader assortment of consumable products, the stakes rose.

"We were gonna beat them or buy them," that manager told me. "They weren't going to win."

Little did anyone know at the time that the ensuing battle would have ramifications on the Amazon/Walmart rivalry for the next decade. And that one of Quidsi's ambitious, risk-taking founders would play a historic role in the battle to come.

JET FUEL

M arc Lore and his cofounder, Vinit Bharara, could not believe what
they were hearing. It was the fall of 2010, and the two entrepreneurs who ran Diapers.com were seated across from a group of irate
Amazon.com executives in a private corner of a trendy restaurant in
New York City's Meatpacking District. On first glance, Lore might
have been confused for a distant cousin or East Coast version of Jeff
Bezos, a business leader he long respected from afar. Both men suffered from male-pattern baldness, which they treated with close buzz
cuts. Each, at that time, also favored a uniform of button-up shirts—
Lore's untucked, while Bezos kept it contained—distressed jeans, and
casual dress shoes. Lore's huskiness and New York–ese accent lent him
a slightly harder edge. The truth, however, was that he was a softie who
avoided discord like he did a normal nine-to-five job.

Lore's cofounder and childhood friend, Bharara, had just returned
to the table from the restaurant's bathroom and a stop at the bar to
grab a glass of prosecco, which he often drank in place of dessert. Bharara then finally built up the courage to share some news he'd been sitting on: a top Walmart executive had phoned the entrepreneurs earlier
in the evening with an offer to buy their startup for around $650 mil-
lion. The problem? The Amazon executives at the table were in town
to finalize their own impending acquisition of Diapers.com and its

parent company, Quidsi—for about $100 million less than Walmart was now offering.

Nine times out of ten, such a decision would be a no-brainer for entrepreneurs on the precipice of their first big payday: take the Walmart money, obviously. But the Amazon executives were not going to make the decision easy. The Amazon team, with tempers perhaps lubricated by an evening's worth of adult beverages, lit into the Quidsi cofounders, suggesting that Amazon would slash prices even further to crush Diapers.com if they accepted Walmart's offer. Amazon had already cut diaper prices by 30 percent in recent months, and now the executives at the table were promising to increase those discounts to insurmountable levels for a startup that was just squeaking out single-digit gross margins on diaper sales, even without a discount.

The next morning, the Amazon execs and the Quidsi cofounders met at the startup's Jersey City, New Jersey, headquarters to continue due diligence in advance of the anticipated closing of the deal. But the events of the prior evening had made an impression. Lore was a highly ambitious entrepreneur, but soft-spoken and conflict-avoidant. To him the dinner-table threats felt like the corporate version of a mafia maneuver: align with us or suffer our wrath. While the Quidsi founders had been left almost speechless by those threats, they shouldn't have been altogether surprised. Lore had long been a student of Amazon and the Bezos way, devouring every one of the company's annual 10-K filings and referring to the Amazon CEO internally as "sensei." Those documents, and insights gleaned by rabid media coverage of the e-commerce giant, told Lore everything he needed to know about Bezos: he was laser-focused on the quickest path to total retail domination. And Lore and Bharara were standing in the way.

In the late 2000s, Diapers.com was a hit in big urban markets like New York City and San Francisco, offering next-day delivery to a new wave of busy working parents who were both digitally savvy and craving convenience. Lore and Bharara knew that fast shipping—within at least two days, as Amazon's Prime service offered—was the key to convincing people to order online rather than making a trip to a nearby store.

In some cities, Diapers.com was beating Amazon on delivery speeds by a full day. Their goal was to break even on diaper sales and then make money on upselling parents on more profitable merchandise like car seats and baby shampoo. But after years of rapid growth, Diapers.com had run into trouble. Threatened by the rising popularity of the upstart diaper website, Amazon executives implemented a lethal attack: a 30 percent price cut on all diapers on the giant e-commerce site. Amazon was willing to lose money on diapers in order to drive a competitor into the ground. The move was ruthless. The move seemed like pure Jeff Bezos.

Amazon's executives knew that Diapers.com was burning cash fast, spending heavily on a successful cocktail of marketing, express delivery, and excellent customer service. And so the price cuts were meant to make life really, really hard for Lore and Bharara. They did. The entrepreneurs were left with a choice: take the risk of spending time trying to secure more capital from venture capital investors—which would be tough under the circumstances—or sell the business to a bigger company before their growth completely stalled. Years later, Lore admitted that the 30 percent price cuts did not feel like normal, above-the-board competition. "It felt very unfair," he told me.

But in late 2010, Lore and Bharara didn't have a ton of options and, for the first time, they were forced to seriously consider selling. They first spoke with Walmart, which had a new e-commerce leader and a renewed desire to make a big splash in the space. Walmart executives in favor of buying the startup loved the fact that Diapers .com had established a real connection with its customers that didn't revolve solely around low prices like Walmart's did. The fact that Lore and Bharara had managed to do this in a category as important to Walmart as diapers and other baby products was a huge plus, too. Of course, the startup's e-commerce technology chops would also be a boon for Walmart, whose technology capabilities trailed Amazon's to an embarrassing degree.

Walmart ended up making an initial lowball offer to buy Quidsi, but it left Lore and Bharara disappointed and determined to get Amazon involved. The pair flew to Seattle to discuss a potential deal with Bezos. A few weeks after the meeting, while Walmart appeared asleep at the wheel, Bezos gave one of his top dealmakers the go-ahead to purchase Quidsi. Amazon ultimately offered to purchase Quidsi in a deal valued at $540 million,[1] and gave the entrepreneurs mere days to sign a letter of intent that would kick off a thirty-day exclusive negotiation period to conduct due diligence and finalize the transaction.

When the Quidsi entrepreneurs notified Walmart of a potential sale to another large retailer that they could not name, the executive who took the call sounded truly stunned, according to a person familiar with the details of the conversation. Shortly after the exclusive negotiating period between Amazon and Quidsi began, Walmart's top e-commerce executive called the entrepreneurs with the $650 million offer on the same day as the fateful New York City dinner. The founders considered bailing on Amazon despite the dinner-table threats, yet they needed assurance from Walmart that the $650 million deal was a sure thing. But when Walmart sent over written deal terms, they contained a clause that gave the retailer an out if there was a material adverse change in Quidsi's business before the transaction was finalized. Basically, the provision gave Walmart the option to back out of the deal if Quidsi's business tanked before the government approved the acquisition. While the clause was standard in M&A agreements, it left just the sliver of doubt needed to help tilt the decision in Amazon's favor. Plus, Lore and Bharara weren't exactly thrilled about the prospect of telling their young coastal staff that they would soon be working for an old-school, Arkansas-based retailer.

What's more, the entrepreneurs weren't willing to find out if Amazon and Bezos's deputies were bluffing on the idea of an all-out price war; they accepted the Amazon offer, giving Bezos a huge victory while crushing the hearts of Walmart leadership. The sale to Amazon made the founders tens of millions apiece and allowed Diapers.com to remain a separate entity with the founders running it, but Lore would later claim that he had felt depressed that Bezos's questionable tactics had succeeded and that Quidsi had sold out. Even so, he and Bharara were still determined to make the most of the opportunity to learn from a company that they had long tracked and, in many ways, still admired. But they never quite fit in at Amazon. Bezos and his executives seemed to have good intentions when they decided to keep Quidsi intact as a stand-alone subsidiary after the sale. But that meant that

Diapers.com continued to compete head-to-head with Amazon even under the same parent organization, and neither side ever truly agreed on the right, differentiated value propositions to customers.

Lore was also miffed when Amazon leadership declined his requests for a substantial marketing budget that he thought necessary to get in front of more young, digital-savvy parents who would help the Quidsi portfolio of shopping websites live up to its full potential. He also struggled to accept the vast chasm between each company's approach to workplace culture. Bezos preached a religion of brutal honesty to his leaders, no matter the impact on personal feelings. Lore, on the other hand, wanted to win, but also liked to be liked—and to make sure others felt appreciated. But that just was never going to be the Amazon way. So, in 2013, less than three years after being acquired by the company, Lore and Bharara left Amazon, and their baby Diapers.com with it.

Months later, my sources began to whisper that Lore was up to something new in e-commerce. "A big swing," as one person described it. Lore wasn't interested in talking, as he made clear to me, politely, when I phoned him for more information, but he promised he would let me know if that changed.

If Costco and Amazon Had a Baby

Lore's new startup would turn out to be Jet.com, an e-commerce firm that raised more than $200 million in venture capital before it even launched to the general public. The Jet model involved online shoppers paying an annual $50 membership fee in exchange for the best prices on the web, across product categories as varied as electronics, toys, and fashion.

"We always said that if Costco and Amazon had a baby, it would be Jet," said Liza Landsman, Jet.com's former chief customer officer, who oversaw marketing, analytics, and the customer experience.

The Jet discounting structure, however, was not simple to implement on the backend nor easy for customers to understand. Some of the savings for customers were supposed to come courtesy of the retailers and brands that sold goods on Jet.com; they'd pay commissions to the startup to list products on the site, and Jet would kick most of those fees back to customers in the form of savings.

Jet also tried to lure shoppers with unconventional methods that would allow them to receive even lower prices: shoppers could earn price cuts if they purchased multiple items in a single order—Jet called this feature the "Smart Cart"—and larger savings if the goods were all shipped from the same warehouse. Jet's executives described these moves as "stripping costs out of the system." In their eyes, these were savings that were hiding in plain sight in the warehousing and shipping operations that powered any online retailer. They believed that if you passed on some of those savings to customers, you could train them to order more items at once, potentially bringing down shipping costs, too.

"It's not like we're smarter with the way we ship stuff," Lore once said.[2] "We're really just exposing the true underlying economics. And when we make that transparent to the consumer in discounts, we're creating in effect more efficient orders."

The savings didn't end there. Shoppers could also earn additional, smaller discounts if they agreed to use a debit card instead of credit, or waived their right to return the item.

Between the savings from the brand commissions that Jet would pass along to customers, plus the "smart cart discounts," the startup estimated the average shopper would save 10 to 15 percent per order, or $150 annually.[3] Building this new type of business model, and recruiting customers who got it, was an uphill battle—and an expensive one. Within months of its launch in 2015, Jet was spending $20 million to $25 million *a month* on advertising, pouring funds into Google search optimization, blanketing buses and subway stops in New York and San Francisco with ads, and even running an expensive national TV campaign. Lore admitted years later that Jet was at one time spending around $40 million a month on marketing.

"We knew we had to get to scale and get to scale fast," he said.

To help attract customers, Jet launched a referral program called Jet Insider that promised 100,000 stock options to the online shopper who courted the most fellow shoppers to sign up for beta access to the site. It worked. At launch, the startup was quickly overwhelmed, in part because of the way it was quietly sourcing inventory behind the scenes. Yes, Jet carried some of its own inventory in its own warehouses—mainly so-called consumable products like cereal, diapers, and shampoo. It also had a small handful of suppliers at launch who were listing products on the shopping site and shipping them to Jet customers themselves.

But about 70 percent of what the startup was selling at launch came directly from other shopping sites. The euphemism that Jet used for this hack was "Jet Concierge," but the startup was simply listing a product on its site that it had no connection to, selling it to a customer, and then ordering the product from a rival to have it shipped directly to Jet customers.

Jet executives thought it was one of the only ways to solve their "cold start" problem until they could attract more selling partners. But in the short term, it made absolutely no financial sense. And it required extra staffing: Jet had a five-hundred-person team of contractors located in the Philippines to help execute these orders from rival sites. But they quickly became overwhelmed when the customer demand far exceeded expectations at launch.

"It was utter chaos," a former executive told me.

If Jet didn't want to disappoint customers, it needed a solution. The company went into triage mode, recruiting and training employees from teams across the company on the right way to place orders from these competitor sites. One former executive told me that about $700,000 of Jet's $1 million in first-day sales came courtesy of this program. And of that $700,000, around $250,000 alone was ordered from a single rival: Walmart.

For the first month following launch, it was all hands on deck. Most teams at Jet were asked to put aside their day jobs and help place orders. The company also bused corporate employees down from the Hoboken, New Jersey, headquarters to the startup's first East Coast warehouse, located in the south New Jersey town of Swedesboro, which did not have enough room or workers to keep up with demand.

"We needed to ship more and couldn't," recalled Joe Gullo, the manager who was hired before launch to run the New Jersey facility. "We were storing items outside during the day. People were working eighteen hours a day. It was, in the truest sense, the startup warehouse nightmare.

"But I was thrilled," he added. "Because up to that point it was unclear if any of it was going to work. Admittedly, though, we were selling people one dollar for eighty cents."

That first summer of 2015, Lore spent a lot of his time doing what he does best: pitching his long-term vision to investors. The pitch went something like this: E-commerce sales in the US only represented around 10 percent of total retail sales, and that percentage was only headed in one direction: up. While Amazon was the clear leader in the space, there was no clear-cut No. 2. Not Walmart, not Target, and not Costco, all of which had long neglected the idea of building a large internet presence. Jet could be that No. 2, and along the way, build a business worth tens of billions of dollars—or more. How would Jet do it? By appealing to shoppers who would rather save money than get every product under the sun from Amazon Prime within a day or two of their order.

Jet's strategy and tactics for creating customer discounts were unique and predicated on the idea that the startup would eventually have enough inventory in enough supplier warehouses that when customers placed large orders, they could be fulfilled out of a single warehouse, bringing packing and shipping costs down. All the startup really needed, Lore stressed repeatedly, was enough advertising money to attract enough customers, which would in turn attract the brands and retailers needed behind the scenes to fulfill the startup's inventory needs and, thus, its discounting strategy.

"It's just math," he would often say. Amazon and Jeff Bezos were famous in business circles for the idea of the flywheel, and Lore believed Jet could create its own, substituting express shipping speeds in exchange for the lowest prices on the web.

With impressive sales numbers after Jet's July launch, Lore received interest from private equity investors with a similar message to the founder: we need you to get bigger, fast.

Lore knew Jet would have to raise hundreds of millions, if not billions more anyway to reach its full potential, so he wanted to take advantage of this opportunity. But that would mean a drastic shift in how quickly the startup's sales would need to grow. Jet execs had been projecting that the startup would hit an annualized run rate of $1 billion in gross sales eighteen months after launch. But because of this investor interest, plus early momentum among customers, Lore slashed that timeline to ten months. Bezos would have been proud.

Around the same time, the startup's investors and executive team began considering a decision that would have seemed foolish just a few months earlier: axing the $50 annual membership fee for Jet customers, which was intended to be the startup's main source of profits as well as a substantial (and steady) revenue stream.

There were a few factors feeding the debate. At the time, Jet was planning to offer customers two buckets of discounts that would total 10 to 15 percent on an average multi-item order. The first bucket offered up-front discounts of around 7 percent on most individual products, which was in essence the reward for the membership fee and a way to lure new shoppers in. But the core of how Jet hoped to set itself apart was its "Smart Cart" savings—discounts of 4 to 5 percent, on the low end, that shoppers earned when they added more products to orders, resulting in more efficient orders for Jet seller partners to fulfill.

In early site tests, Jet executives noticed that when the startup didn't discount individual items off the bat, but just offered customers the Smart Cart savings of, say, 4 to 6 percent, they still completed a purchase at a similar rate as customers who had received both buckets of discounts, totaling 10 to 15 percent. Therefore, they didn't need the original savings of 7 percent that the annual membership was providing for them. There were other factors, too. Many of the retailers and brands that Jet recruited to sell through its new marketplace were intrigued by an alternative to selling on Amazon, but didn't love the perception that Jet was a discount site. Perhaps more importantly, they did not appreciate Jet pricing their merchandise below their desired up-front retail price.

Landsman, the marketing and customer experience chief, had her doubts about the membership shift. Nearly one million people had signed up for Jet's prelaunch waiting list and had just been converted to members on a free trial basis. How would they react to a key change in the Jet value proposition so early on? And could the startup execute the membership about-face before all of those early customers began being charged for the service? Having to issue a rebate to hundreds of thousands of shoppers could be both operationally and optically distracting.

Lore had heard the arguments for and against the membership fee for months and had initially stuck to his gut that the model could work. But as the CEO discussed the topic more with the investors who sat on Jet's board of directors, there was concern that a subscription would cap the company's sales growth and potential valuation. These financial backers were already committed to pumping hundreds of millions, if not billions, into the startup, and so they needed the company to be a colossal home run. Training customers to learn a new way to shop would be hard enough. Add an up-front subscription fee to the equation and that uphill battle looked even steeper.

"You have to sink a serious amount of marketing money in if you're going to steal customers away from someone else," a former Jet.com executive said. "And if you have a membership model, it gets even worse."

Lore knew what it would take to land those private equity investors he'd flirted with over the summer, and it was clear it would be easier to hit the $1 billion sales goal quicker without the membership fee. After listening to all sides, Lore made the call: the membership fee would be sacrificed before it ever saw the light of day.

Still, the decision put Lore and Jet in a precarious position. Without the membership fee, the company was losing its main source of profits. Now the company would have to grow to a massive scale since big online retailers often sell low-priced consumable goods for tiny profits per order. But that's easier said than done: Jet had to convince shoppers who might already be satisfied shopping on Amazon.com or Walmart.com or Target.com to visit Jet.com in the first place. Once they did, they had to hope that Jet's unique discounting structure would be both easy enough to understand and attractive enough to keep customers coming back again and again. Some inside Jet wondered all the while whether Amazon was paying special attention to the young startup.

Turbulence

Less than a week before Jet.com launched in July 2015, Jeff Bezos's company held its first Prime Day—a twenty-four-hour discount extravaganza for its tens of millions of Prime members. Amazon portrayed the event as a celebration of its twentieth anniversary, but some Jet executives wondered if the timing had anything to do with their impending launch. (Former Amazon executives deny it did and, on this, I take them at their word.) Then, shortly after launch, Jet employees watched as Amazon's pricing technology followed Jet prices both up and down. It was not uncommon at the time for Amazon's technology to match major competitors on prices, but a startup that had just hit the scene? That was different. That felt personal.

"That would make sense when we were at a billion [gross merchandise volume], but they did it right out of the gate when we were at $2 GMV," Landsman said. "That did not feel totally programmatic, because there's no point to price-match someone who's not big enough in the market to matter yet."

But inside Amazon, executives noticed the attention Lore was garnering for Jet, even while the shopping site was still in beta.

"Marc was really good for both Quidsi and Jet at getting visibility to what he was doing," said Greg Greeley, the nineteen-year veteran of Amazon and the vice president who oversaw the Amazon Prime program when Jet launched. "Marc had been with us long enough to know we took that pricing very seriously. On the other [hand], maybe he was testing us—how much damage can he inflict and if that was going to help him get more attention."

Indeed, in Jet's first few months of beta testing before its public launch, product pages on Jet featured Amazon's price for the same item to prove that Jet had the lowest price on the web.

"Anyone who is doing that is inviting customers to compare," Greeley continued. "And so by definition, Amazon has no choice but to take that very seriously."

Jet was also trying to overcome another outside force, but this one wasn't a competitor. It was press coverage from the *Wall Street Journal* in 2015 that raised questions about various Jet.com business practices, including a program in which Jet rewarded customers with merchandise credit if they clicked through from Jet.com to buy items on other retail sites. While Lore's ambition, stated goals, and history with Amazon made for a good media narrative, his strong storytelling skills had one flaw.

"You know what Marc is like when he's telling a story—he's all about the narrative arcs and the big picture," a former Jet.com executive said. "But the rounding errors of, 'Is he getting the decimal points and data points exactly right?' He doesn't give a shit about that."

Those traits can give credence to Lore's supporters and critics alike. For his biggest fans, Lore is the visionary and eternal motivator who gets the absolute most out of his employees because he not only paints a picture of an extraordinary future that, together, they can make possible, but has a strong mathematical mind that makes it all seem possible.

"Unlike a lot of pie-in-the-sky founders, he's connected to the numbers," one venture capitalist told me.

And Lore makes people want to believe.

"My grandmother had a saying, roughly translated from Yiddish: 'People who could talk clouds out of the sky,'" Landsman said. "And I always thought this about Marc."

But many in the venture capital industry were skeptical of Lore. One of the reasons, even if investors wouldn't admit it publicly: his background and pedigree did not match those of Silicon Valley legends. Lore never launched a startup in San Francisco, didn't know how to code, nor did he attend Stanford or the Massachusetts Institute of Technology, or drop out of college for that matter. After graduating from college, Bucknell University in Pennsylvania—the first in his family to do so—Lore spent the first few years of his professional life on Wall Street, working in risk management and eventually running himself into the ground in the pursuit of riches.

"My family was full of mercenaries," he said years later. "I didn't know anything else."

His dream was to make six figures by age twenty-six, seven figures by thirty-six, and eight figures by forty-six. He didn't have grand Silicon Valley visions of changing the world—he just wanted enough of a fortune to buy the world. (He achieved the first milestone but, a year later, collapsed at work of exhaustion and figured there had to be a better way. He finally listened to his entrepreneurial intuition and never looked back.)

His parents were twenty-one and twenty, respectively, when they had him, raising him and his two younger siblings first on Staten Island, the least-loved New York City borough, with a large Italian American population, and then New Jersey from middle school on. Lore was broad-shouldered and burly in his Diapers.com years and his look was more distressed denim jeans and shoes than khakis, hoodies, or sneakers. His accent also carried hints of his Staten Island and New Jersey upbringing. The *Wall Street Journal* highlighted this in one of its pieces on Jet.com, which some Jet executives read as a personal dig. The reporter wrote that Lore's "Staten Island, N.Y., roots come through whenever he says 'toilet paper.' (It sounds like 'TAW-let paper.')"

The *Journal*'s coverage of Jet.com was more damaging than that. One of the first pieces focused on the concierge service Jet quietly employed at launch that allowed shoppers to buy products from other retailers while on Jet.com, even when the retailer was not partnering with Jet or even aware that its products were advertised on the marketplace. The article was published two days before Jet's public launch and shined a light on what seemed to be a completely unsustainable model. A few weeks later, the newspaper published another piece, about retailers who were outraged when they learned that Jet was listing them on its shopping site under a so-called affiliate program called Jet Anywhere. The program implied that these retailers and brands were partners of Jet even when they weren't. In fact, Jet simply signed up as an affiliate partner through a third-party company that worked with all types of e-commerce sites.

"That's a no-no," a former e-commerce chief of a large US apparel brand said. "You want to be a partner? Then come to me directly."

Landsman, Jet's former marketing chief, characterized the impact of the *Journal*'s reporting as "catastrophic." Retailers and brands that were once likely to sell on Jet fled for the emergency exits.

"Home Depot knew it was going on, but as soon as that [story] hit, it was, 'We have to stop this,'" according to another former executive referencing the story about Jet's early concierge service. "And that happened over and over again."

Until that point, Home Depot had led some Jet.com executives to believe that they were on board with selling goods through the site. Losing them was a big blow. The company also had serious conversations with Best Buy about funneling some of their listings through Jet.com.

"That was going to be our big electronics source," the former executive said.

But after Lore traveled to meet with Best Buy's then-CEO to try to close the deal, the electronics giant decided against the partnership. Bed Bath & Beyond also balked once the press attention reached a fever pitch. Then there was REI, the outdoor-gear retailer. When its leadership team caught wind of Jet including their logo on its Jet Anywhere page, a top executive insisted on a phone call with Jet. But if a conversation requires two people to talk, this would not be a conversation.

The REI executive "was just nasty, saying, 'I don't know you! Your strategy is all wrong and I'd never ever stoop to your level to work with you!'" the former Jet executive remembered.

REI blasted a message out to a wide range of outdoor brands warning them against working with the nascent startup. Legal warnings rolled in from apparel and fashion brands, too. Jet employees tried to make the most of the opportunity.

"For every one of the letters we got from a brand's legal team, we would reach out to them and tell them we would love to talk," one former Jet employee said. "From that, we'd try to convert them by explaining to them how we work. They became sales leads conversations and we turned a few of these."

When the fiftieth cease-and-desist letter arrived, Jet's general counsel rewarded the employee assigned to respond to it with a celebratory beer.

But the challenges of getting big-name brands and retailers on the marketplace extended beyond the reaction to negative press. Jet executives knew that if they were going to build the Costco for the digital age and beat out Walmart and Target as the No. 2 US e-commerce destination, Jet needed to have the best prices on things people buy repeatedly: consumer goods like toothpaste, toilet paper, and tampons. The startup was okay with losing money on these sales to beat competitors on price, in a move that even Jeff Bezos would have to respect. It also stocked them in its own warehouses so it could guarantee two-day delivery speeds that would be competitive with Amazon Prime. But those bargain-basement prices on consumable goods meant the company needed to make strong profits in other product categories, such as home décor, sporting goods, and apparel.

While some apparel brands did appreciate the appeal of an online marketplace not named Amazon, the idea of having premium apparel sit alongside grocery items or toilet paper on the Jet website was not appealing to many clothing execs. Jet employees pitched brands on having more price control than they would have on Amazon and other marketplaces, as well as visual merchandising capabilities that would better represent their brand than the tech giant could or would. They also tried selling them on the company's unique discounting structure, which in hindsight was probably a mistake when pitching premium apparel or fashion brands that associate discounts with diluting their image.

The team did have some successes though. Getting Cole Haan on board was a coup, even if it took a ton of manual backend work by Jet employees just to get them up and selling on the site. Signing up Yoox, an Italian online retailer of discounted luxury fashion, was also a big win.

Ultimately, though, Jet struggled to get enough attractive apparel and fashion brands on board, and former employees blame that in part on who the core Jet customer was. It also didn't help that other than the two-day-delivery promise on consumables that Jet stored in its own warehouses, deliveries from fashion brands or apparel retailers could take a week or longer to arrive at customer doors when being shipped from their own facilities. Despite what Lore preached publicly about how many online shoppers were willing to wait a while in exchange for discounts, it did not always seem to be true for those purchasing apparel.

Project Cheetah

In the fall of 2015, as Jet's first holiday season approached, the company's future was already being called into question. Executives who commuted from New York City to Jet's modern Hoboken headquarters—a high-rise on the opposite bank of the Hudson River—joked with each other that they should only be buying weekly, instead of monthly, transit passes, seeing as they might not have a job a few weeks later.

As Jet pumped even more money into advertising to boost sales in the early fall, Lore returned to his conversations with the private equity firms he had flirted with during the summer. He was in for an unpleasant surprise. One firm that had verbally agreed to invest $30 million in Jet was now pulling out. Without that investor, the whole funding round was in danger of crumbling. Lore needed to do one of the things he did best, and quickly: he needed to convince other investors to trust him with more money.

That fall, Lore hit the road armed with "simple math," as he put it, and a promise to make it come true: if Jet could just raise enough money over the following years, it could invest more in marketing and reach $20 billion in gross sales by 2020, allowing it to start turning a profit. At one point during this stretch, Lore pulled back-to-back all-nighters, and, on a cross-country flight, his body fought back. The multimillionaire entrepreneur vomited all over his seat.[4] On another occasion, Jet executives arrived at the Hoboken headquarters one morning to find a stubble-faced man stretched horizontally across a bench in a conference room. It was Lore, "fresh" off a red-eye.

But in late 2015, facing down a month or so of cash in the bank,

Lore finally succeeded and secured hundreds of millions of dollars in new investments led by Fidelity, the mutual fund giant.

"You've probably never had the opportunity to see Marc pitch when he's fund-raising, but he's like the equivalent in fund-raising of the Beatles," Landsman said. "I've seen very staid, conservative VCs who, when Marc pitches, turn into gushing schoolgirls."

But the investments couldn't fix Jet's main problems: the company was losing money. Tons of it. And the shopping site didn't have enough repeat customers who were sticking around. For those employees in the know, it was depressing. Lore had been intentional about building a flat and transparent culture at Jet to motivate employees in a way that was the opposite of the "carrot and stick" approach the CEO says he experienced at Amazon after the Quidsi acquisition. Jet did not include standard noncompete clauses in employee contracts, freeing workers to pick up and go work for a competitor if the startup did not live up to its end of the employer-employee bargain. Every Jet employee was paid the same amount for a given position, and all Jet employees had access to an app that divulged the company's top-line financials.

"They did something that no other company had done at the time: complete salary transparency," said a former employee, Marcie Cheung. "I came in as an associate director and I knew that all ADs were paid the same salary; this idea blew my mind and had a huge impact on me."

Despite the transparency and collaborative spirit, by the summer of 2016, some employees who had been with Jet since the earliest days inside its original Montclair, New Jersey, office were growing disillusioned. When Lore gathered the growing company for his regular pep talks, new employees were mesmerized. But some long-haulers rolled their eyes.

"There was a sense of futility," one early employee said years later. "You couldn't stop because if you stopped, everything would fall apart. We ran fast and loose and it was like barreling down a hill at full speed and you couldn't trip. But the music had stopped. In short, the theory wasn't proving out."

The theory, essentially, started with the idea that Jet would attract a big enough collection of brands and retailers to sell on the site that it could use their warehouses to help blanket the country. These selling partners would also set rules on the backend to help Jet's pricing system decide whether to award a certain merchandise sale to them or another merchant, based on factors like the location of the customer placing the order in relation to their warehouse. (In reality, few brands or retailers even had the personnel to handle such a role.) The goal was that Jet would have enough inventory coverage nationwide that when a customer placed a multi-item order, the startup's technology could route it through a single warehouse or a couple of facilities that were located near each other or near the shopper. This would reduce shipping costs, and Jet would reward the customer with discounts.

"I will say I believed in that promise long after I actually should have because the beauty of the simplicity of that idea, and the idea of reengineering the supply chain was really compelling," Landsman, the chief customer officer, said.

The startup did indeed provide discounts as customers added items to their cart. But all too often, the price had little to do with real supply chain savings and was not even correlated with the price at which a brand had agreed to sell an item.

"Practically, the way it worked was we would just take massive losses," a former employee said. "We would have rules that were preset that dictated how the consumer pricing would work. And, on the backend, we'd give it to the best bid we could but it wasn't based on what the retailer was offering. There were many cases where the retailer would come to [the chief revenue officer's] team, and it was, 'I'm the head of e-commerce and my CEO went on your site and ordered something and you guys paid us more than what the customer paid for it.'"

Yet Lore still believed he could build Jet into a stand-alone business. Call it the entrepreneurial distortion field, or call it conviction. Either way, Lore continued to spend considerable time out of the office and on the road, selling his vision to potential partners and investors.

He also looked for ways to bulk up Jet's sales quickly. In March 2016, Jet purchased an e-commerce site called Hayneedle, which was known for selling outdoor and indoor furniture. The site had been around for fourteen years and was doing more than $300 million in annual gross sales, but growth was stagnating and the site was losing money. Jet paid just $90 million for the company, which instantaneously doubled Jet's total gross sales numbers overnight. Even better, while Hayneedle's overall business was unprofitable, almost every product it sold was contribution profit-positive, meaning there was money left over after subtracting variable costs—such as the wholesale cost of an item and the packaging required to ship it—from the sale price. At Jet, on the other hand, executives were starting to feel some heat for selling so many items at a loss.

In the spring of 2016, one of Jet's longtime investors and board members made an introduction to a potential savior: Doug McMillon, Walmart's CEO. McMillon had taken over as chief executive in 2014, several years after Lore had spurned the retail giant's offer to buy Quidsi, so they didn't know each other. The two sat down for a meeting inside the Quail Room, the conference room at Walmart's home office adorned with Sam Walton's quail-hunting photos. At first the discussion focused on a possible investment; Lore was adamant that if Jet was able to keep raising new funds, and pump them into giant ad campaigns, enough customers would end up sticking with Jet and its discounts that the math would eventually work itself out.

That June, leaders at Jet's New Jersey warehouse were instructed to prepare the facility for a special visit, with no hint as to who would be walking in the door. On the day of the tour, Lore arrived at the warehouse accompanied by a group of Walmart executives. As Jet leaders led the group through the massive facility, showing off the startup's processes and efficiency, one of the Walmart leaders broke off from the pack. Jet employees, communicating across the warehouse on walkie-talkies, eventually tracked him down in an unexpected spot.

"We shipped a lot of adult products like [sex] toys and had them sequestered in a cage, because they were also high-theft," Gullo, the warehouse leader, said. "And Walmart did not sell that type of stuff. We found him in there just looking around."

This one difference between Walmart and Jet would be a precursor of more dramatic cultural differences that would eventually emerge. Still, Lore and McMillon clicked right away, but the Walmart leadership team didn't want a potential deal to be a normal venture capital-like

cash-for-equity arrangement. The brick-and-mortar titan offered to secure lower shipping rates for Jet from FedEx, since the retailer did so
much business with the giant shipping carrier. Walmart later offered
to also help Jet get lower wholesale costs on inventory purchased from
Unilever, the massive consumer packaged goods company. This kind of
inducement happened several times, until McMillon floated a more
straightforward deal: buying Jet outright.

At Walmart, McMillon knew his company had to do something
drastic, and fast. So did Greg Penner, the former venture capitalist who
had married into the Walton family and encouraged company leaders
to embrace e-commerce in the early days. Penner had risen to the
Walmart chairman role in 2015, taking over for his father-in-law, Rob
Walton. Without Penner's endorsement, the pursuit of Jet probably
wouldn't have gone anywhere. While a CEO like Bezos might be able
to push through a deal that his board members weren't fond of because of his founder clout or the fact that he also held the chairman
role, the dynamic was much different at Walmart.

"We've had a great tradition of our chairmen working closely with
the CEO," Penner has said.[5] "So my office in Arkansas is right next to
[McMillon's], and he and I talk every day. I tend to play a more active
role, probably, than most chairmen."

The uphill battle facing Walmart was plain to see for both leaders, as
well as for Lori Flees, Walmart's head of corporate development. When
Flees arrived at Walmart, the retailer's online business accounted for
less than 3 percent of total e-commerce sales in the US, compared
to Amazon's 33 percent. Moreover, its trajectory was pointing in the
wrong direction, with revenue growth decelerating quarter after quarter, while consumer spending online was heading in the other direction. Plus, Walmart was actually losing market share in the US in
online and store sales combined—something that Flees found many
company leaders weren't aware of, because they were used to operating
in their own silos. Flees, a no-nonsense longtime strategy consultant
who went to Harvard for her MBA and played on the club ice hockey
team there, believed that something drastic needed to be done. Inside
Walmart, the plan to acquire Jet was first referred to by the code name
Project Cheetah.

"The whole thesis was it would make us faster," Flees, who oversaw mergers and acquisitions, told me. "My response was always, 'If we don't do this, what are we going to do to go faster?'"

In Lore, you could imagine McMillon squinting and seeing a version of a modern-day Sam Walton, an entrepreneur who wanted to find new ways to save money for customers every single day. Mc-Millon also knew the credibility that Lore had developed within the e-commerce community. With him at Walmart, a halo effect could attract fresh technical talent, filling the retail giant's e-commerce division with new life and energy. It would also serve as a declaration to Wall Street investors that the brick-and-mortar giant was *finally* taking its digital future seriously.

Also, by then it was unclear whether Walmart's current global e-commerce chief, Neil Ashe, was ever going to be the leader to make a dent in Amazon's widening lead in online sales. Ashe was hired in 2012, two years before McMillon became Walmart CEO, and had been a longtime executive in digital media, not e-commerce or retail, when he got the job. The head of the most important future sales channel for the world's largest retailer hadn't led a large e-commerce operation before.

On the other hand, Lore had spent the last fifteen years living and breathing e-commerce. What's more, Lore almost joined Walmart when the giant retailer made the bid for Quidsi a few years earlier, before Amazon swept in to steal the deal. Lore also knew Amazon from the inside out. For Lore, the question this time around of whether to sell Jet.com to Walmart was easier to answer than it had been the first time, back in the Diapers.com days. Would he rather spend the next couple of years on a fund-raising treadmill for the small chance that Jet could become the next great independent titan of retail? Or should he tap into Walmart's cash machine, leverage its huge store network to bolster online delivery, and make enough money along the way that his great-grandchildren's great-grandchildren couldn't create a financial worry for themselves even if they tried?

"It was like we were fighting this war but, all of a sudden, you get the allies' planes and tanks to back you up," Lore recounted years later.

Lore was interested, but he knew McMillon might need to sell his board of directors on the deal, in part because of how expensive it would be. So Lore went into salesman mode—but with a slightly different tack. He combed through every available annual report that Walmart had published since going public, and wove his learnings about Sam Walton's innovative ways across a PowerPoint presentation that he voiced over to present his vision for what his company and Walmart could accomplish together.

"I knew at the time that I was a big part of the acquisition . . . but I wanted them to know that I [also] had a big vision for how Jet and Walmart could merge together and really make a formidable run at Amazon," Lore said.

The pitch seemed to work, and Walmart board members supported the deal.

"I thought it was a great idea because it felt like we were flailing to some degree," said Linda Wolf, the former CEO of the ad agency Leo Burnett who served on Walmart's board for more than a decade. "And we really needed strong leadership."

Unlike with the Quidsi acquisition talks year earlier, the negotiations with Walmart this time were fast and furious, though a media leak may have helped move things along. On the morning of Wednesday, August 3, 2016, negotiations were still ongoing when the *Wall Street Journal* reported that Walmart was in talks to purchase Jet.[6] Landsman and other Jet executives were scheduled to spend that day slotting all of Jet's employees into the right corporate compensation categories at Walmart. The setting was the executive's Manhattan loft apartment so no leaders would be late to a small party Landsman was hosting on her roof deck that evening for the startup's summer interns. While the execs scrambled to complete the task, Lore locked himself in one of the only private empty spaces in Landsman's loft: the bedroom of Landsman's then fifteen-year-old daughter. There, Lore cemented the final details of the acquisition over the phone with Walmart's CEO.

Though the negotiations moved quickly, there were complications. One of Walmart's stipulations was that Jet stop selling top consumable products—items like toothpaste and packaged snacks—below the price of the same items on Walmart.com and, most importantly, those in Walmart stores. As a result, Jet leaders had to craft countless different permutations of future business projections for Jet.com based on different pricing and marketing adjustments.

On Sunday night, August 7, I broke the news that Walmart would announce its $3 billion acquisition of Jet.com the following morning.[7] Lore would be named the CEO of Walmart's US e-commerce business. The next morning, Walmart made it official. The world's largest retailer was staging the largest e-commerce acquisition ever, paying $3.3 billion for a cash-burning, wobbly operation that was barely a year old.

No matter. When the deal was finalized that September, McMillon had gotten his man. And Lore was about to secure a war chest large enough to take another crack at Amazon—and Jeff Bezos.

HOMETOWN BOY

Long before Doug McMillon recruited Marc Lore to force Walmart out of its comfort zone, the Walmart CEO had to learn to do the same to himself. In the 1990s, McMillon, then a young merchandising leader, met with his boss and longtime Walmart merchandising exec, Don Harris, to fill him in on a potential deal with Disney that he was about to sign. Harris was a Walmart lifer or, in his own words, a "Walmart brat," whose father, Claude, was Walmart's first buyer and a member of the company's executive leadership team alongside Sam Walton. The younger Harris would follow in his father's footsteps and go on to serve on the executive committee as well.

Back when McMillon first joined Walmart as part of a leadership training program, the younger Harris, a senior buyer at the time, was asked to show McMillon the ropes—choosing what products Walmart should sell in its stores, starting with the seasonal candy category. Though McMillon was hand-selected for the program, his earnestness and eagerness shone through immediately.

"There are times when you meet people who just get it," Harris recalled. "He was completely unflappable, completely humble, didn't come in thinking he was hot stuff or walking with any kind of strut."

Years later, Harris found himself working alongside McMillon again, this time as his boss. Harris was the executive vice president overseeing Walmart's entire general merchandise business; McMillon ran the largest product division for Harris, overseeing toys, electronics, and sporting goods. On this day, McMillon was briefing Harris on a big deal he was about to ink with Disney. Under the terms of the agreement, Walmart would get its hands on some of Disney's most popular movie inventory, but there was a catch: the brick-and-mortar retailer would have to carry some of Disney's less popular titles as well.

By then McMillon had developed a favorable reputation among big Walmart suppliers for being more amenable to win-win negotiations than his cutthroat predecessors had been. "He realized that in order for something to be good for Walmart, it helps if the other guy is also happy," Moe Nozari, a former top executive for 3M, the parent company of Ace bandages and Scotch tape, told me. So to McMillon, naturally, the Disney agreement seemed like a good one. Both sides were getting what they wanted, after all.

But while Harris had long been an admirer and internal champion for the younger McMillon, he couldn't have disagreed more with the terms that McMillon was about to agree to.

"'I thought our job was to buy an assortment of goods that customers *want*,'" Harris recalled, decades later, having told McMillon. "'I mean, seriously, you're gonna allow them to dump their warehouse on you? I don't care if they give it to T.J. Maxx or somebody. But when did we start buying stuff that we know customers don't want?'"

Seated across from McMillon in 2022 inside the same wood-paneled office that each of his predecessors once inhabited, the CEO chuckled as I brought up this flaw, if you could call it that, of niceness.

"I still like to think I'm a nice person," McMillon told me, flashing his down-home, "Please, after you," smile, yet not disagreeing with Harris's assessment. "But I was criticized for that in the beginning."

McMillon has come a long way since then, in more ways than one. When I met him inside Walmart's squat brick home office on a sunny 70-degree late winter morning, the CEO was dressed in an ensemble more reminiscent of a New York creative agency leader than the chief executive of a retailer that has become a symbol of America's working class. He sported an untucked but crisp white button-down shirt, tailored navy-blue chinos, and black suede sneakers from the Los

Angeles designer James Perse that retail for $395. An Apple Watch adorned his left wrist, and a Tesla, I had been told, was his vehicle of choice. The idea of McMillon holding the same role as a predecessor known for driving a dilapidated pickup truck and donning trucker hats could understandably seem downright laughable.

But contradictions like these partly explained why the Walton family and Walmart's board chose McMillon to replace his predecessor, Mike Duke. The new CEO needed to lead the company through a period of necessary, if not desperate, transformation as Amazon continued to suck up market share, talent, and consumer adoration. To thrive, Walmart needed to head in a much different direction, and McMillon personified an intoxicating mixture of Walmart DNA and higher-minded ambition.

"We needed a forty-something CEO with a tech bias because Mike wasn't the right guy for where we needed to go," Don Harris told me. "Nothing against Mike; I love him to this day. But it was time."

If you were to artificially concoct a company ambassador for a powerful, yet controversial and floundering, titan of American capitalism, Walmart could have done a lot worse than McMillon. At six foot two, with a short salt-and-pepper cut, he looked like he could have played Coach Taylor in *Friday Night Lights*, if acting had been his thing years earlier. When he spoke, it was hard to imagine him capable of raising his voice much above what was necessary for a "Dinner's ready!" invitation to the kids. His temperament was that of someone who wouldn't hesitate to inform a stranger that a sliver of spinach was wedged between their two front teeth, but somehow do it in a way that didn't make them yearn for a sinkhole to swallow them up whole. Plus, for Bentonville long-timers, his religious beliefs seemed like icing on the cake.

"Great faith. Great grace. Very Christian young man," was how Burt Stacy, who ran the Bank of Bentonville when McMillon was a summer intern in the 1980s, partly described the Walmart CEO.

To those whose universe centers in northwest Arkansas, McMillon was the model of a company golden boy, and one tasked with resurrecting his lifelong employer from a long, dark hour.

What Would Sam Do?

The Walton family placed myriad challenges in front of McMillon when he became Walmart's fifth CEO in 2014 at the age of forty-seven, the youngest Walmart chief executive since Sam Walton himself. Striking the balance of investing in the low-profit future of Walmart e-commerce while nurturing the profit-boasting store business that employed more people than any other retailer, was at the top of the list.

But Walmart's—and thus McMillon's—hurdles extended far beyond that. How do you mesh the best of the low-key, sweat-the-details, hit-your-numbers Bentonville belief system with the flashy, shoot-for-the-moon ambition of those tech startup folks? How do you move a highly successful—and immensely prideful—organization further away from a top-down, centralized, decision-by-committee structure and more toward a mindset where small teams are empowered to imagine, and act on, new visions of what the Walmart of the future should be? How do you achieve buy-in from both old-school and new-school leaders on a unified path forward when their incentives are divergent? How do you jump-start sales momentum in your gargantuan store network that has been stagnating for too long while winning back in-store shoppers from rivals like dollar-store chains and other discounter competitors? And how do you convince Wall Street investors that they should stick along for the ride, even though your stock price increase over the prior five years was only half of the S&P 500's?

The issues McMillon faced also extended outside US borders. McMillon inherited federal investigations into allegations that Walmart intermediaries in Mexico, India, Brazil, and China were guilty of bribery on behalf of the retail giant's foreign subsidiaries. (The company paid $282 million in a settlement five years after McMillon became chief executive. The CEO ran the company's international division during some of the alleged misconduct but was never personally implicated in wrongdoing.)[1] And in the promising market of India, where Jeff Bezos and Amazon were announcing billions in investments, Walmart had just abandoned plans to open retail stores because of government regulation. McMillon was being offered the opportunity of many lifetimes with the CEO appointment, but there was a catch. Many catches, in fact.

"The startup thing sounds cool to me, but I haven't heard one yet that is more challenging than what we're trying to do," McMillon told an audience of Stanford Graduate School of Business students in 2015. "I mean, if you want hard, try to take a fifty-two-year-old business that's at this size and change it. That's hard. And it's worthy. I mean, creating a situation where 2.2 million people stay employed, and have a life. That's a big deal."

Of course, there were many reasons why the Walton family had entrusted McMillon as the steward of Sam Walton's empire, of which the family continues to own around 50 percent. It starts with McMillon's almost-too-good-to-be-true, Bentonville-centric backstory.

Born Carl Douglas McMillon in 1966, the future CEO moved to Bentonville from Jonesboro, Arkansas, when he was sixteen. A noncompete agreement had forced his father to relocate the family to set up a new dental practice.[2] McMillon knew next to nothing about Bentonville, which sits about six hours east of Jonesboro, where his parents had raised him and a younger sister up to that point (a younger brother was born after the family's move to Bentonville). But on a trip to break the news about the move to his then-girlfriend, her father predicted what would be in store for the youngster.

"You're gonna end up working for Sam Walton."

"And I said, 'Who?'" McMillon recalled years later.

"You shop at Walmart, don't you?" the father asked.

"Yeah."

"Well, you're gonna end up working for that company because that's all there is in Bentonville," his soon-to-be ex's dad predicted.[3]

Sure enough, McMillon spent the summers before and after his senior year of high school loading and unloading boxes at the local Walmart distribution center, making $6.50 an hour, which was at least a better wage than the town McDonald's was offering at the time. The work was bumpy from the start, literally; McMillon rear-ended his boss's car the first day on the job. (As he later told it,[4] the teenage McMillon was following behind his boss in his old Honda Civic and accidentally accelerated at a stop sign while reaching to turn down the volume on a boom box.)

When he wasn't in class or playing real-life bumper cars with his superiors, McMillon played point guard for the Bentonville High basketball team, sharing a love for the sport that his father, Dr. Morris McMillon, instilled in him. The eldest McMillon ran a weekly pickup game nearly every Sunday afternoon for almost forty years[5] before his death on Thanksgiving Eve 2020, just seven months after he was diagnosed with a brain tumor.[6]

"Glioblastoma is undefeated, so you know what the outcome is gonna be," McMillon told me, his eyes welling, composing himself for seven seconds that felt like seven minutes, before responding.

In his final months, the elder McMillon stressed to his family the service aspect of the life he lived.

"Some dentists make a lot of money," McMillon said. "If you study Dad, Dad didn't make a lot of money. And he's like, 'I just felt like I couldn't overprice them.' So he had a life of service that became even more clear to all of us through that process. He's buried over here in the cemetery, not far from Sam Walton. When I drop by there, which is frequently, and think about them, that service aspect—are you *helping* people today?—is what hits me."

After high school, McMillon attended the University of Arkansas, in Fayetteville, just a half hour's drive south of his new home in Bentonville. He worked at the Bank of Bentonville during summers, where he met his future wife, Shelley. On one Fourth of July during this time, the bank's president, Burt Stacy, the best friend of Walmart's second CEO, David Glass, asked McMillon to dress up like Uncle Sam for the festivities. Sure enough, McMillon donned a red-white-and-blue top hat, matching wide-legged pants, and a blue tailcoat, and greeted folks outside the bank's entrance, where popcorn was being handed out for free.

"Someone asked me what I was doing," McMillon would tell Stacy years later, "and I told them, 'I was doing what I was told to do.'"

After graduating with an accounting degree in 1989, McMillon pursued an MBA at the University of Tulsa. Between the first and second years of the two-year program, the story goes, he phoned Walmart executive Bill Fields to accept an offer for a buyer-trainee program at the company. Fields told him there was a job for him right away as an assistant manager at a Walmart store right there in Tulsa. Despite fears of how he would juggle his second year of school with the job, McMillon wasn't going to pass up the opportunity and made it work.[7] It was the beginning of a trend.

The first day on the job, McMillon found a Post-it note amid a pile of paperwork, showing the price of Walmart fishing line alongside a lower price next to the name "Kmart." In his telling, the note was from Sam Walton himself, who had retired as CEO in 1988 and would die in 1992 from multiple myeloma, a blood cancer.

A series of promotions over the next decade would follow. The main thread tying them together? You could call it overachieving, or butt-kissing. McMillon called it volunteering.

"When there was a project or my boss was out of town and somebody needed to go to a meeting," he told Duke University graduate students in 2016,[8] "I would say, 'I'll go.'

"I would find myself in these situations where sometimes I didn't always know the answer [but] I got comfortable, as we're encouraged to at Walmart, in saying, 'I don't know, but I'll find out and I'll get back to you quickly," McMillon added. "It's a good formula for success inside our company. So, people saw me handling a responsibility one level up, which made it easy for them to promote me."

McMillon was also unwaveringly curious, and a true lover of the retail trade. Don Harris, the longtime Walmart merchandising executive, said he could quickly tell that for his understudy, "the notion of buying and selling merchandise at a profit was something that was fun.

"If you don't have that gene," he added, "it's really hard to enjoy the business."

When he was just thirty-nine, in 2005, Walmart named McMillon CEO of Sam's Club, the Costco rival named after Sam Walton. To Walmart insiders with ambition of their own, it sure seemed like the Walton family was turning the company into McMillon's personal IDP, as it was known internally—an Individual Development Plan. Sure enough, four years later, in 2009, McMillon was appointed to the top Walmart role responsible for the company's businesses abroad, as CEO of Walmart International, where he was exposed to both the immense opportunity and humbling complexity of the next great retail markets of China and India.

That exposure, even if helmed from an office in Arkansas, was one key reason some powerful company voices were confident he could navigate the flurry of change threatening the retailer's future.

"I told the board that I thought that he would be the best CEO since Sam," Lee Scott, who served nine years as Walmart's third chief executive, told *Fortune* magazine in 2015.[9] "I think he's prepared so much better than we were. And his view of the world, his understanding of the context of Walmart within that world, his age and youth in an environment that's changing so quickly—all of that I think is going to give him more energy to embrace change rather than try to simply cope with change."

His charm and friendliness are said to have been another factor in the Waltons choosing him as Duke's successor. Kathryn McLay, the CEO of Sam's Club and, according to some insiders, a dark-horse candidate out of three potential successors to McMillon, told me that the CEO is "extraordinarily personable." If there were such a grading system, McMillon would likely score an A+ when it comes to what Walmart refers to as CBWA, or Coaching By Walking Around. His memory of faces, names, and stories, up and down the hierarchy of Walmart staff, is literally unbelievable to many. Even from his elevated perch, he was seen as a listener who talks *with* people, not down at them.

Kevin Systrom, the cofounder and former CEO of Instagram, who served on Walmart's board from 2014 to 2018, once referred to McMillon as "intensely friendly," adding that he had never met another business leader in Silicon Valley or afar who matched the depth of friendliness in the Walmart CEO. Jeff Bezos, McMillon was not.

"Intensely friendly in the sense that his focus is on *you*, like there's no other thing going on in his mind when he's talking to you," Systrom said.[10] "He's not distracted. He's not thinking about a meeting he has next. He's one hundred percent focused on you."

That attention and charisma extended to larger group settings. Talk to enough Walmart veterans and you're bound to come across many who bring up McMillon's world-class orator skills. One former Walmart corporate manager compared his speaking ability to "early Barack Obama level."

Scott Hilton, a former Jet and Walmart.com executive, said that while he and other leaders might nail 60 percent of a presentation, even with a teleprompter, McMillon could recite an entire talk without even a glance at a screen, sometimes with just a single once-over of a script beforehand. McMillon chalked up his oration skills to often being put on the spot for answers in Friday afternoon executive meetings as an up-and-coming company leader.

"A little bit of training years ago, but not much," McMillon said in our 2022 discussion. "Just at-bats."

"I used to always say 'Doug should be president,'" said Jenny Fleiss, cofounder of Rent the Runway, whom Marc Lore would hire at Walmart to incubate and run a Walmart-owned startup called Jetblack.

Moe Nozari, the former top executive at 3M, was not at all joking when he told me in early 2022: "I wish he was the president right now. Doug's extremely charismatic and he has a high level of intellect that doesn't rub people the wrong way." (Later, McMillon shook his head side to side before I could even finish my query about potential interest in running for public office. "I don't see that," he said. "That doesn't look like a very fun process.")

McMillon's skill set was why it was so frustrating to many internally who believed that Walmart didn't take advantage of the CEO's abilities enough. Instead, inside the Bentonville home office, new e-commerce hires were shocked to discover just how often Sam Walton still came up in conversations and meetings, nearly two decades after his death.

"Someone said, 'What would Sam do?' and I looked around and it wasn't a joke," one former e-commerce manager told me.

But the "What would Sam do?" mindset is not all that surprising when you consider what longtime employees have been staring at every single workday for several decades in some cases. Photos of Walton—and quotes attributed to him—adorn Walmart walls both inside and outside the home office. In the early 2000s, the level of

Walton adulation was even shocking to a group of Russian software engineers, who had joined Walmart in a dot-com acquisition.

"They saw these pictures of Sam Walton everywhere and were like, 'This feels like Russia, with big pictures of Russian leaders,'" a Walmart employee from the time told me.

Even McMillon himself has poked gentle fun at the adoration, once telling a reporter, "Sometimes I wonder if he really said all that stuff," as the duo passed a sign inside a Walmart warehouse that featured a quote attributed to the founder.[11]

But years later, in our sit-down interview, McMillon still maintained that all the Walton talk has a forward-looking purpose—a crucial one.

"The reason that we should still talk about Sam Walton is because of the characteristics that he had; it's not about hero worship or being too stuck in the past," McMillon told me. "It's about servant leadership works. Listening to associates, having a sense of urgency, some of the things like the Sundown Rule." (The Sundown Rule is the directive that Walmart employees should respond to any customer or vendor request or complaint by the end of the day it is received.)

"Being authentic and human and treating customers in a way like you'd want to be treated," McMillon continued. "Those values are timeless, and they still work."

Of course, it's fair to wonder what else the company's biggest cheer-leader was supposed to say. McMillon never did actually work for Walton, unless you wanted to count those summer gigs as a high school student. McMillon's first full-time job at Walmart, as the assistant store manager in Tulsa, began the year after Walton handed the CEO role to David Glass. You could imagine that fact might release a leader, even subconsciously, from some of the mental shackles that could have influenced McMillon's CEO predecessors to not stray too far afield from a future Walmart that Walton may have himself wanted.

Yet, even several years after McMillon moved into the CEO office that Walton himself once inhabited, the refrain of "What would Sam do?" remained—bafflingly, to some—alive inside Walmart headquarters.

"You have Doug, a very charismatic guy, living in a modern era," a

former Walmart executive told me, his voice pregnant with exaspera-
tion. "If you're a modern company, you really need to shift off of what
Sam said. I get it—Sam was an iconic leader; Sam wrote the book. But
Sam is dead."

Social Capital

In the summer of 2016, Americans across the country got an up-close
introduction to Doug McMillon even if they couldn't previously tell
his face from the neighbor down the street's. The CEO starred in a
thirty-second commercial that ran for three months on TV and social
media and was a first for a Walmart chief executive.

"I'm Doug," he says, looking directly into the camera as he stands in
front of a Supercenter produce section. "Here at Walmart, we're committed to taking care of the people who take care of you."

McMillon highlighted a $2.7 billion investment the company had
recently announced focused on training its store workforce and improving minimum hourly wages for its workers, first to $9 an hour, and
then $10 the year after that. Still, at $9 an hour, store workers would
have to log more than 1,000 hours of work to take home what Mc-
Millon earned in a *single hour* at the time.[12] No critic was arguing that
workers stocking shelves should get pay equal to that of the executive
responsible for making decisions that impact more than 2 million
employees and hundreds of millions of customers. But that outrageous
a disparity certainly called into question the authenticity of the company's "servant leadership" mantra, no matter how kind McMillon appeared to be.

"The amount of money that Doug McMillon makes is outrageous
compared to what workers are getting paid in stores," Cynthia Murray,
a Walmart store worker of twenty-two years and a leader with the
worker organizing group United for Respect, told me in 2022.

Back in 2016, McMillon's debut TV ad gave a glimpse of his Instagram account, where the CEO—with the help of his staff—features
frontline staff he meets on regular visits to company stores across the
country.

"I grew up in Walmart, I am a product of Walmart, I am proud of Walmart," McMillon once told a student audience.[13] "And I understand Walmart in a way that those of you that don't work there don't."

By the time he took over as CEO, Walmart was already nearly a decade into a reputation makeover. For much of the 1990s and early 2000s, Walmart was viewed as the big, bad bully of retail, known for cutthroat negotiations with brands that forced more US manufacturing jobs to China, resulting in bargain-basement prices that were great for consumers but terrible for vendors and the Main Street shops unable to match them. Critics also targeted the company for its low wages, anti-union stance, and environmental impact. Walmart found itself at the center of an especially embarrassing firestorm over a company policy that essentially locked in store employees who worked overnight shifts.[14]

But under former Walmart CEO Lee Scott, the executive team reached a point in the mid-2000s where it decided to no longer ignore or roundly dismiss its critics, and instead underwent a wide-reaching listening tour—a shrewd but wise approach that Amazon still hadn't adopted more than a decade later as scrutiny of its own labor and business practices mounted.

"You might be surprised about what we heard," Scott said in a 2005 speech.[15] "Many of these individuals and groups see things differently than we do, but they also have ideas. In fact, many of our most vocal critics do not want us to stop doing business, but they feel business needs to change, not just our company, but all companies."

It was an awakening, albeit a self-serving one. And, according to McMillon, it started with a natural disaster. A month before Scott's talk, Hurricane Katrina had struck New Orleans, killing more than 1,800 people in Louisiana,[16] plus hundreds more throughout the Gulf Coast, and displacing more than a million others. On a conference call with Walmart executives days later, as the business leaders watched news coverage of the desperate conditions of those who survived, Scott recommended a new approach to his leadership team.

"'What if, instead of doing the things we just kind of habitually do that may help a little bit, we recognize how significant this problem is and we just throw everything we've got at it,'" McMillon recalled Lee saying years later, pointing to the call as an inflection point for Walmart as a corporate citizen.[17] "We decided to do that, and we stopped counting what we were sending, and we sent not only goods but we sent a lot of money and we sent our people."

Less than a year later, Walmart hired a former adviser to President Bill Clinton, Leslie Dach, to help remake the company's image—not merely through PR campaigns but with bold new business practices that, at Walmart's size, could have real impact. The company, for the first time, set large renewable energy goals and, in 2011, committed to source $20 billion in products for its US stores from women-owned businesses over five years.

The changes in mindset and actions took years. Top leaders had to reverse their thinking about ignoring the opinions of outsiders who didn't know their intentions. That view could be traced all the way back to Sam Walton himself. But Walmart emerged from Dach's tenure with a much better public image than when he joined. In 2007, Walmart had a score of –5 on a scale of –100 to +100 of YouGov's BrandIndex Buzz, according to the *New York Times*.[18] When Walmart announced Dach's departure in 2013, that number had risen to around 10, "in line with the discount retail industry as a whole," the *Times* reported.

Yet there were two significant areas where Walmart did not accomplish what Dach had hoped during his time at the company: wages, and guns. Following Dach's departure, McMillon decided to make big moves in those areas, even if they were more reactionary than progressive, with some critics and many employees still labeling them as insufficient.

On wages, McMillon and his US stores CEO, Greg Foran, recognized that if they were going to limit employee turnover and improve the customer shopping experience, they had to increase pay. But by the time Amazon raised the bar with a $15 minimum hourly wage announcement in the fall of 2018, Walmart was still only offering $11 an hour to its lowest-paid workers.

On guns, Walmart removed assault-style rifles like AR-15s from its

US stores in the summer of 2015. A company spokesman at the time said the move was made because of waning consumer interest, not the national gun debate. But gun control activists were nonetheless pleased by the move.

In 2018, Walmart stopped selling guns and ammunition to customers under the age of twenty-one. A year later, shortly after a gunman killed nearly two dozen at a Walmart store in El Paso, Texas, McMillon announced that the company would curtail selling the type of ammunition used in the assault rifle at the massacre, as well as all handgun ammunition. Walmart was one of the largest sellers of ammunition in the US at the time, and the company said they expected the decisions to cut their market share in the space from 20 percent to as low as 6 percent.[19]

The move was met with strong criticism from gun supporters but McMillon must have understood the trade-off. While Walmart long carried a reputation for serving rural communities where gun control policies were unpopular, the CEO had to know that the company's ambition in e-commerce meant it would attract more customers from bluer states, where support for gun control runs high. With the acquisition of Jet in the New York City area, and Walmart's longstanding e-commerce outpost in Northern California, Walmart's employee base was also evolving in a left-leaning way. If McMillon wasn't going to take a stand after a massacre in one of his own stores, when would he? Plus, McMillon already had enough corporate problems to deal with.

The Amazon Dilemma

Of the many corporate dilemmas that Walmart faced under McMillon, the decision about when to chase Amazon from behind versus when to chart its own path was a consistent topic of debate. The first step, of course, was acknowledging that Amazon was a problem to begin with.

In September 2009, five years before McMillon became Walmart

CEO, the *New York Times* published a feature story about Amazon with the headline "Can Amazon Be the Wal-Mart of the Web?"[20] The story, and its title, did not go unnoticed at Walmart. The CEO of Walmart.com at the time, Raul Vazquez, snapped back in a subsequent interview with the *Wall Street Journal*, "If there is going to be a 'Wal-Mart of the Web,' it is going to be Walmart.com."

By the time McMillon took over in 2014, Amazon had made it clear that *it* was indeed the Walmart of the Web. And then some. Rather than deny Amazon's success, or ignore it, McMillon, a self-proclaimed "gadget geek" who was an early adopter of the Apple Newton and the Palm Pilot,[21] showed some admiration for what Bezos and company had built.

On one of his first days as CEO, McMillon joined a longtime Walmart truck driver named Ricky Oliver on a haul from a Walmart warehouse in Mississippi to one of its stores three and a half hours across the state.[22] The driver was candid with McMillon about where Walmart.com was lacking in comparison to Amazon, and the new CEO was receptive in receiving the criticism. At the end of the chat, McMillon told Oliver that he would soon send him a book that had been published just that fall: *The Everything Store*, by the journalist Brad Stone, part biography of Jeff Bezos and part exploration of Amazon's ascent. McMillon also gave a copy to each of his company officers after he was promoted to CEO. McMillon was not shying away from Amazon's impact.

"Clearly, Amazon is teaching the world what's possible," McMillon told one interviewer that same year.[23]

Still, McMillon balanced that reality with a healthy dose of confidence in Walmart's ability to fight back. Take, for example, a meeting I learned about in the course of reporting for this book. Shortly after McMillon took over as CEO in 2014, he paid a visit to Google cofounder and CEO Larry Page, and a few other executives from the tech giant, on one of his pilgrimages to Silicon Valley. Despite significant cultural and business model differences, Google and Walmart had one big reason to work closely together: a shared rival in Amazon. (Amazon was Walmart's rival for obvious reasons, but the threat to Google was not as clear to many outsiders just yet. "Many people think our main competition is Bing or Yahoo," Google chairman Eric Schmidt said in a speech in Europe that year. "But, really, our biggest search competitor is Amazon.")

During the meeting, Page was straight with McMillon about his business worldview, according to people familiar with the discussion: Traditional companies like Walmart had no realistic chance at a successful enough pivot to the digital world to take on an internet giant like Amazon. Especially not on their own. They needed a Silicon Valley savior like Google to give them even a fighting chance. One person I spoke with told me that this was just Larry being Larry; he had no intent to disparage Walmart or to insult McMillon, and this was the same version of a sales pitch he gave to many corporate titans of yesteryear; he was just telling it like he saw it.

But another person privy to the conversation told me that Page's remarks went over with McMillon as well as gun control proposals do with the National Rifle Association. It was at that point that Walmart stopped considering partnering with Google on a cloud-computing deal, this person told me. What's more, the two companies, despite the common threat that Amazon posed to their futures, would not partner in any significant way for several years, until well after Walmart's Jet acquisition.

The following year, on a call with Wall Street stock analysts, McMillon made a more public proclamation that seemed to highlight his view of Walmart's chances to overcome Amazon.

"Is it easier for an e-commerce company to build out a massive store network and create a customer service culture at scale?" McMillon asked rhetorically. "Or are we better able to add digital and supply chain capabilities and leverage our existing stores? We like our chances."

Internally, however, McMillon took a different tact at times. On several occasions over the years, the CEO broke down, in detail, the brilliance of Amazon's business model to company leaders and even the board of directors. He talked up the existential threat that it posed to the fifty-six-year-old retail giant he so loved. He proclaimed that if

Walmart didn't invest in drastic change going forward, it could soon end up as one of the once-great retailers that had since faded into irrelevance—a list of which McMillon carries on his phone as a constant reminder. You can either choose to disrupt yourself, or be caught flat-footed when disruption chooses you. If Walmart didn't adapt quickly, he liked to tell those before him, it was unlikely the retail titan would live to see its centennial.

You had to wonder: How much of McMillon's rhetoric was spoken with candor and how much was messaging to some inside Walmart who doubted the threat Amazon posed? When McMillon took over, and in the years that followed, the top boss faced varying views of the risk level of Amazon from his executive teams and rank-and-file staff. While you could break them down into two large sections of believers and nonbelievers, each section contained multiple factions.

Among the nonbelievers, some doubted Amazon's retail operation would ever be consistently profitable and trusted that the money-losing would come back to haunt them in an undetermined significant way. Others in the group thought that Walmart would be saved by the fact that Amazon was not a significant player in the grocery industry, which was the brick-and-mortar retailer's strength and represented more than half of all Walmart sales.

On the opposite side, some employees and executives did recognize the Amazon threat but believed that with the right digital strategies, ones that played to Walmart's strengths and advantages, the Amazon risk could be neutralized at best, or minimized at worst. McMillon appeared to fall in this camp. But there was another, smaller group that was obsessed with the Amazon threat, to an extent that puzzled and concerned Walmart newcomers who had previous experience working inside the Bezos Borg.

"I don't think there was a day that went by where I didn't hear about Amazon," a former Walmart logistics executive who previously worked at Amazon told me. "Jeff [Bezos] says don't worry about competitors, worry about customers—if you take care of the customer, the other stuff works out."

McMillon, for his part, tried to strike a balance. In meetings with his leadership team, he would flag other company results or news announcements as a way of keeping his staff on their toes and guarding against complacency. He also made efforts to command digital literacy among his direct reports, so the company "was evolving with a sense of pace and paranoia," according to Kathryn McLay, Sam's Club's CEO. The goal, in her view, was to stress the "importance of this colossal battle that we're in to make sure that Walmart remains relevant."

McMillon, a CEO in title, was, in practice, Walmart's internal narrator of the retail revolution. He could only hope his executives didn't tune out the story, because unlike his Amazon counterpart, Jeff Bezos, McMillon rarely got involved in the thousands of daily decisions that percolate inside an organization the size of Walmart.

"I don't make every decision in Walmart [and] don't wanna make every decision in Walmart," he once said. "If I do my job well, I'm not making very many decisions because the team is doing it."

When you're dealing with the level of leader like the ones who report to McMillon—several who've run their own large companies elsewhere—making decisions for them could come across as undermining, which runs the risk that you'll—to use a sports phrase that McMillon is likely familiar with—"lose the team."

Yet in time, significant disputes between Walmart leaders with different priorities, different goals, and different incentives would threaten the progress the company was making to better compete in the new world of retail that Amazon was leading. Some executives who were otherwise strong supporters of McMillon found themselves praying to the altar of Sam Walton for their CEO to start making decisions and step in. But whether it was McMillon's stance on empowering his leaders by leaving the vast majority of decisions to them—the CEO admitted to me that he's had to overcome his own "tendency to be slower on decisions because I'm trying to build consensus"—or what some described to me as his natural aversion to conflict, he allowed internal rifts to widen. To many newcomers, it seemed like the pace of change that had been improving under new Jet leadership was starting to slow.

"Doug is a coach," one longtime Walmart partner told me. "Not a player."

The question was whether the hands-off approach was a strategic decision in and of itself, with intended consequences that only Mc-Millon had mapped out in his mind, or the sign of a leader who had spent too much time inside the Walmart machine to recognize the fallout that might come next.

THE 4 TAKEOVER

On August 9, 2016, Doug McMillon appeared at Jet's startup-chic Hoboken headquarters looking more the part of an e-commerce startup CEO than the chief executive of the country's largest employer. Both McMillon and Marc Lore wore blazers, but McMillon paired his with jeans, while Lore opted for dress pants.

McMillon had traveled to New Jersey to announce Walmart's plans to acquire Jet and to appear on CNBC alongside Lore in their first television interview together.[1] While viewers might not have noticed the style swap, it was a small but telling sign to some insiders of the respect each leader had for the other's background and expertise. The old-school retail titan and new-school e-commerce impresario were going to make this marriage work.

McMillon and Chairman Greg Penner had promised Lore and his executive team the keys to Walmart's US e-commerce kingdom. And from the time the deal closed in September of that same year, the new royalty didn't waste any time shaking things up.

"They gave us carte blanche," Jet.com chief revenue officer Scott Hilton, who would also take over as Walmart.com's chief revenue officer, told me.

Lore instantly became a regular at New Jersey's Teterboro Airport, where he would board weekly flights on a Walmart private jet to the

Bentonville home office to consult, strategize, and try to build consensus among the rest of Walmart's leadership.

His Jet cofounder Nate Faust became a regular on United Airlines flights out of Newark Airport—his role didn't come with regular access to Walmart's private fleet of jets—but his destination was San Bruno, California, where Walmart's existing e-commerce operation was based. There his first task was to move whatever mountains he needed to get Walmart's e-commerce division and warehouses ready for the first new launch that Lore and team would unveil just four months later: free two-day shipping on orders of $35 or more.

Just a few months earlier, before the Jet acquisition, Walmart had announced the national rollout of a two-day shipping program that required customers to pay $49 a year for the perk. No more. This was a new day with new leaders. It was a Jet takeover. The mission was rapid growth—and, like in the early days of Jet, Lore didn't want a membership fee standing in the way.

In a statement at the time, Lore called the new offering "table stakes." Some long-timers in the physical retail division, however, knew Lore's reputation for money-losing growth and heavy spending, and felt that this "table stakes" example was likely just the beginning of a string of costly moves designed to goose online sales.

"Everyone wanted to throw up," a former executive told me.

They were right. Under Lore, Walmart dramatically increased its advertising spending to fuel top-line sales growth and began an acquisition spree. That same month, Walmart announced the purchase of ShoeBuy, the operator of a Web 1.0 shopping site. The next month, Lore was at it again, with Walmart announcing the acquisition of Moosejaw, a retailer with ten stores and an online shopping site first launched in the early web days that was known for a wide assortment of outdoor gear and apparel.

The streak continued in March 2017 with the acquisition of Mod-Cloth, one of the first movers in the era of venture-backed fashion brands that were native to e-commerce rather than physical retail. ModCloth sold both its own brands and others and had developed something of a cult following for its focus on vintage-inspired women's clothing years earlier. But in late 2016, amid a turnaround effort, its

CEO had trouble raising additional venture capital as the company stared down debt payments coming due. Jet and Walmart were there with open arms and an appetite for another distressed asset.

The e-commerce shake-up entailed more than just acquisitions, though. That same month, Lore unveiled his plans for an incubation arm inside Walmart that would spin up its own startup companies. Some longtime Walmart executives rolled their eyes at the idea, but it was atop the list of must-dos for Lore. It would be called Store No. 8—an homage to Walmart's eighth store, based in Morrilton, Arkansas, which Sam Walton used as a testing canvas for new ideas. Lore hired Jenny Fleiss, the Rent the Runway cofounder, that spring to lead the first new internal startup: a text-message-based concierge service called Jetblack that would eventually launch to a group of wealthy New York City moms. There was officially a new Walmart on the block.

The beat of e-commerce announcements was becoming steady. Some longtime colleagues had questioned whether Lore would quickly tire of big-company bureaucracy. But the rapid pace of announcements seemed to energize him instead. He was Walmart's biggest cheerleader, both internally at town hall events and externally at one industry conference after another.

It didn't hurt that Lore had quite the financial incentive to be excited about the work. Walmart had agreed to pay him $477 million over five years for his ownership stake in Jet. And that was just the cash. Lore was also awarded more than 3.5 million Walmart restricted stock units to be paid out over five years, but with 30 percent of that total back-loaded into year five. Those units were worth more than $256 million at the time of the acquisition.[2] While the sale of Quidsi to Amazon had made Lore a fortune, the sale of Jet to Walmart would catapult his wealth to a whole new stratosphere. (Of course, while Walmart was doling out this compensation bonanza for Lore, the average hourly rate for full-time company workers was just $13.38, or around $27,830 annually for those who worked forty hours a week.)

Lore and his teams also looked for ways to take advantage of Walmart's existing store footprint—an advantage that Amazon executives had long feared. In April 2017, Walmart.com began offering a

5 percent discount on a selection of ten thousand items if customers agreed to pick them up at a store instead of selecting delivery to their home—in what was a new twist on the old Site to Store service.[3] These orders would be more profitable for Walmart.com since they didn't require paying a shipping carrier like FedEx to ferry the boxes to a customer's home; Walmart trucks were already carrying goods from warehouses to their Supercenters, and these online orders would go along for the ride.

There would be some bumps, though. The selection available for discount was restricted because there was no way Walmart's US store chief, Greg Foran, a New Zealander with sharp elbows and a dry wit, was going to allow online customers to get a better deal on merchandise found in stores than shoppers who did the shopping themselves. It would be one of the early signs of more friction to come.

Even still, the discounts served as a way to potentially beat Amazon on price and reclaim the section of consumers' brains reserved for price perception and the retailer best at it. Not surprisingly, perhaps, the new discount option also set in motion one of the first big battles between Walmart e-commerce under Lore and Amazon, his old nemesis-turned-employer-turned-nemesis.

Amazon's internal price-matching software regularly matched Walmart.com merchandise prices. But an internal debate erupted at Amazon over whether the matching tools should also match the discounted prices that Walmart was awarding its customers who chose the pickup option instead of at-home delivery. Should Amazon stick with its matching-all-the-time pricing philosophy and suffer heavy losses, since it still had to pay to ship the discounted item to a customer's door? Or should it come up with a new pricing tenet to include this rare exception and not match a lower Walmart price that the rival was giving out for pickup orders?

"You don't know how firmly you hold your convictions until you test them," Doug Herrington, Amazon's current CEO for its worldwide consumer business, told me years later. "And this was a good test of those. Some products actually spiraled down—some customers got the most amazing deals in the history of packaged goods during that time period."

Herrington and other Amazon executives instructed their teams to stand firm. If Walmart was offering online shoppers the lowest price anywhere, even if it was part of a special pickup program, Amazon was going to train its spying algorithms on those prices, too. Inside Walmart, pricing teams watched the digital sparring with fascination. At times it looked like Amazon was blinking when prices got too low, either making an item in question only available to Prime members to stem the losses, or even labeling it out of stock. Walmart employees, suspecting something was up with the out-of-stock incidents, then ran tests where they would raise the price on an item if Amazon marked the same item out of stock.

Sure enough, the items would almost immediately reappear on Amazon.

"At some point, it looked like they were using 'out of stock' as a way to say, 'All right, go back up with the price,'" a former Walmart executive told me.

As this battle raged, Lore was about to make another move, one that would signal a new day in Bentonville—or at least in Hoboken. In June 2017, Walmart made a $310 million deal for Bonobos, an upscale men's fashion retailer that had started out online but utilized a network of showrooms to help customers get fitted in-person before ordering merchandise to their doors. Bonobos was run by a charismatic founder named Andy Dunn—a well-known commodity in the New York City tech scene and one of the founding fathers of the digital-native consumer brand boom. Dunn had coined the term *digital-native vertical brand*, or DNVB, and Lore would charge him with building out a portfolio of such brands under the Walmart umbrella, either through acquisition or incubation, where Target had outflanked Walmart for years by creating breakout brands that connected deeply with customers.

In the background, another innovation Lore had championed fiercely was being tested, and it was ruffling some feathers internally. It was a feature that allowed shoppers to more easily reorder frequently purchased goods that they usually bought in Walmart stores. Behind the scenes, that meant Walmart was using the credit or debit card numbers of their in-store shoppers to track and identify them when they shopped online. Walmart financial leaders were furious when they heard about this tracking method, and some of the e-commerce employees working on the project shared their concern.

"We always had in our mind that we are hugely violating people's privacy," a former employee told me. "Someone going to the Walmart store to shop has no idea how we are taking [their] data and putting it into the e-commerce side."

But the initiative was a top priority of Lore's from the start—it was, he thought, the entry point to getting more of Walmart's massive in-store customer base to shop online—and so the employees working on it fell in line. Lore, for his part, could not even fathom the problem with his approach. Though the credit card data was being shared between two different shopping channels, the data remained within the same company. Did Walmart leadership really still consider the stores division and e-commerce division to be two separate companies? Regardless, why would customers look at it that way? What decade was this?

The debate made it all the way up to Walmart chief financial officer Brett Biggs, who was concerned the tracking system might violate agreements with Visa and MasterCard and cost Walmart billions, according to someone who heard his concerns. But Lore didn't back down, and the new feature rollout went public in July 2017.[4] It's not clear how the concerns were resolved, and Walmart declined to offer specifics.

"With any project or initiative at Walmart, stakeholders are encouraged to identify and share their concerns," Walmart spokesperson Erin Hulliberger said. "Walmart appropriately addresses concerns as they are raised."

What *was* clear was that this was still the honeymoon phase of the Walmart/Jet marriage, and the new top dogs were not yet used to being told "No."

The pace of action and change was astounding for a company like Walmart. Walmart's management structure was historically a centralized one, and a common symptom of that was slow decision-making, as well as decisions by consensus. But that wasn't happening now, even if things were at times sloppy behind the scenes. After the Moosejaw acquisition closed, for example, a young Jet employee was charged with training Moosejaw's employees on Jet's systems. The employee was given little notice and ended up slapping together a presentation the night before in a crummy hotel room in Detroit. This might not have been "move fast and break things," but it was at times "move fast and fake things."

Either way, in Bentonville, large swaths of the rank and file felt invigorated by the moves. It felt like the company was getting more media coverage than ever before. And, for a change, much of it was positive.

A New Narrative

Thanks to Lore, the digital dinosaur was waking from its slumber. Walmart might not have been considered a true Amazon rival yet, but it wasn't a laughingstock in technology circles anymore, either. Talented founders and engineers who might have ignored Walmart recruiters or M&A execs just a year or two earlier were now taking offers from the company seriously.

Each move on its own might not have seemed impressive, Lore admitted to me years later. "But if you look at the sum total of all the decisions, it changed the narrative, and that brought in incredible talent," he said. "And that was what I was trying to do."

Doug McMillon also paid close attention to the narrative that was building both in the press and among shareholders. In the summer of 2017, some e-commerce employees were told that the CEO had been tipped off about a new Amazon delivery program that was set to launch imminently. The goal for Amazon was to take its promise of delivery convenience to the next level by allowing Amazon Prime members to opt in to get deliveries placed inside their home, to guard against porch-pirate thefts. Customers had to own or purchase a smart lock that opens without a physical key, as well as an Amazon indoor security camera that would allow for real-time monitoring of the delivery, and the delivery person, as it happened.

McMillon wasn't going to let this juicy tip go to waste. A small group of Walmart e-commerce employees were told that McMillon wanted Walmart to beat its rival to the punch. In a matter of about six weeks, Walmart created the outlines of a similar program. On September 22, 2017, Walmart published a blog post titled "Why the Future Could Mean Delivery Straight into Your Fridge," announcing a small pilot test of in-home delivery in Silicon Valley that would include delivery people unpacking perishable goods and placing them in a customer's refrigerator.[5] Tech blogs, which had grown accustomed to covering more innovation at Amazon than at Walmart, ate it up. McMillon would later give executives the green light to expand the pilot and turn it into a stand-alone business inside the Store No. 8 startup incubator.

By the time Amazon announced its Amazon Key program, on the other hand, it was more than a month after Walmart's announcement.

"It was a good fuck-you moment," one former Walmart e-commerce manager told me. "We had a lot of really great press and we beat them to the punch on in-home delivery. The story was then that Amazon follows Walmart. We were leading and Doug really wanted to be leading on certain things."

To be sure, no one inside Bentonville headquarters or on Wall Street was confusing Walmart for Amazon. But those moves were making waves.

McMillon's involvement in helping to shape this new narrative had started even earlier. On the day the Jet acquisition was finalized, for example, Walmart published a blog post under his name with a headline that imitated media trends of the time: "Five Big Reasons Walmart Bought Jet.com."[6]

At the top of the list, McMillon wrote: "Jet.com created a unique, transparent way for customers to shop, helping them make choices that lower their prices as they shop—from building smarter baskets to opting out of free returns and using debit cards. This has helped Jet.com win fans among savvy shoppers and will help us put the power to save in more shoppers' hands.

"Look for that on Walmart.com," McMillon added.

Jet had indeed created a unique shopping experience in which customers earned discounts as they added more merchandise to their orders. The startup dubbed this feature the "Smart Cart." Internal data showed that the more items a customer added to their online shopping cart, the more likely they were to add *another* item to their cart, a former executive told me. That wasn't the way e-commerce typically worked, and that should have been a good thing for Jet, and for Walmart. Packing more items into a single online order can reduce costs and give a mass retailer a better chance at earning a profit, since different product categories carry different profitability characteristics.

No, the discounts that the Smart Cart offered Jet customers often had little to do with actual lower logistics costs, which is what executives boasted about publicly while Jet was still an independent startup. But the technology behind the Smart Cart did largely work, and Walmart's massive store and warehouse networks could have helped lower those costs and bring the true promise of the Smart Cart to fruition on Walmart.com. At least in theory.

But some Jet executives already knew that the terms of the acquisition prevented Jet.com from selling a lot of its most popular merchandise for a lower price than Walmart. That would make the original Smart Cart model tough to keep alive, even on Jet.com. To do so under those circumstances, Jet executives ended up crafting a cocktail of solutions that included raising prices on some goods, swapping out some items for similar ones that weren't the exact pack size of what was sold at Walmart, and even rejiggering how Smart Cart savings were shown on Jet.com so they wouldn't be displayed next to items that Walmart also sold.

But if items couldn't be priced cheaper on Walmart's websites than in its stores, there was seemingly no practical way that the Smart Cart would ever make its way to Walmart.com too in its original form, since some of Jet's workarounds like raising prices wouldn't work under the Walmart brand and its commitment to everyday low prices. (Shortly after the acquisition, Walmart's US CEO, Greg Foran, and Jet executives had debated over a complicated pricing agreement to limit the friction between the e-commerce sites and the profit machine that was Walmart's chain of Supercenters. One Jet executive cheekily dubbed it the Treaty of Versailles.)

In short, some insiders were realizing that the Smart Cart as originally constructed didn't have any real future on Walmart.com. Still, a year after the deal closed, Walmart executives were continuing to

talk publicly about the innovation as one of the keys to the $3.3 bil-
lion deal.

"Over the next year, you'll see the Smart Cart technology on Jet
migrate onto Walmart.com," Lore told investment analysts at a conference in the fall of 2017.[7] In early 2018, McMillon repeated a similar
expectation on a call with Wall Street analysts, saying, "You'll start to
see Smart Cart functionality move over to Walmart."

What they apparently were reflecting at the time—whether it was
clear to outsiders or not—was an internal broadening of what the
Smart Cart phrase meant. Several former Walmart e-commerce executives told me that, internally, they began using the term "Smart Cart"
more loosely to include other website features that influenced customers to take actions that helped strip costs out of Walmart's existing
systems, while providing some benefit in return to the shopper. The
discount offered to online customers if they picked up their order at a
local Walmart store rather than having it delivered was one example.
When Walmart introduced a next-day-delivery offering for orders of
$35 or more in 2019, some executives also considered that a Smart
Cart perk. In order to make the economics of next-day delivery work,
Walmart only offered it on items that could all be shipped out of the
same warehouse, thus limiting supply chain costs that the company
might incur when items in a single online order have to be packed and
shipped from multiple facilities. Still, this was not what many outside
the top executive suite thought to be the Smart Cart innovation.

"I think they missed out in a huge way by not implementing Smart
Cart," said Joe Gullo, a supply chain leader who worked at Jet and then
Walmart following the acquisition.

But during 2017, the first full year that Jet executives were in charge,
the future of Smart Cart still seemed bright. So did Walmart's digital
future in general. On the day that Walmart's acquisition of Jet was
finalized in September 2016, Walmart's stock price closed at around
$73 a share. By the middle of November 2017, it had briefly traded as
high as $100. For some of Walmart's top executives in its store divi-
sion, the stock price and the resulting boost in their personal fortunes
helped stem some of their doubts about the expensive growth plans
that Lore and team were enacting.

That holiday season would be a big one for the Jet team. While they had been through one Walmart holiday season already after the deal closed in September 2016—a rough one in which a key automation system in Walmart's e-commerce warehouses broke down during the Black Friday weekend—many of the strategies and plans were already decided by the time they had joined. So the fall of 2017 would mark the first holiday showdown against Amazon and other rivals with Jet folks in full control of Walmart's US e-commerce division. Their credibility was riding on it.

But there were conflicting demands being placed on the new leaders, several former employees told me. Some US Walmart store leaders wanted the e-commerce division to match the blowout, doorbuster mentality of shopping holidays inside Supercenters.

"Most senior [store] managers were addicted to winning holiday and just burning the house down," Hilton, Walmart.com's revenue chief at the time, said in reference to the negative impact that these holiday discounts had on e-commerce profits.

Meanwhile, Walmart finance executives were pressuring Lore to rein in his division's losses, which were coming in higher than planned. After registering quarter after quarter of e-commerce growth of 50 percent or higher in the first three quarters of 2017, Lore surprised some of his employees by telling them to take their foot off the gas heading into the holidays.

"It was a very anti-Marc way of doing things," a former employee told me.

Walmart chief financial officer Brett Biggs indirectly messaged a planned slowdown to Wall Street at an investor day that October, when he said the company would register $11.5 billion in US e-commerce revenue for the full year. To do some quick back-of-the-envelope math, that would mean fourth-quarter e-commerce growth was set to decelerate into the 20s percentage range.

When Walmart released results for the holiday quarter in February 2018, investors seemed shocked that US e-commerce growth had decelerated to 23 percent from 50 percent in the third quarter, and 60 percent in the three months prior to that. The stock dropped nearly 10 percent—the largest decline in more than two years—knocking more than $30 billion off the company's value.[8] Meanwhile, Amazon recorded 38 percent revenue growth across its varied business lines for their own holiday quarter. That rapid growth was coming off a substantially larger e-commerce sales base, too.

"The majority of this slowdown was expected as we fully lapped the Jet acquisition as well as creating a healthier long-term foundation for holiday," Walmart's McMillon would say on the earnings call.[9]

But there were issues on top of the planned pullback. McMillon discussed them briefly, pointing to "operational" problems related to not having enough space in facilities for both popular holiday gifts and everyday merchandise, which hurt the company's ability to keep in stock those items customers order year-round.

Some Black Friday merchandise sold out by Thanksgiving, according to news reports from the time.[10] And in a key West Coast warehouse in Chino, California, automation system issues led to holiday orders being shipped out slower than normal. The company also wasn't used to the volume of product that Walmart.com was pumping out and underestimated how many packages they could ship out of their doors each day. If new e-commerce executives asked leaders at the warehouse facility in Bethlehem, Pennsylvania, for example, what kind of daily volume they could do, they may have said 200,000. In reality, it may have turned out to be somewhere around half that amount. The inability to accurately forecast shipping volume wouldn't bode well for the leaders of these warehouses inherited by Jet executives.

Inside the company, the bad press from the e-commerce revenue slowdown was fuel for longtime execs who had wanted the company's web division to match some of the blockbuster sales happening in stores.

"The negative media attention drove some store execs crazy," a former Walmart e-commerce employee told me.

But the stock sell-off also had a different kind of impact internally within the e-commerce division.

"It was a big wake-up call for the organization that, 'Holy shit, e-com can move the [stock] market,'" the employee said.

Lore and company would continue to try to use that fact to their advantage during the honeymoon phase. Lore's strategy "to win" in e-commerce included three legs. The first was "nail the fundamentals"—

the unsexy grunt work that was code for making improvements to Walmart.com so that it became "a good enough" alternative to Amazon. Amazon, of course, was way ahead in merchandise assortment, delivery speed, search engine technology, customer reviews, and most everything else.

So, the e-commerce division decided it needed to continue to chip away at these advantages with incremental improvements. "Have it," "Find it," "Display It," "Price It," and "Deliver It" was Lore's shorthand for the metrics used to judge Walmart.com's progress. This was the defensive part of the Walmart strategy to battle Amazon.

The other two sides of Lore's strategy triangle were Walmart's offensive plays. The places Walmart could *win*. They were "Innovate for the future" and "Leverage unique assets."

The first of those two buckets involved experimentation that created a lot of the sizzle that Lore and team were advertising their first year in power. One example was a test where Walmart store employees would deliver customer packages on their way home from work. Another involved a partnership with Google to let shoppers reorder goods from Walmart by simply giving a voice command to a Google smart speaker. The Store No. 8 startup incubator was the flagship of this strategy, with the group touting the exploration of how technologies like virtual reality would impact the retail industry in years to come.

Yet the unsung heroes of Walmart's e-commerce growth during the honeymoon—and the weapon that Amazon executives had long feared in their once-uphill battle against the brick-and-mortar retail wrecking ball—was actually the existing Supercenter stores themselves. Everyone at Walmart, including Lore, knew that great swaths of the US drove by Walmarts on a daily basis. That, coupled with the retailer's standing as the largest grocer in the US, offered something Amazon would have trouble competing against. Even before the Jet acquisition and Lore's arrival, Walmart was already offering a curbside pickup option for online grocery orders at nearly four hundred Supercenter locations in the US.

By the time Lore and his teams had spent about a year inside Walmart, the grocery pickup rollout had expanded to nearly one thousand locations, and the majority of that work was being executed by teams overseen by Greg Foran. The service had the highest customer satisfaction score of any main offering at the company.

The narrative around Walmart as a digital laggard was changing. The press and investors were paying attention. Rank-and-file employees were energized. And Lore was getting credit for this revival. Whether that would be a good thing in the long run was an altogether different question.

PRIME ATTACK

Long before Doug McMillon was CEO of Walmart, and before Marc Lore had even a glimmer of the idea for Quidsi or Jet.com, a former pharmaceutical manufacturing executive named Jeff Wilke was busy laying the foundations for perhaps the most disruptive innovation in retail since the Supercenter: Amazon Prime.

Jeff Bezos had recruited Wilke, a thirty-two-year-old who oversaw sales, marketing, manufacturing, and R & D at the Pharmaceutical Fine Chemicals division of AlliedSignal, to Amazon in 1999 to replace Jimmy Wright. Wright was the hard-charging former Walmart logistics executive who had succeeded in rapidly expanding Amazon's warehouse footprint, but in a way that was more old-school retail than new-school e-commerce. Wright's Amazon facilities were a sight to see at the time, "with blinking lights on aisles and shelves to guide human workers to the right products, and conveyor belts that ran into and out of massive machines," according to Brad Stone's *The Everything Store*. But Wilke and others determined that the equipment and processes implemented by Wright, and those who preceded him, were not suited for the type of continuous and efficient flow of merchandise orders through a warehouse that Amazon now desired. Wilke and company needed to completely overhaul the operations.

Wilke's task was a gargantuan one: to reinvent Amazon's systems and processes to be able to rapidly ship out items within a few hours. To accomplish this, he partnered with another Walmart veteran, Rick Dalzell, the Amazon CIO and former Walmart executive who had been at the center of the Walmart-Amazon lawsuit in 1999. Dalzell and his technical teams helped transform Wilke's warehouse process changes into computer code that would be at the core of Amazon's logistics prowess for decades to come.

"What helped the most was that Rick had been an IT exec at a large, sophisticated company," Wilke told me shortly before his retirement from Amazon in early 2021. "And I needed such a partner to implement the process work that I knew was going to be important for the company to scale."

In 2001, the big changes inside Amazon's network of warehouses— what it calls fulfillment centers—began. Software code was rewritten and fulfillment center layouts changed. The new processes incorporated techniques from the lean manufacturing methodology, of which Wilke was a disciple, and which aimed to maximize productivity while minimizing waste—or unnecessary steps. The new system was called FastTrack.

By 2002, there were signs the new system was working. Previously, it took a full day between when an Amazon customer placed an order and when the box left the fulfillment center. Now that twenty-four-hour turnaround had shrunk in best-case scenarios to a mere three hours. A year later, Amazon began messaging those quick turnaround times to shoppers. Right on the website, a message declared: "Want it delivered tomorrow? Order in the next five hours and 25 minutes." That promise had a profound effect: more shoppers started paying for expedited shipping.

Then, with a maniacal focus on operational excellence that even an old-school Walmart executive might begrudgingly applaud, Wilke demanded that his warehouse managers email him at the close of every day explaining the reason behind each and every late shipment. (Of course, this organizational addiction to speed and convenience would eventually help produce a pace of warehouse work for the tech giant's lowest-paid employees that some found brutal.)

"We did that for almost a year to make sure that the processes worked and then we were confident launching it externally," Wilke told me in 2018.[1]

By late 2004, when Bezos green-lit the idea for Prime—code-named "Futurama"—Wilke didn't even need to be in the room. Most of the hard logistics work was already done. And, unbeknownst to just about anyone anywhere at the time (including Amazon's own employees working on the secret project), Prime would catalyze Amazon's e-commerce dominance for decades to come.

When Prime did launch in 2005, Walmart had little reason to consider this new membership program a threat. For one, the titan of retail's profits were larger than Amazon's revenue. Whether you were a Walmart executive in 2005 or 2015, you might happily ignore the threat of Prime for another very simple reason: the cost. Prime cost subscribers $79 a year from 2005 until 2014. That was a significant investment for the average Walmart customer, who had a household income of $53,000 in 2014, while Amazon Prime members in the US had an average household income of nearly $70,000.[2] Would Walmart's core customer base really cough up that much money up front, just for the right to order even more merchandise from Amazon?

Many Walmart leaders didn't think so. Walmart was going to keep doing what it had done so well for so long: squeeze suppliers down to the penny to get their lowest wholesale cost, pay rank-and-file store workers a legal but barely survivable wage, and pass on the savings from those tactics and others to customers in the form of everyday low prices. The Walmart belief was, you shouldn't have to guess if you are getting a good deal when you walk into a Walmart Supercenter; you *know* you are. And if you really wanted to join a retail membership program, Walmart customers could join Sam's Club, Walmart's answer to Costco.

When Amazon upped the cost of Prime to $99 a year in early 2014,[3] the threat could have become even easier to ignore for Walmart executives. A bigger price tag for Prime would be considered an even bigger splurge for the average Walmart customer. How many would really take Amazon up on that offer?

Inside Amazon, however, top leaders trusted that the value they were providing was more than worth the new price. They had already added an entertainment perk to the Prime bundle a few years earlier, when Bezos surprised his video executives with the idea that the company's new streaming video service, which lacked great content, should be free for Prime members. Bezos wanted to take a page from Netflix's lucrative playbook, which first introduced its streaming service as a free bonus to existing DVD-rental subscribers. Bezos believed that Netflix had succeeded despite the fact that its early collection of streaming shows and movies was more lackluster than blockbuster. Bezos wasn't above copying a competitor's tactic—if it was a good one.

"I remember Jeff used those exact words: it's an, 'Oh, by the way,'" former Amazon executive Bill Carr told me in 2018. "'Yeah, Prime is seventy-nine dollars a year. Oh, by the way, there's free movies and TV shows with it.'" And how much could consumers complain about the quality of movies and TV shows if it's free?[4]

The move worked. The entertainment perks of Prime not only helped accelerate membership growth; they also gave existing members another reason to stick around if they were placing fewer merchandise orders and were considering canceling their membership.

When Amazon announced the Prime membership fee increase in 2014, they knew they were giving members more bang for their buck than when Prime first launched, with additional features planned to be revealed in the future. Amazon leaders had a goal of reaching 100 million global members, and a fear that shipping and video content alone might not get them there.

"I started going to every business leader at Amazon and said, 'Hey, Prime is this opportunity to provide our premium customers the best of Amazon,'" former Amazon Prime VP Greg Greeley told me in 2018.[5] "'What is it in your business unit that you think we could include in Prime as a way to drive more engagement, not only for *your* business, but to add to the flywheel of all things Amazon?'"

Later in 2014, the company introduced Prime's music streaming service, as well as Alexa and the first Amazon Echo speaker (half price for Prime members at launch, of course) to use with the new music service. Amazon also unveiled Prime Now, which offered two-hour delivery for no extra cost on a small subset of popular goods in New York City, followed by other urban areas over time.

Amazon executives tried to be cautious about these additions; they were acutely aware of the risk of adding hollow "benefits" that came with certain credit cards, or a AAA subscription. They understood the impact those kinds of perks had on diluting the value of the overall offering. But they believed the new additions would help convince customers that Prime was just too good to pass up.

"We want Prime to be such a good value, you'd be irresponsible not to be a member," Bezos wrote in his 2015 annual shareholder letter.[6]

Use It, Abuse It, Lose It

For a large subset of Americans, however, Prime's $99 up-front cost was a nonstarter. Amazon executives understood this. They had long debated making Prime more accessible to more people by offering a monthly payment option instead of the annual fee. Not only would that require less up-front money for customers to pay, but it would also let costumers weave in and out of the membership as their income allowed. When Amazon surveyed customers who signed up for a free trial but declined to pay for the membership at the end, the up-front annual cost was a top reason why.

"To them, they're buying shipping, right?" Greeley told me. "It's like, 'Well, I don't know how much stuff I'm going to buy in the future.'"

A main concern among executives who opposed the monthly option was that customers would subscribe for a month leading up to the holiday shopping season—putting even more pressure on the company's logistics operations during Amazon's peak season—and then cycle out of the service come the new year.

But as Amazon added more perks to the program, more executives became confident that the upside of making Prime more financially accessible to more people outweighed the downsides. By 2016, Amazon Prime was having great success attracting wealthy and upper-middle-class Americans. That was important—Prime customers shopped more frequently and spent more on Amazon than non-Prime customers did. That's because the program did something fascinating to the consumer brain that many all-you-can-eat memberships do: it ignites the desire to want to use it frequently so as to get your money's worth, at the expense of spending with other retailers.

In the earliest days of Prime, this behavior was problematic precisely because Prime's first heavy users were those already frequently paying extra for express shipping, which often required shipping products by airplane, which cost Amazon about ten times as much as shipping by truck. With Prime they began shopping even more, and the annual membership fee was falling short of covering the shipping costs associated with their orders.[7]

From the perspective of a profit-obsessed company like Walmart, this might have been seen as a death knell for a program like Prime. Yet, at Amazon, Bezos had promised to focus on the long term, even at the expense of short-term profits. The Prime show would go on.

"Jeff just saw the strategic benefit of Prime and he saw the value to customers," former Amazon executive Julie Todaro told me in 2019.[8] "Whereas, I think at some companies they would say, 'Yep, customers are doing what we want, but it's a little too expensive. So let's kill it.'"

Over time, as Prime's popularity grew, some shipping costs came down because the customer demand that Prime encouraged gave Amazon good reason to build more warehouses closer to more customers, allowing for more shipments sent via trucks than aboard costlier planes. That warehouse expansion accelerated when Amazon began cutting tax deals with state governments in the early 2010s, making the company more willing to build facilities in states it had previously avoided.

But if Amazon execs wanted to mint more Prime members in the back half of the 2010s, they needed new ways to attract less wealthy Americans. At the time, 60 percent of US households with income of at least $150,000 had Prime memberships, according to research from Cowen and Company. On the other hand, only about 40 percent of households that made between $40,000 and $50,000 a year had a Prime membership, and just 30 percent of those with earnings of less than $25,000.

So, in March 2016, Amazon dipped its toes in the water with a monthly Prime subscription option for Sprint wireless subscribers. Later that year, the company opened the option up to all US customers.

Monthly Prime members would pay a premium for the luxury of paying for their membership month by month—Amazon charged $10.99 a month for Prime, which worked out to $132 a year, compared to the annual fee of $99 for those customers who paid for a year of Prime all at once. But for those who couldn't, or wouldn't, pay $99 all at once, Prime membership was finally a possibility.

That same year, Walmart announced the closing of more than 150 US stores, raising the question of whether the timing of Amazon's launches had something to do with their brick-and-mortar competitor.[9] Amazon Prime's boss at the time, Greg Greeley, insisted that the timing of the move to introduce the monthly Prime option had nothing to do with their rival. But the former Prime boss did admit that he was aware that "as soon as [Walmart] closed those stores, they expanded the number of retail deserts that were out in the world."

At the time, Amazon was very interested in figuring out how to appeal to shoppers in retail deserts, many of whom struggle to make ends meet. By early 2017, Amazon Prime membership growth was fastest in US households with less than $50,000 in annual income.[10] That year, Prime attracted the most paid members in a year in its then-thirteen-year history. The monthly payment option for Prime memberships had helped Amazon's cause.

Amazon executives have long seen three methods to adding more members to Prime, according to current Prime boss Jamil Ghani. One is international expansion. Another has been by adding more perks to the program. But a crucial third lever, and the one that perhaps was the biggest threat to Walmart, has been to make Prime more accessible—that is, cheaper—for more people.

In the wake of Amazon's introduction of a monthly subscription option for Prime in 2016, the company continued to unveil new ways to attract customers with less disposable income. In 2017, Amazon began a test to let customers buy groceries online using food stamps—a program the company would later roll out widely just in time to reap the rewards of the human and economic devastation wrought by the Covid-19 pandemic.

(When the program rolled out nationwide in 2019, Amazon gave those customers using food stamps free access to the Amazon Fresh grocery delivery service, which was added to Prime that same year as a free perk and was otherwise restricted to Prime members. The decision to give those on food stamps free access to Fresh without a Prime membership was hotly debated at the executive level. The leader in charge of Amazon initiatives aimed at "underserved populations" [UP] remained steadfast that it was simply the right thing to do. That executive was a former company lawyer named Kristina Herrmann, and she had a powerful ally on her side: the then-chief of Amazon's North American retail business, Doug Herrington, for whom she had previously served as a "shadow," or chief of staff.)

In early June of 2017, Amazon stepped up the Prime onslaught by providing a 45 percent discount to the membership service to US customers on government assistance programs. Instead of paying $10.99 a month for Prime, eligible shoppers would pay just $5.99 for a Prime membership. In March 2018, Amazon added Medicaid recipients to those eligible for that discount. Now working-class and low-income Americans could access Prime every month for less than the cost of a movie ticket. There was some concern that the discount program might cannibalize their full-price membership business, if existing low-income Prime members could now qualify for the lower-priced fee. But the discount idea moved ahead, nonetheless. Herrington often reminded the "UP" team that the work they were doing "was on the side of the angels," which would become a rallying cry for Herrmann and her staff.

"Was there some discussion about Walmart? Yeah, probably," a former company insider told me. "But it wasn't the driving factor. Fundamentally, Amazon was trying to do the right thing for this customer segment."

For Walmart executives who thought the Prime conflagration wouldn't rage all the way to Bentonville, the introduction of the monthly Prime subscription in 2016, and then the discounts for those on government assistance the following year, should have set off fire alarms. But even at that point, some longtime Walmart executives still didn't see Amazon as a particularly noteworthy threat, in large part because of Amazon's weakness in the arena where Walmart held its biggest strength: perishable groceries.

Though Walmart did not start out as a grocery merchant, the invention and massive expansion of the Supercenter in the 1990s and 2000s catapulted it to become the largest seller of groceries in the country. By comparison, Amazon was still not a large seller of fresh groceries, despite having first launched the Amazon Fresh grocery delivery service a decade earlier, in 2007. Even Amazon's acquisition of Whole Foods in 2017 would leave some Walmart long-timers shrugging; the overlap between customers of the bougie organic grocer and the low-priced mass retailer, they assumed, was minimal.

But even before he joined Walmart, e-commerce lifer Marc Lore understood the threat Prime posed to just about everyone in retail, including Walmart. He was acutely aware that Walmart's existing subscription service, ShippingPass, came across as an ineffective substitute to Prime, whether it was intended to be a competitive offering or not. Walmart had started offering ShippingPass in the spring of 2015, first as a membership program that offered unlimited three-day shipping at a cost of $50 per year. Shortly before the Jet acquisition, Walmart's existing e-commerce leaders shaved the price to $49 and improved shipping speeds to two days instead of three.

But the two-day shipping speed was still only available for a catalogue of goods that was a fraction of the size of Amazon Prime's catalogue. The main reason for the discrepancy was the fact that third-party merchants who sold goods on Amazon could pay Amazon to store and ship their products through a program called Fulfillment by Amazon, or FBA. Merchants who paid FBA fees qualified their merchandise for Prime shipping and the crucial Prime badge on the Amazon shopping site. It was a critical reason for Prime's growth.

But Walmart didn't have a competitive offering to FBA for third-party merchants who wanted to sell on Walmart.com—not yet, anyway. That meant Walmart could only offer the shipping speed on the 2 million or so items that Walmart's e-commerce division purchased and stored itself. Yes, ShippingPass was half the price of Amazon Prime, but it had none of the nonshipping perks like entertainment or music, and it did not come close to matching the product catalogue of Amazon's Everything Store.

Not surprisingly, Lore's first big move was to axe the knockoff Prime program in early 2017, and he issued a rather dismissive statement in doing so: "In today's world of e-commerce, two-day free shipping is table stakes," he said.[11] Two-day shipping on the same catalogue of goods from Walmart.com would now be free—no membership necessary—as long as customers ordered at least $35 of goods. At the time, a source told the *Wall Street Journal* that the ShippingPass program had been intended "to test and ramp up its logistics and online warehouse network on an easier to manage, limited number of shoppers."[12] To many, though, that explanation sounded like an attempt to save face over a failed membership program.

Even with the move, there would be little reason for Amazon Prime customers to shop at Walmart.com for anything other than perishable groceries, like dairy products, produce, and meat. But perhaps making two-day shipping free on many popular, nonperishable products—everything from toys to video games to packaged goods like soap and cereal—would at least keep those Walmart shoppers who hadn't been sucked into the Prime vortex from doing so, while Walmart came up with a real plan for a membership program that would inspire loyalty and extinguish the flames from Amazon's indirect attack.

Walmart Prime

Lore wasn't dead set against a membership program at Walmart.com; he was dead set against one that wasn't worth paying for. So in the spring of 2018, as Jeff Bezos announced that Prime had surpassed 100 million members globally, Lore's e-commerce strategy team crafted an internal memo that touched on the idea for a new membership program that Walmart should pursue.

"If we want to win, we need to be the primary digital destination, and we already have something that can do so: same-day delivery of the full store assortment," the memo read. "It's a value prop[osition] others can't match," it continued, citing the advantage of having fixed costs for such a program paid for by the revenue Walmart stores already generated from their in-store customer base.

Members of this new service would pay "an affordable" $98 a year for unlimited same-day deliveries of Walmart's full store of products, including both perishable and packaged groceries, as well as general merchandise. That same spring, Amazon increased the annual price of Prime from $99 to $119 a year, which included deliveries from Whole Foods and a small selection of mainstream groceries through a service called Prime Now, but not the full selection of Amazon's more affordable Amazon Fresh grocery service. Prime members who wanted access to Fresh's full online store of groceries had to pay an additional $15-a-month fee. That meant Amazon customers subscribing to both Prime and Amazon Fresh were paying $299 annually, *combined*. With that comparison in mind, Walmart executives were right in considering a $98 annual fee focused on same-day grocery delivery "affordable," even if the service lacked the entertainment perks of Prime.

Lore's team felt even more confident about the membership idea because they knew Walmart customers loved the closest comparable offering at the time. Walmart called that service Online Grocery Pickup, or OGP for short. It had rolled out years earlier, prior to the Jet acquisition, and allowed customers to place grocery orders of $30 or more on Walmart.com or Walmart's dedicated grocery app, and then have a Walmart associate bring the goods out to the customer's car when they arrived. Grocery pickup might not have had the business-world sex appeal of grocery delivery, which was all the rage in Silicon Valley and among tech investors at the time. But in large swaths of the country, where minivans far outnumbered delivery vans, the model made a lot of sense—for customers and for Walmart.

Walmart executives working for the company's Asda grocery chain subsidiary in the United Kingdom first honed the model on the other side of the Atlantic, where it's referred to as Click and Collect. But they only did so after losing boatloads on an unsuccessful grocery delivery initiative, which resulted in the company pulling out of the UK online grocery market for a period of time. As a result, Asda ceded first-mover advantage to their giant rival Tesco—and significant customer loyalty along with it.

So, when some of those same executives, including current Walmart

International CEO Judith McKenna, moved into senior roles inside Walmart's US division years later, they kept a promise to start first with a pickup service instead of delivery.

The service started expanding from a small test to a wider rollout at Walmart stores in the US while Neil Ashe, the company's previous global e-commerce leader, was still in charge prior to the Jet acquisition. But even though they weren't the ones to first get it off the ground, Lore and his executive team recognized the strength of the program, which was clear in its usage and customer satisfaction metrics. Of the 2 million customers who were using the grocery pickup service at the time, around 1 in 4—nearly 500,000 people—used it at least twice a month, the memo said. Moreover, customer satisfaction scores were through the roof—OGP was far and away the service that Walmart customers loved the most.

To make the new $98 same-day delivery membership more economically viable, the e-commerce strategists called for combining Walmart's two separate shopping apps—one to order perishable groceries and the other general merchandise—so customers could order more profitable items, like clothing, alongside less profitable groceries like a gallon of milk. At the time, the "orange" branded grocery app was used by customers to order fresh groceries for pickup or delivery, both of which were largely run by the US stores division. The main "blue" app, on the other hand, was run by Lore's e-commerce division and consisted of general merchandise like toys, TVs, and clothing.

The idea of combining the apps had festered for years, even before Lore and his team took over Walmart's e-commerce operation. Shortly after the Jet leaders arrived at Walmart, Walmart's US stores leader, Greg Foran, had tentatively agreed to the merging of the apps, much to the surprise of his staff, according to a former Walmart e-commerce executive. But Foran backed away from the verbal commitment as the technical timeline to execute the app merger grew longer than first promised. The memo made the case to revisit the app consolidation idea once again.

Lore had his team include one last tidbit in the memo to try to prod leadership to move aggressively on the latest membership idea: a new metric, and a made-up one at that. It was called "first place wallet share," meaning the percentage of customers who spent more with a given retailer than any other. Over the course of five years, the memo said, Walmart's "first place wallet share" had declined from 25 percent to less than 22 percent. Amazon's, during the same time, had more than tripled—from approximately 4 percent to more than 12 percent.

"Let's lean into same-day delivery . . . and win," the memo said.

By the fall of 2018, the membership idea had gained enough traction that Walmart CEO Doug McMillon included it in a board meeting presentation. But when Walmart closed out its fiscal year at the end of January 2019, Walmart was still without its answer to Prime. McMillon was juggling big personalities, differing incentives, and a long list of potential blockbuster bets to prioritize. All the while, the Amazon Prime wrecking ball continued to swing.

6 NOT READY FOR PRIME TIME

For all of Prime's success, there was one glaring weakness in the product assortment Amazon offered to members: perishable foods like dairy, produce, and meats that grocery stores—and Walmart—specialized in.

Aware of this shortcoming, Amazon had been working on catching up to its megacompetitor for quite some time. All the way back in 2005, Doug Herrington—formerly of Webvan—joined the online retailer at the executive level, where he pitched Jeff Bezos on the idea for a nationwide grocery delivery service.

Herrington requested a $60 million investment to launch the program, but Bezos only agreed to a scaled-down $7 million beta test in Seattle. No one inside or outside of Amazon was having much luck figuring out how to make online grocery delivery services profitable back then, so Amazon's top leader prioritized major investments in other areas. By 2012, though, Herrington made clear his frustration about the service not being available outside its home market, and did so in quite the Amazon way: with a strongly worded internal memo.

"We can't reach our $400 billion aspirations with today's business model, and there's good reason to fear we won't make the necessary transformation," Herrington wrote, according to journalist Brad Stone's book *Amazon Unbound*.

The memo would earn Herrington a green light on a small geographic expansion of Amazon Fresh from its only existing market of Seattle to parts of Los Angeles and San Francisco. But even for Prime members lucky enough to be in those locations, the service still came at the steep price of $299 a year, versus the $79 annual fee that Amazon was charging Prime members at the time. In short, the vast majority of Amazon customers didn't even have the option to purchase perishable groceries from the online retailer, and that Achilles' heel would no doubt limit the company's ambitions for world domination if it wasn't rectified.

Yet as Amazon continued to tinker with pricing and delivery methods for fresh groceries, another category of grocery store purchases was perhaps just as important to Amazon's future, and one that would seemingly be easier to penetrate: so-called consumer packaged goods (CPG), or "consumables," for short.

This broad retail category encompasses essentially any type of non-perishable food, household, or personal health product that you use or consume, and then toss in the trash (or recycling bin). Basically, stuff that needs regular replenishment, and would typically be stored in a pantry, cabinet, or underneath a sink. Think bottled beverages like soda and water, chips, cereal, and canned soups in the food category. Or soap, deodorant, and shampoo in personal care. Or Clorox spray and paper plates in the home supply category. These goods are often not sexy nor inspiring. But they are core to daily American life. Thus the market was huge: at around $850 billion in US sales every year. This was Herrington's opportunity to pursue his biggest goal.

If Amazon wanted to reach the same retail heights as Walmart—let alone surpass it—the company would have to figure out how to sell more of the same low-priced consumables that customers most frequently purchase from standard grocery and big-box stores. These items, in an ideal world, would keep Amazon customers coming back to the online retailer over and over again. And the more they might do that, the less they'd be tempted to enter the doors or website of Amazon's old-school competition.

"Selling a book or a TV is great and super helpful," Herrington, now CEO of Amazon's entire global e-commerce and physical store businesses, told me in late 2021, "[but] how many times do I buy a book or TV each week versus how many times do I buy a packaged goods item, or some toilet paper or some food?"

CRaP Is King

By the early-2010s, Amazon had become a go-to destination for several CPG products, including coffee K-Cups, bulk packs of cereal and candy, and especially diapers, despite being less than profitable. Amazon was unafraid to use diapers as loss leaders to attract new parents to its website and hopefully make more profit from them over their lifetimes. It was a key reason why Amazon was so intent on either decimating, or acquiring, Marc Lore's Diapers.com.

For lower-price points, though—say consumables that cost $10 or less, which make up a majority of CPG categories—things got a lot trickier for Amazon, and the company was having trouble making a real sizable dent in that market.

Herrington knew the challenges of the sector all too well. He had previously consulted with CPG companies as a partner at Booz Allen Hamilton, where he worked for nearly a decade. Then, during the dot-com boom of the late 1990s, he oversaw marketing for Webvan, the online grocery startup that delivered same-day orders before going belly-up in 2001 in the wake of rapid, unprofitable expansion. Different Webvan veterans had different versions of what went wrong. But no matter the reasons for Webvan's demise, Herrington long remained undeterred about the power of the idea even if the economics of the business at times seemed unsolvable.

At Amazon, Herrington quickly garnered respect from his staff without instilling fear, a common tactic used by Bezos and other hard-charging business leaders. Those who worked for him told me that Herrington—who once had aspirations of becoming a US senator—was competitive, but even-keeled and affable. Upon joining Amazon in 2005, consumables "was an almost nonexistent category with . . . twenty people working on it," he told me in 2021. "I was vice president of a very small empire when I came in, but the aspiration was, 'Let's try to improve this experience for customers.'"

Herrington told his then-small staff that he wanted their culture to be one of a bias toward action, "with a calm and quiet confidence," according to Justin Leigh, a former product manager in the group.

Relative to other Amazon leaders, Herrington was "more mild-mannered, fair, empathetic," said Andrea Leigh, Justin's wife, who rose to the level of general manager at Amazon during a nearly decade-long career there that included stints on grocery and consumables teams.

That confidence would be put to the test often. The challenges of selling groceries online, whether perishable or shelf-stable, are plentiful. Grocery stores have notoriously low net profit margins to begin with, typically between 1 percent and 2 percent.[1] That's even when customers are the ones doing all the work of driving to the store and shopping themselves. But if you add in the costs that a retailer spends to sell those same items online—massive warehouses, delivery trucks, and the staff to handle those orders—the economics can quickly turn downright ugly, and upside down.

That was a big reason why, by 2013, the Amazon Fresh grocery delivery service was still far from a sure thing. It was clear, however, that customers *were* willing to order nonperishable groceries such as consumables online if the pricing was similar to what they were paying in physical stores.

The problem for Amazon was that Prime, for all its benefits, had trained Amazon shoppers to place orders one item at a time. Need a new baseball glove for your kid? Search, click, buy. Need a new humidifier filter for dry winter days? Search, click, buy. There was a certain beauty in this simplicity that rivals marveled over.

But that simplicity actually worked against the company's best interests when it came to low-priced consumer goods, and especially ones that were heavy (and therefore expensive) to ship. If you're an online retailer, you want customers buying more items per order when it comes to low-priced merchandise so there's a better chance that the order total can cover warehousing and shipping costs. A key factor in Amazon's present-day success was a significant blocker to its future ambition.

"Our units per order were very, very low, and that's counter to what you need for groceries or consumables," said Jennifer Pann, an eighteen-year veteran of Amazon who oversaw grocery supply chain and inventory-planning teams.

Up to that point, Amazon had come up with largely imperfect solutions for selling consumables like deodorant or soda without destroying the company's finances. At times, these goods were available only as so-called add-on items that could be ordered in addition to a separate, larger order—maybe alongside a Kindle or a few books, for example—which gave Amazon more revenue per order to try to turn a profit. At other times, Amazon, or merchants who sell as third parties on the Amazon Marketplace, would price the goods much higher than grocery stores, with the fulfillment and shipping costs essentially baked into the product price. On other occasions, Amazon would make the economics work by selling, say, a six-pack of deodorant instead of a single stick, since the higher price point could maybe, just maybe, make up for the shipping expense that Amazon would have to pay to get the order from one of its warehouses to a customer's doorstep.

Each of these options came with a trade-off, and for a company that prides itself on its vision of being "Earth's most customer-centric company," those trade-offs were a threat to what Amazon officials considered paramount: customer trust. So, in 2013, Herrington began dabbling with an idea to overcome the profitability challenges, and hopefully help Amazon better compete with Walmart and other big retailers in the grocery and CPG categories. Herrington's new idea all started with one of the most common purchases that shoppers make, regardless of the store: Diet Coke.

Win the Pantry

"What do we have to do to be able to deliver a twelve-pack of Diet Coke to anybody in the US for the same price [as in a] Target or Walmart?" Herrington recalled as the spark for the new service.

Why the obsession with Diet Coke? Well, twelve-packs of Diet Coke come with common CPG challenges. The price point is low, at around $5, but the weight is substantial, at about ten pounds. Shipping it by FedEx truck could cost more than the product itself. Amazon's internal name for items like that pack of Diet Coke is CRaP: "Can't Realize a Profit." Memorable in a way.

The hope was that someday, Amazon Fresh would grow into a nationwide service and make these points moot by giving Amazon the ability to sell CPG goods alongside fresh groceries in large, frequent customer orders. But that wasn't the reality back in 2013–14, and Herrington and team were impatient.

As a result of this, the former Webvan exec and other Amazon staff began brainstorming a new service that would eventually launch with the name Prime Pantry, and be exclusive to Prime members. Herrington wrote the original Pantry PRFAQ document, a type of internal memo documenting how a new Amazon product or service might be received by the press in an ideal world, as well as how the company should answer likely questions about the new service. A near-final draft of Herrington's memo began with an imaginary *New York Times* article under the headline "Amazon's Prime Pantry Phenomenon":

> *"Done," Nicole Sherwood smiled proudly, laying her iPhone on the table. "I just finished off my Pantry order with a 12-pack of Diet Coke for $3.99 and a box of Honey Nut Cheerios for $3.59. Those prices are a lot better than Safeway's—even better than I can get at my local Target or Wal-Mart. And it will be on my doorstep by Thursday, so no more trying to squeeze in a trip to the club store this weekend, between the kids' soccer games." She shakes her head. "I don't know how they do it, but I'm hooked."*

Getting past the cheesiness of the faux news article, the memo made clear that the primary appeal of Prime Pantry was supposed to be the prices. More specifically, prices on everyday pantry and household goods that might even beat the in-store prices of a certain family-owned, Arkansas-based retail behemoth.

"So what's all the fuss about?" Herrington's memo continues. "The price. Items in the Pantry store are typically equal to or lower than Wal-Mart and your local club stores."

These were items like twelve-packs of Diet Coke, canned foods and bagged snacks, detergent, toothpaste, and toilet paper. With a bigger order total, Amazon might have a better shot at being able to afford the packing and shipping costs associated with making a bigger splash in the CPG space, and competing more fiercely in an area that was Walmart's strength.

On the backend, though, it was a complicated mess. Amazon needed to make sure every item available through Pantry could be shipped out of a single warehouse closest to a given customer, to cut down on costs. If that sounds familiar, it's because it was a key to another business that Amazon had purchased a few years earlier: Marc Lore's Quidsi, which owned Diapers.com.

"When we bought Quidsi, we learned that their cost structure was a lot better than ours for fulfillment," said Pann, the longtime Amazon veteran with expertise in grocery inventory planning.

But even with that warehouse constraint and others, Amazon leaders were still concerned about making the financials work. At the time, Amazon wasn't swimming in profits like it would be in future years. As a result, it was decided the service would also have to come with a fee of $5.99 per Prime Pantry order, even though Prime members were already paying an extra $99 a year at the time for faster shipping speeds and access to Prime's streaming music and video catalogues.

It was a curious decision and, unsurprisingly, not everyone was thrilled about it. At the time, Greg Greeley was the head of Amazon Prime and thus the biggest internal advocate for Prime customers. Greeley told me he argued against such a cost, believing it would be a nonstarter for many Prime members who expected to receive all of their orders with no additional shipping fee. Instead, he was more in favor of adding an order minimum to the program to incentivize multi-item orders that could cover Amazon's costs on their own.

"There was a lot of debate," Greeley told me years later. "I'll leave it there."

At Amazon, debate is encouraged if not expected. It's even codified in the company's Leadership Principles. Among them: "Have a backbone; disagree and commit."

"Leaders are obligated to respectfully challenge decisions when they disagree, even when doing so is uncomfortable or exhausting," it reads. But, the principle concludes with, "Once a decision is determined, they commit wholly."

That last sentence is key. Greeley ended up committing to launching with the added $5.99 fee, even though he did not believe it was the ideal solution and had, as the head of Prime, veto power to block it.

Years later, Herrington told me that the group opted for a per-box fee versus, say, a $50 order minimum, because they feared customers might order $50 worth of items like bottled water, which would require multiple boxes instead of just one, and result in shipping costs that almost certainly would lead to unprofitable orders.

"If you want to order fifty dollars' worth of water, that's fine, it's going to take five boxes [with a $5.99 fee per box]," Herrington recounted to me in late 2021 of the model that Pantry ended up launching with. "[But] if you want to be a little bit more clever about this, you can probably get your water, some chips, some of this and some of that" and get it all shipped in one box for $5.99.

Stephenie Landry, the executive with day-to-day responsibility for the creation and launch of the Pantry program, was a rising star in Amazon's retail division. She had worked as a chief of staff of sorts—known as a technical adviser or "shadow" internally—for Jeff Wilke, Herrington's boss and Bezos's deputy who first oversaw the warehouse overhaul that made Amazon Prime possible. (Wilke later rose through the ranks to run Amazon's entire core retail business globally, a position that Herrington was named to in 2022.) Landry had led the original Amazon Fresh grocery delivery test back in Seattle in the mid-2000s and had a hand in managing several other services that launched under Herrington.

The user experience that Landry ended up crafting was a new one for Amazon: the Pantry web page showed a digital representation of a brown shipping box, and as customers added items to their Pantry shopping cart, the page updated to show shoppers what percentage of the box was filled. It was novel, but potentially confusing.

What was invisible to the customer was the calculations Amazon was doing on the backend to decide what constituted a full box: either goods that weighed forty-five pounds or took up four cubic feet of space, whichever happened first.

In the early years of the service, Amazon highlighted two key benefits offered by Prime Pantry:

"Save on the Essentials—Low prices and additional savings with hundreds of coupons," giving shoppers small discounts that the CPG brands were often expected to offer.

"Shop Everyday Sizes—No more buying in bulk. Buy what you need, when you need." In the past, Amazon shoppers interested in buying tuna fish from the online retailer might have had to resort to buying a twenty-four-can pack when they only wanted a few cans, because a pack size like that was the only way it made sense for the company to sell the low-priced product.

Behind the scenes, a small Prime Pantry "project team," in Amazon parlance, helped hone the idea and plan out the execution, before responsibility for the program would be handed over to a separate team that would run the service on the backend once it launched. But problems were identified when key internal experts like Pann, the inventory specialist, were looped in just a month before launch and realized the plan on paper had no chance of being successful when put into practice. There were many issues that boiled down to a gross underestimation of how long it would take to sell through the goods Amazon was ordering by the pallet from CPG brands. Amazon was purchasing this merchandise by the pallet to make it more efficient for Amazon warehouses to receive them, but Amazon sold through various types of consumable goods at differing rates, and that caused problems. While a pallet of laundry detergent might consist of 150 containers that could be sold through in a couple of weeks, a pallet of tuna cans might include 1,500 units that would take months to sell through one by one.

"They just took this very academic approach of like, if we buy it in bulk and we ship it to customers in [singles], it'll work out," Pann told me. "But nobody put pen to paper in the sense of, 'What does that mean?'"

It was just math, as Marc Lore would say, and the math most definitely did not work. Even with last-minute adjustments to the operations plan, the work going on behind customers' computer screens was bumpy from the start. Vendor relations staff had to corral CPG brands and convince them to join the new program, which was no easy task. To make the shipping economics work, even with the additional $5.99 fee, Amazon had to figure out how to tweak its technology to funnel each Prime Pantry order to the right Prime Pantry warehouse so that the order could make it to the customer's home by truck and not have to be shipped via plane. It was, in short, a logistical headache of grand proportions.

On the front end, some customers were turned off by the additional $5.99 shipping fee. They were already paying for Prime, after all. Others were confused or frustrated by the quantity minimums required to ship a single Pantry box, according to various Amazon executives. To make matters worse, Amazon made customers use different virtual shopping carts for Prime orders, Amazon Fresh orders, and Prime Pantry orders, respectively, and at times displayed different prices for similar items depending on which Amazon service they were being ordered through.

"It was complicated, and I'm not proud of where we ended up," Greeley, the former Prime boss, admitted to me. "Having a different cart with a different search or worse—and this is the thing I hated—different prices. It was the Walmart trap. Even knowing the program, I could get stuck [wondering], 'Why is this price different?'"

CPG Bully

Amazon continued to tweak the Pantry business model to try to attract more customers, all while attempting to make the economics work. At the same time, in typical Amazon fashion, it continued to invest in other ways to sell consumables to customers, even at the risk of redundancy.

There was Prime Now, a two-hour delivery service in metro areas that launched in late 2013 to combat the threat of Instacart and the now-defunct Google Express. Landry, the up-and-coming executive who oversaw the Pantry launch, would eventually move over to run

Prime Now full-time. Then there was Amazon Fresh, the longtime grocery delivery offering that shipped perishables as well as shelf-stable goods out of Amazon warehouses. And there was still the regular Amazon.com storefront, through which Amazon continued to sell some CPG goods that either didn't need the Pantry model to be profitable or were too important to Amazon to lock behind the Pantry wall.

In early 2017, I began hearing from nervous executives at CPG companies like Unilever, PepsiCo, and Kimberly-Clark that Amazon and Walmart were engaged in an all-out pricing war, and some of America's most popular consumable brands had become caught in the crossfire.[2] One of the main issues, they told me, was that Amazon's price-matching algorithm was identifying the lowest price per unit or per ounce for a given product—even if it was in a huge bulk-size pack at Costco—and then applying it across the same type of good on Amazon, even when the pack size was much smaller. This, they explained, had a long trickle-down impact.

Say Costco was selling a forty-pack of juice boxes for $12, or around 30 cents per juice box. But Amazon was selling a much smaller pack of the same item, such as a six-pack. Amazon's algorithm would match the per-box price of 30 cents from the Costco forty-pack and apply it to the six-pack on Amazon, even though that would mean Amazon was charging just $1.80 for the six-pack, with seemingly no possible way of turning a profit when factoring in shipping costs. Walmart would see this and assume that the juice box brand was giving Amazon a better wholesale price and would pressure the brand to cut the wholesale price for Walmart so Walmart could match Amazon's price.

The saga didn't end there. Even though these newly unprofitable products were partly the result of their own price-matching technology, Amazon employees would often ratchet up the pressure on CPG brands for better wholesale prices as well, unafraid to kick popular products off the site as leverage. For example, on a random Friday in February 2017, all Pampers diapers sold by Amazon disappeared from the site. The talk of the industry was that Amazon executives may have kicked the entire Pampers portfolio off Amazon.com during a negotiation over wholesale prices, which would be a very big deal in the retail world. Neither company would confirm or deny the speculation when I inquired at the time, but former Amazon employees later told me the speculation was quite plausible because Amazon had been known to boot top CPG brands like Tide off the site as leverage during annual negotiations. Lore's mafia analogy didn't seem so crazy after all.

These one-sided negotiations, according to executives, reminded many in the CPG world of that other major retailer: Walmart. The CPG conglomerates that produce the toothpaste, snacks, and shampoo that would typically keep customers coming back to big-box or grocery stores again and again had grown accustomed to such dealings with the Bentonville bully, which saw every penny of cost saved through tough negotiations as a penny that would go back into consumers' pockets. To Sam Walton and the Walmart leaders who followed him, that was the retailer's entire reason for being: savings. Anyone standing in the way of those savings should either submit or retreat.

But in negotiations with Amazon, top executives from large CPG companies say, the tech giant also developed a reputation in the 2010s for making uniquely unreasonable demands despite repeatedly failing to hit projections. Separate from the ramifications of the pricing battle involving the regular Amazon.com storefront, there were several years where Amazon Fresh failed to launch in as many new geographic areas as employees had promised some of the CPG companies that supplied it with the inventory to sell. But, like clockwork, Amazon staff would show up at negotiation sessions the following year with corporate amnesia—little acknowledgment of its failure to hit its numbers, and the same aggressive demands of up-front investment dollars that the CPG companies would need to commit to have their products included in the customer offering.

"For the most part, they've underdelivered on promises for years, yet continue to ask for astronomical levels of supported investment with promises to deliver something that doesn't happen," a top executive of a popular snack brand told me. He requested anonymity to speak freely about the relationship with Amazon, because his company has no choice but to continue doing business with the tech giant.

Inside Unilever, the maker of brands like Hellmann's, Dove, and Vaseline, tensions with Amazon reached a boiling point in the mid-2010s. During a meeting between the two companies, one of Amazon Fresh's midlevel leaders made what Unilever execs considered to be ridiculous financial demands and backed them up with even more ridiculous reasoning:

"'You need to understand that Jeff Bezos says we have to operate this business at a profit, so that's why we have to ask you for these investments,'" the Amazon Fresh manager said, according to someone who was present at the meeting. "This was a really smart person who had spent time at McKinsey and had a really big, fancy degree."

One Unilever executive was flabbergasted by Amazon's "logic" and confronted the Fresh manager in front of several dozen staff members from both companies, who were in attendance.

"So that means we can't make money for you to make money?" the Unilever executive asked. "You're basically saying that your model doesn't work."

The Amazon Fresh manager's face lit up red as the CPG executive predicted what might come next. Eventually, he said, the brick-and-mortar grocery giants were going to get their act together and transform into formidable digital-savvy foes. At that point, Amazon would have a considerable problem on its hands.

"Nobody's going to want to play with you," the executive told them, "because you were such a pain in the ass."

Years later, Amazon would be forced to confront just such a reality as the Covid-19 pandemic swept the world. As a result, Walmart and others attracted new customers to their online grocery services, and thus more interest from CPG brands.

In an interview, Landry, the Amazon VP responsible for the company's global grocery delivery services, appeared perplexed by the litany of complaints that CPG industry execs relayed to me. It seemed hard to believe that she hadn't heard some version of them over the years. But what was believable was her claim that she doesn't spend much time worrying about such critiques.

"We have been engaged in trying to invent something that didn't exist in a big way before," she told me in 2021, "and I find that our vendors have wanted to participate in creating that future and have been very happy to work with us."

Pantry's Closed

In early 2021, Amazon announced that the Pantry service would be shut down and, in typical Amazon fashion, put a positive spin on the news.

"As part of our commitment to delivering the best possible customer experience, we have decided to transfer Amazon Pantry selection to the main Amazon.com store so customers can get everyday household products faster, without an extra subscription or purchase requirement," a spokesperson said in an email.[3]

Amazon's grocery offerings had come a long way between the launch of Amazon Pantry in 2014 and its shutdown in 2021. And that progress made Pantry less of a priority by 2021 than it was in the mid-2010s. But I was curious—I wanted to see how much of the Amazon spokesperson's statement held true; that is, would the same twelve-can pack of Diet Coke—which was so pivotal in the creation of Prime Pantry—really be available to customers at a good price, "without an extra subscription or purchase requirement," after Pantry's selection was supposedly folded into the main Amazon.com storefront?

So, in December 2021, I searched Amazon for that twelve-pack of Diet Coke that Herrington told me had started it all. The top search result showed a price of $16.27. I did a double take. The item would be shipped and sold by a third-party Amazon merchant that was almost certainly baking the shipping costs into the product price itself. At the same time, it didn't appear that Amazon was carrying the Diet Coke on its own, and when I specifically searched the Amazon Fresh selection instead of the broader Amazon.com grocery catalogue, a message indicated that Diet Coke cans were out of stock.

Even though we don't regularly buy soda in our household, the $16.27 price sounded high. And it was. Reports from 2014 show that Amazon was selling the same Diet Coke twelve-pack for less than $4 through Prime Pantry shortly after launch.[4] As for comparable prices in 2021, I found a local New Jersey Walmart Supercenter near me was selling the same twelve-pack for almost $10 cheaper than the Amazon merchant. For that price, I could order it online and pick it up at the Walmart Supercenter, or add it to a larger Walmart.com order of at least $35 to have it shipped to me for free. Even if I wanted Walmart to deliver the twelve-pack to me on its own, with nothing else, it would cost $12.27, including a $5.99 shipping fee, or about $4 cheaper than through Amazon. Either way, this 2021 snapshot signaled that Amazon still had more work to do to make mainstream grocery brands available to online shoppers at affordable prices, no matter what the company communicated to the press when Pantry folded.

"I've had many failed innovations here," Herrington told me in 2021, reflecting on Pantry's demise, "and I think it was probably a bridge too far [to involve] the customer in the challenges of the consumables grocery product category."

Landry said it seemed that "customers just didn't want to think in that way," and that Pantry's limited selection—about two thousand items at launch—was problematic. "They wanted to be able to add what they wanted."

Not surprisingly, both executives said the arc of the Pantry life cycle represents a feature of the Amazon method of invention, rather than a bug in the system: come up with a proposed solution to an identified problem, test it at scale, learn stuff along the way, and fold it when necessary—while keeping open the possibility that the idea could one day be resurrected.

"All of these things that we're working on are very likely to come back in slightly different forms based on consumers' willingness to try new things," Landry told me. "Technology developments, making the experience better, there's just so many different factors at play. None of these ideas are necessarily bad ideas if they didn't work at the time; it just might be that the execution or the time isn't right."

Others I spoke to, however, had a slightly different view: that Pantry stood out from other Amazon failures not for where it ended, but where it started: with concerns about profit and losses—something that former Amazon employees who later took jobs at Walmart would tell me was a key obstacle to innovation at their new workplace, and something they didn't often encounter at Amazon.

"It felt like one of the first times that we didn't start with the customer [in mind]," a former Amazon senior manager told me years later of Prime Pantry.

Still, Amazon had another card up its sleeve in the CPG and grocery wars, and a nearly $14 billion one at that. On a Friday morning in late spring 2017, Amazon put Walmart on notice that it was doubling down on grocery sales, and its ambitions were no longer strictly digital.

7
AMAZON SENDS A WAKE-UP CALL

On Friday morning, June 16, 2017, my phone lit up with a flurry of text messages and push alerts. Amazon was acquiring Whole Foods for $13.7 billion, the companies had announced, in what was Jeff Bezos's brashest bet in a very long line of them.

While the announcement was stunning in some respects, it did not come completely out of nowhere. Amazon had long struggled to sell consumables and fresh groceries profitably, and it would be easier to do that with physical stores. Also, in April of that year, Bloomberg reported that Amazon executives had pondered the idea of acquiring Whole Foods a few months earlier, but never developed a formal plan to make an offer for the company.[1] Yet as public filings would later reveal, around the time that article was published, Whole Foods CEO John Mackey was feeling pressure from an activist investor who wanted the underperforming chain to consider selling, and had a liaison reach out to a top Amazon official.

By the final Sunday of the month, Mackey and a few deputies were on a plane to Seattle to meet with Bezos and other executives in the Amazon CEO's boathouse. The Amazon contingent included one of the corporate development leaders who had threatened Marc Lore and his Quidsi cofounder at that fancy New York City dinner years earlier when the duo had broached the topic of selling Diapers.com and the rest of their company to Walmart instead of Amazon. Doug Herrington, the longtime internal proponent of grocery delivery and, for better or worse, Amazon's king of CRaP, also attended the Whole Foods summit.

Less than a month later, the two sides would agree on Amazon paying a purchase price of $42 a share, and business history was made. After a decade of developing mostly middling grocery initiatives that had yet to break through in a big way, it seemed like the Amazon team was waving a large white flag accompanied by a mea culpa: physical retail isn't dead. But Amazon rarely makes a move only for defensive reasons. The acquisition was also received by grocery store executives, including at Walmart, as a warning flare: Amazon was coming.

Checkers vs. Chess

June 16 was supposed to mark a celebration of sorts inside Walmart, too—at least for Marc Lore and Andy Dunn, the cofounder and CEO of the menswear brand Bonobos. Dunn and Bonobos had gained a certain level of business-world fame for being one of the first fashion brands to hawk its line of goods first and foremost online, and later expand into the physical world, rather than vice versa. That same morning, Walmart announced that it was acquiring Bonobos for $310 million.[2]

Unlike distressed websites like ModCloth, which Walmart snatched up for less than $100 million, Lore knew Bonobos would be more expensive but envisioned the startup playing a more strategic role in the Walmart digital transformation plan. For starters, Lore saw Dunn, the charismatic founder, as the leader who could oversee a growing portfolio of acquired and incubated startups inside Walmart. There was also hope that the Bonobos deal would serve as another poster child in the "this ain't the same Walmart" narrative-building exercise aimed at future hires and Wall Street investors.

Despite this vision, and Lore's strong standing as Doug McMillon's digital prophet, the Bonobos acquisition idea was far from a sure thing.

"Everyone thought he was crazy," said Walmart executive Lori Flees, McMillon's head of mergers and acquisitions.

In early 2017, at Walmart's year-start meeting for executives, Lore was exasperated that his strategy was not resonating with those he would need buy-in from to close such a deal. Flees, who oversaw Jet's integration into Walmart after encouraging McMillon to make the deal, tried to help. She spent three hours on the phone with the e-commerce boss Lore, each chatting from their respective hotel rooms, listening to the entrepreneur vent and counseling him on how to explain his Bonobos idea in a way that would resonate with the retail traditionalists in Bentonville.

"My role was a bit of a translator," she told me. "I felt like my job was helping him understand where [Walmart] was, and why his idea was crazy from their viewpoints."

Flees herself was not a proponent of acquiring Bonobos, but still felt a responsibility to help Lore make the best internal pitch he could. And that pitch needed to focus at least in part on profits, as many tough conversations inside Walmart do. But it would also help to offer a vision of Bonobos as the foundation of a new portfolio of attractive name-brand merchandise that consumers could only buy at Walmart, and not from their Seattle archrival.

"The argument that had to be made . . . was how do you get to better economics on the e-commerce side," Flees told me, referencing the robust profit margins of the apparel industry that Bonobos competed in compared to the slimmer margins of consumables, while also creating "some differentiation in what you're offering relative to what Amazon is offering."

Lore's pitch worked. On Friday, June 16, 2017, Walmart officially announced the deal for Bonobos, alongside an interview with the *New York Times*.[3]

The timing was almost laughably terrible for Walmart because of Amazon's Whole Foods deal that went public the same day. For every Walmart advancement in recent years, Amazon always seemed to be one step ahead. This time was no different, and the sting was felt deeply within Walmart's e-commerce division.

"That was a really scary moment for the organization," a former

Walmart strategy leader told me years later. "I remember everyone saying, 'Okay, Bonobos versus Whole Foods—we are playing checkers, they are playing chess.'"

It sure looked that way from the outside, too. The Walmart-Bonobos deal seemed like a fine and interesting bet. But the Whole Foods acquisition was an altogether different board move—an industry-rattling affair that, despite the organic grocer's modest 4 percent share of the overall US grocery market, signaled Amazon's firm intent to become a giant player in the sector that Walmart was long used to dominating. To make matters worse, Walmart's stock price dropped nearly 5 percent following the news of the deal,[4] while Amazon's stock gained more value from the announcement than it cost the company to purchase Whole Foods. In a way, Amazon got Whole Foods for free.[5] It almost seemed unfair.

"My heart sank," said Scott Hilton, the former Quidsi and Jet executive who took over as Walmart e-commerce's revenue chief after Jet was acquired. "I thought it was a great acquisition."

Silver Linings

For Marc Lore, though, there were some silver linings—or potential ones—in the wake of the deal. Lore is an optimist by nature, and possibly necessity; the entrepreneur has often stressed that founders need to focus on the tiny chance their idea will pan out, rather than the odds heavily stacked against them.

For starters, Lore felt a certain level of relief over what the deal wasn't—an acquisition of a large mainstream grocer that competed more directly with Walmart on selection and prices—than what it was: a deal for a grocer with less than 5 percent grocery market share in the US, and one that caters toward well-off consumers who typically don't make up the core Walmart customer base.

"If they had bought Kroger," said Lore, "we were screwed."

Lore also predicted the deal could turn into a distraction for Amazon since it marked its first large-scale entrée into physical retail—as well as specialty types of grocery products like organic foods, and fresh meat and fish—that the company knew little to nothing about.

Perhaps the brightest of the linings, though, was the opportunity the deal gave Lore to stress to his counterparts on Walmart's physical retail side that Amazon wasn't standing still—and that Walmart needed to innovate with equal or superior urgency. From day one, Lore and his deputies used whatever piece of external news or announcement they could to urge Walmart leaders to green-light faster and bolder moves as part of the company's digital transformation. This event would be no different.

The Whole Foods deal, Lore later told me, "was a great catalyst."

Lore would make his case—albeit via video conference—at an executive gathering of around twenty Walmart officials that took place within a few weeks of the Amazon/Whole Foods announcement in June 2017. The location was a meeting room above the Walmart Museum and Sam Walton's original 5&10 store in downtown Bentonville. While the strategy meeting was already planned before the acquisition announcement, the Whole Foods deal would now become an important topic of conversation. Part of the discussion involved educating attendees on the organic grocer, whose customer demographics and typical store locations differed greatly from Walmart's. Whole Foods—with its "Whole Paycheck" moniker—typically appealed to higher-income households in cities and in suburbs with dense populations of well-heeled shoppers. The average Walmart customer, on the other hand, comes from a household that brings in less income, and lives in those rural areas where the retailer has a much larger presence.

Greg Foran knew that customer well; he oversaw the company's massive four-thousand-store retail footprint in the US and had been tasked by McMillon with the gargantuan assignment of reversing the chain's disappointing performance in the US. Foran, a New Zealander and the former chief of the supermarket division of Woolworths in Australia, often reminded his colleagues that the most profitable Walmart model was the traditional Walmart model: customers drive to the store themselves, shop for their goods themselves, and transport those goods home themselves. He did, however, warm to the online grocery pickup model. But e-commerce leaders didn't believe that Foran was a strong supporter of the grocery *delivery* model and its challenging economics.

With both store and digital leaders assembled, Lore stressed the urgency of expanding Walmart's online grocery offerings as quickly as possible, by whatever means (and in whatever forms) necessary. At the time, about nine hundred Walmart stores offered grocery pickup as a free option for web customers, but Lore and his deputies wanted to see the nationwide rollout accelerate even faster. Lore also stressed, more than anything else, that while Walmart's pickup business offered a strategic advantage, grocery delivery was the next battleground and the company needed to step up its expansion.

Walmart was already on its way to leaning into online grocery, store leaders would later tell me, as a potential game-changing advantage over Amazon, and Doug McMillon had previously labeled online grocery as one of his top enterprise-wide initiatives—with Foran and his team overseeing the store execution of it even before the Jet team joined the company. As a result, Lore's words fell on mostly receptive ears. Years later, countless former Walmart executives and employees pointed to the Amazon/Whole Foods tie-up as an inflection point. A wake-up call even.

Only a week after Amazon announced the finalization of the Whole Foods deal, Walmart issued a press release announcing that its grocery pickup service would soon be available at its one thousandth Super-center. In what seemed too coincidental to be, well, a coincidence, Walmart said that pickup locations No. 995 through 1,000 would all be located at stores in a city that was especially important to Amazon: its hometown of Seattle, Washington.

"In Seattle, the company will be giving away Google Home devices to the first 250 Online Grocery customers in the market," Walmart said in the press release.[6]

A few months later, Walmart made another online grocery announcement, but this time it pertained to grocery delivery instead of pickup. The press release noted that delivery of groceries would soon be available from Walmart Supercenters "coast to coast," with a geographic expansion from six metro areas to one hundred by the end of 2018.[7] Up until that point, the rollout of grocery delivery was more methodical and strategic. But after the Whole Foods deal, the feeling among e-commerce leaders was that there was company-wide alignment on a more straightforward tack: "Screw it: everywhere, everywhere, every-where," as a former executive described it to me.

"I am extremely confident they would not be on that path if Amazon had not acquired Whole Foods."

The Battle from Within

If someone was to trace the history of Walmart's endeavors in online grocery, they might understand the company being a bit gun-shy when it came to committing to a big grocery delivery initiative. Walmart's first real experience with selling groceries online at any meaningful scale actually came courtesy of one of its subsidiaries: the UK grocery store chain Asda. And it didn't go well.

Walmart bought Asda in 1999 for more than $10 billion and would own the chain for two decades, until it sold off a majority owner-ship stake in the business in 2021 amid a restructuring of its inter-national assets. Asda began offering grocery delivery as early as 1998, but quickly found that its model—delivery from small warehouses—wasn't financially sustainable and was terribly hard to execute well without regularly disappointing customers. The company's two ware-houses were still processing fewer than five hundred orders a day by 2000,[8] while its rival Tesco sped ahead. Asda eventually backed away from the online grocery market altogether in the wake of the delivery abomination, until launching with a new online grocery model in 2011 called Click and Collect—or what Americans might refer to as "buy online, pick up at store." By the time that service ramped up, though, Asda was staring uphill at far more popular rivals.

"Tesco got first-mover advantage," Asda veteran and current Wal-mart International CEO Judith McKenna told me in late 2021. "And once they locked up the loyalty, it's the devil's own job to move them on." (Years later, Amazon would hire one of Tesco's own to lead a key new grocery initiative.)

Despite trailing Tesco, Asda pushed forward in online grocery since the opportunity was enormous and consumers expected the offerings.

When Doug McMillon took over as Walmart CEO in 2014, he traveled to the UK with Walmart board members to witness firsthand Asda's progress. Some of the company's innovations included grocery pickup lockers featuring three compartments with different temperature settings—chilled, frozen, and room temp—as well as pickup points inside the London subway system.

McMillon came away impressed and, having decided that online grocery would be a key initiative for Walmart during his tenure, he and his deputies tapped a collection of Asda leaders to relocate to the US. Together, they had one central goal: to build a national online grocery service in the US that finally took advantage of Walmart's massive store footprint. With Supercenters located within ten miles of 90 percent of the US population, Walmart had the ability to beat Amazon on speed for both grocery pickup *and* delivery orders—and perhaps could do it more cost-effectively. It was an advantage that Amazon executives had long feared Walmart would identify and leverage, but one that the traditional retailer had long underutilized.

With McMillon as CEO, that began to change. Between 2014 and 2015, two former Asda chief operating officers took on key Walmart US roles. One was McKenna, who had also spent time as Asda's chief financial officer, giving her expertise into the financial pitfalls that an online grocery business could instigate.

"We made every mistake under the sun," McKenna said of Asda's early online grocery initiatives. "But we learned a whole pile."

The other was an executive named Mark Ibbotson, who quickly developed a reputation as someone employees tried to avoid when standing between him and a goal or task for which he was responsible. Viewed by some as the "muscle" for Greg Foran, CEO of Walmart's US store business, Ibbotson had a penchant for military analogies that aligned with his execute-by-any-means-necessary mentality.

"He was definitely tough and into power," one former e-commerce executive told me of Ibbotson, "but he was also really effective at getting stuff done."

Together, McKenna and Ibbotson made a pact based on their Asda experience in the UK.

"If we ever got a chance to do grocery over again, we'd start with pickup first and delivery second—not the other way around," McKenna told me.

Prior to the takeover by former Asda executives, Walmart had dabbled in grocery delivery in a couple of test markets with its own delivery trucks. But the results were mostly disappointing, according to one former team member. Walmart was often spending a minimum of $20 per delivery order—an unsustainable cost—and the execution itself left much to be desired. But the Asda executives were confident that the Click and Collect pickup model that was common in the UK could also be popular in the US, considering the nation's car culture, and the popularity of drive-through restaurants in the suburbs and small rural towns.

Walmart first launched online grocery pickup in early 2014,[9] with a small team of e-commerce employees building the online ordering experience, and counterparts in the physical store division overseeing the initiative's actual real-life execution. The e-commerce team dedicated to the online grocery initiative got to move faster than they were used to at Walmart, in part because they were working separately from the Walmart.com team.

"They gave us a lot of independence," a former product manager said. "We really believed at the time that we had an opportunity to finally beat Amazon in one area."

McMillon saw the competitive advantage, too, but he knew he needed a respected veteran leader to bridge the gap between the digital and physical retail teams that the company desperately needed to work well together. He chose Michael Bender, a top store operations executive with a reputation for rallying an organization around a unified goal. McMillon's goal then, according to Bender's recollection, was to move Walmart toward a place where it wasn't "just able to mimic what Amazon is doing" but "to think differently," too.

The role, which Bender compared to something like a corporate "secretary of state," was not an easy one. He had to achieve consensus between key leaders on both the e-commerce and store sides of Walmart, on everything from the speed of the rollout to which division got internal credit for online grocery pickup sales. There was also work that needed to be done to convince regional and local store leaders that online grocery could be an advantage for them and the company, rather than a costly distraction.

To help get buy-in from the store managers whose staff would actually handle these orders, Bender and others decided to assign internal credit for online grocery sales to the physical store division, rather than the e-commerce division.

"We tested that and found out that, yes, that gets the attention because the store manager says, 'If you're doing something to help me improve my sales, improve my inventory and in-stock position, I'll listen,'" Bender told me. "'If you're doing something that's against that, or I don't see the benefit of, then I may not pay as much attention to that.'"

Leaders of the initiative also had to encourage store managers and executives to accept the possibility that online grocery pickup orders might cannibalize more profitable in-store sales. This was not just old-school paranoia; it was plausible, or even likely. But McMillon had stressed his view to his leadership team from the time he named online grocery as a top company initiative.

"Doug was very clear from day one [that] it might cannibalize, but we want to keep customers within our ecosystem," said Kieran Shanahan, who ran online grocery for Asda in the UK and then was tapped as VP of online grocery for Walmart in the US in 2014.

But as early positive customer feedback and heartwarming customer testimonials accompanied strong financial results and milestones being met, store managers became some of the initiative's most important internal advocates. And a recommendation from one store manager to another could, in many cases, be more powerful than any top-down directive, even at a company as hierarchical as Walmart.

There were other key decisions, too. One was whether Walmart would charge online customers for the grocery pickup service. After all, the service involved a Walmart associate essentially shopping for the online customer and then bringing the order outside to the customer's car. The company also had to set up specialized training programs for its workers, utilizing much of the Asda playbook.

As a result, there was a debate over whether the customer should bear any cost, and the company even tested charging a nominal fee. Among those in favor of keeping the service free, though, was Mc-Millon, the CEO. Other leaders responsible for the program also did not want to give customers any reason to avoid trying out the service, especially considering the three stated goals of the initiative: "attract new customers to Walmart, deepen existing [customer] relationships, and then use the service to change perception of Walmart," according to Shanahan.

It was decided: the pickup service would be offered to customers for free. And once a Walmart store location exhibited consistent performance with its online grocery pickup service, it wouldn't be that much more work to hand off the order to a delivery person rather than placing the order in a pickup customer's car.

But before any of that could occur, Walmart first needed to develop the will to make a big play in grocery delivery services, too. Amazon's blockbuster acquisition of Whole Foods helped provide an impetus. But for better or worse, it would still be executed in the typical Walmart cost-conscious way.

"They settled on the middle ground of 'We're going to roll [grocery pickup] out as fast as we possibly can, and we're going to add delivery,'" an executive familiar with the meeting told me, "'but we're not going to go as far as even barely [unprofitable] to drive unnatural growth.'"

Outside Walmart, the rest of the grocery industry was also figuring out how best to react to Bezos's chess move. Inside CPG conglomerates like the Coca-Cola Company, where the vast majority of sales still came from physical retail stores, there was a newfound appreciation for the strategic importance of online sales.

"That is the first time a lot of people in Coke started taking Amazon seriously," one source told me.

A crop of young, on-demand delivery companies also found themselves in the spotlight. Instacart, the grocery delivery startup, had counted Whole Foods as its biggest partner, so the Amazon acquisition could have been crippling. But in the wake of the deal, dozens of grocery chain partners desperate for a delivery ally flocked to Instacart and more than made up for Whole Foods' eventual departure. Instacart competitor Shipt also found itself an increasingly attractive partner for grocery chains. On the day the Amazon/Whole Foods deal was announced, Shipt founder and CEO Bill Smith was on vacation. But not for long.

"People were bouncing back and forth between 'Is this horrible news, or is this amazing news?'" he told me about fielding the dozens of calls and texts he received about the announcement. "I was in the camp that it was good news, because you couldn't buy Coca-Cola at Whole Foods. You can't get Cheerios. Whole Foods doesn't have the products that most American consumers buy regularly."

Within two weeks, multiple large grocery chains contacted the startup about partnering with it or acquiring it. One of them was Target. By July the two sides were engaged in acquisition talks, and a deal was reached in the fall. In December, Target announced the deal and said it had paid $550 million in cash to acquire the startup.

"I think when the Whole Foods/Amazon deal happened, it created urgency," Smith told me.

According to Smith, representatives for his company had a few conversations with Walmart before the Target acquisition, but nothing serious ever came of them. He always figured the Bentonville retailer would build a grocery delivery network on its own.

As for Amazon, Smith said he had a few calls with an M&A employee there prior to the Whole Foods acquisition. But Smith turned down an offer to visit Amazon officials in Seattle to discuss a potential deal more in-depth.

"I think they were just sniffing around for information," Smith said. "My investors told me they do that with everybody—all kinds of companies. They'll call them and they want them to come into Seattle and talk to them about the business. And they just take all the information and they use it themselves."

Prime Dreams

By the time Amazon decided to go all in on Whole Foods, company leaders had made a few key decisions. One was that if the opportunity presented itself, they would be open to acquiring a physical retail chain. For all their progress in transforming online shopping from a niche into common daily behavior, they couldn't ignore that some 80 to 90 percent of commerce transactions every second of every day still occurred inside physical stores, and they knew the ratio was even more lopsided when it came to fresh groceries. If Amazon wasn't innovating in physical retail, especially in a retail sector as important to consumers as grocery, was the tech giant really living up to its promise to be the world's most customer-centric company?

Once that was decided, they made a dream list of potential grocery chain targets. Whole Foods was toward the top, but it seems likely that Trader Joe's might have been, too. Several company executives had long been admirers of the quirky grocery chain whose reputation for innovative, relatively low-priced packaged foods—not to mention an unusually friendly staff—coalesced into a cult following in communities across the US. Bezos himself had yearned to strike a delivery partnership with the grocer years earlier, when Amazon's two-hour delivery service, Prime Now, launched, but was denied.

A takeover of Trader Joe's was never going to happen. And once Whole Foods founder John Mackey felt backed into a corner in the wake of flagging sales and a pot-banging activist shareholder, Amazon was happy to listen—especially considering their own dearth of expertise in organic grocery and refrigerated supply chains.

"When John said he was ready, I think we were all like, 'Yeah, this just makes sense,'" said Greeley.

One obvious reason a Whole Foods deal made sense for Amazon was that it was simply a grocery chain, and owning a grocery chain offered Amazon a rather old-school solution to its CRaP problem that consumables leader Doug Herrington, and other execs, were so adamant about eventually solving.

"The most important add that we had to make was in support of the very freshest items—the items that were just too low-price to support delivery one at a time," Jeff Wilke, the longtime Bezos deputy, told me. "And that's what happens in a grocery store."

But the Whole Foods chain also possessed another characteristic that made it appear to be a solid fit for Amazon: geographic overlap between its store locations and the cities and towns where a large percentage of US Prime members lived. For that reason alone, Greeley was ecstatic.

"We knew that Prime would be a part of it from the get-go," Greeley said, "because Jeff [Bezos] had been very supportive of me saying [that] every business in this company needs to have a Prime offering, or a really good rationale as to why not."

Once the deal was in the works, Greeley immediately set out to brainstorm creative ways to bring the Prime loyalty program to the organic grocer. He had hoped to announce at least one of the new Prime perks alongside the deal's finalization in late August.

The list included such ideas as reserving five to ten parking spots up front for Prime members at Whole Foods locations; discounts on Whole Foods gift cards on Amazon.com; a 5 percent cash-back offering for Whole Foods shoppers who paid with the Prime Visa credit card; and, just for fun, a free giveaway of prime rib.

In the end, none of the ideas were green-lit before the deal was finalized. Some of them would have required the two companies to work together in-depth prior to the deal closing, which could be deemed an illegal behavior known as "gun-jumping." Company leaders feared that other ideas would simply give off the appearance of gun-jumping. (The prime rib giveaway never happened, but butchers at a Whole Foods location in California did take it upon themselves to mold ground beef into a Prime logo to celebrate the acquisition closing.)

The Prime Visa card discount was eventually announced about six months after the acquisition closed, in February 2018.[10] That same month, Amazon finally unveiled something the whole industry had been waiting for (and fearing, in some cases): free same-day delivery of Whole Foods groceries for Prime members, through the Prime Now rapid delivery service.

Around that same time, Greeley was looking for a new challenge, having run Prime for more than four years. He discussed several ideas for a new role with his boss, consumer head Jeff Wilke, as well as with Jeff Bezos himself, Greeley told me. One of the proposed roles involved overseeing the integration of Whole Foods into Amazon. As Greeley and the Jeffs were kicking around different options, Business Insider published multiple stories, beginning in December 2017, documenting significant stocking issues inside Whole Foods stores.[11] The two Jeffs had seen enough, and sent Greeley a note.

"'I know you've been thinking about these four different ideas and we've—I mean you've—decided that it's going to be Whole Foods,'" Greeley recalled the note saying, with a laugh.

What the Jeff duo didn't know at the time was that Greeley was also seriously considering leaving Amazon, having been offered a job by another growing company. Within a few weeks of Greeley's taking on the Whole Foods role in early 2018, he would accept a top executive role at Airbnb, the home-rental company, to help transform the travel startup sensation into an enduring, large corporation capable of eventually going public. Bezos and Wilke would need to find another leader.

But neither Greeley nor the Jeffs were aware of another company that was training its eye on Amazon executives to help with its own transformation. A company that, twenty years earlier, had sued Amazon for poaching its executives: Walmart.

8
AMAZONIFICATION

While Walmart store leaders felt a newfound urgency to expand the online grocery business following Amazon's Whole Foods acquisition, Marc Lore's e-commerce leadership team was still evaluating the best ways to compete online when it came to shipping goods from warehouses, not stores. With logistics issues that were impossible to ignore, top supply-chain executive Nate Faust concluded that an overhaul was needed, and it started where e-commerce orders do—in the warehouses where staff pick and pack the shipments before sending them off to online customers' doors.

His reasoning was rather straightforward: that 2016 holiday season, the first one after the Jet acquisition, was a borderline disaster, and problems emerged during the 2017 holidays, too. When Walmart announced its financial results for that period, the company revealed a drastic deceleration in the growth of its online sales, which spooked Wall Street investors, cratering the stock price. Walmart CEO Doug McMillon told stock analysts at the time that much of the pullback in sales growth was planned. Walmart's year-over-year growth numbers were no longer benefiting from incorporating Jet.com's sales numbers, since Jet had by then been part of Walmart for more than a year. Sources told me that Lore had also been pressured to pull back on losses in an attempt to better balance out sales growth with profits.

But McMillon did reveal that some "operational" issues also played a role in that deceleration. Those issues were varied, according to former executives, but included seasonal inventory taking up too much space and blocking out merchandise that customers bought frequently year-round, as well as significant miscalculations by existing warehouse leaders over how many packages they could ship out each day during the peak holiday shopping season. Walmart's warehouse automation systems also experienced issues in both 2016 and 2017.

"Conveyors were a problem, we didn't hire enough people, there was no forecasting," a former e-commerce leader told me. "We needed new talent."

Nate Faust recognized this and quickly began looking outside the company for help. Perhaps not surprisingly, his eyes drifted toward a company with significant e-commerce expertise, one he knew well from his time working there following Quidsi's sale years earlier.

"[We] just hired a lot of Amazon people," a former top Walmart supply chain executive told me, "and the Amazon people started to hire other Amazon people."

In late 2017 and across 2018, a wave of Amazon warehouse and transportation leaders began taking over inside Walmart e-commerce facilities across the country. If Amazon had proven one thing to competitors and consumers alike, it was that it knew how to get packages to customers quickly—first under longtime Bezos deputy Jeff Wilke, and later under his deputy, Dave Clark, a hard-charging former warehouse manager once nicknamed "The Sniper,"[1] who would go on to replace Wilke as CEO of Amazon's worldwide consumer business in 2021.

Amazon's warehouse strategy succeeded for a bevy of reasons: part process innovation, part automation, and part surveillance, with a technology system that tracked worker movements and performance down to the second.

"I knew that every single time we developed a tool, we are just adding pressure," a former Amazon data science engineer focused on warehouse metrics told me.[2] "The pressure to be consistent and perform every single second there is tremendous."

That was by design. Amazon's longtime obsession wasn't about making life better or easier for its employees; it was about making life better for customers. Seemingly no matter the internal ramifications. And in Amazon's view, it seemed for long stretches of time, there was no correlation between the two. The business results of Amazon's approach—rapid growth of Prime memberships and continuous market share gains in e-commerce—suggested that the company was succeeding in its goal. After all, no one at Amazon was being judged on how nice they were.

Jet leaders, on the other hand, liked to talk up the more humane treatment of its employees. Marc Lore once told me he would err on the side of social cohesion even if it led to slower decision-making—much to the shock of the Walmart public relations official in the room. Conversely, one of Amazon's Leadership Principles includes the section "Leaders have conviction and are tenacious. They do not compromise for the sake of social cohesion." But funny things happen when your back is against the wall and the pressure is on.

Recruiting warehouse leaders from the leading e-commerce company to a notorious digital laggard wouldn't be easy. This led Walmart e-commerce leaders to do something that wasn't particularly popular among some long-timers at Bentonville's home office: paying big money to flip Amazon employees to the dark side. To court them, the former Jet leaders running Walmart e-commerce green-lit what some insiders saw as extravagant pay packages, with cash and sign-on bonuses for warehouse managers totaling $300,000 annually or more—around double what Walmart's existing warehouse staff made, though some Walmart e-commerce warehouse leaders who remained were given big pay bumps, too.

When they arrived, Amazon leaders were given free rein on all kinds of decisions, from heavy spending to procure equipment replacement parts to overhauling performance-tracking systems and worker schedules. But in at least one notable case, the new work culture some Amazon leaders imported to Walmart ran into resistance.

If You Can't Beat 'Em

Jeremy Knight joined Walmart in 2013 as a maintenance mechanic at the company's Porterville, California, distribution center, repairing conveyor belts and forklifts and doing general preventive maintenance to keep things running smoothly. Distribution centers (DCs) are the Walmart warehouses that store merchandise before it gets shipped to stores. The Porterville DC was the oldest on the West Coast, having opened back in 1991.

"It was a great place to work," Knight told me. "It felt like everybody was working together for a common goal."

Weekly lunch cookouts were the norm if the warehouse's safety metrics were good. When a piece of trash or broken pallet found its way onto the floor, you could bet that the first person who passed it would pick it up and toss it in the garbage.

"I know these sound like little things, but the people in Porterville cared," Knight said.

Knight eventually moved on in 2016 for a new opportunity at a newly opened Walmart warehouse in Chino, California. But this facility was a not a distribution center; it was a fulfillment center (FC), which meant it was dedicated exclusively to the packing and shipping of online orders, rather than store-bound merchandise. Under Walmart's previous e-commerce boss, Neil Ashe, the e-commerce division had finally gotten the green light to expand a network of warehouses exclusively dedicated to online orders, rather than having to carve out space in the old-school distribution centers that were mainly used to hold goods headed to Walmart stores.

The Chino FC's first general manager was a Walmart veteran who previously ran safety and security for distribution centers. Now, in Chino, he was running a 1.2 million-square-foot e-commerce facility and oversaw a workforce of more than one thousand people. Despite these pressures, the Walmart veteran could often be found on the warehouse floor interacting with workers, according to Knight, either checking in on questions or concerns, or sometimes even packing boxes himself.

But there were downsides to longtime Walmart leaders running new e-commerce warehouses. An obvious one was a lack of experience in e-commerce logistics. The other was a tendency for Walmart lifers to become a bit set in their ways.

"With that kind of tenure comes complacency," a former Walmart e-commerce logistics leader told me. "And there was a lot of that."

In late 2017, the Amazon takeover began when a new general manager took over in Chino. He increased performance tracking, which former employees admitted was necessary because of lackluster productivity rates—but there was a catch. Several former employees and executives told me that workers were often set up to fail: one of the biggest issues that workers on warehouse floors faced was significant overcrowding of inventory, resulting in widespread difficulties when it came to tracking inventory accurately and knowing which items were where. The Chino Walmart warehouse was in such disarray that, at one point, seventy pallets' worth of merchandise were unaccounted for in the company's inventory management software. In real life, the goods existed, and took up lots of space. But if a customer were to look up the product online, Walmart.com would be out of stock.

The new GM from Amazon also instituted a different type of worker shift schedule—called a waterfall—that was common inside Amazon warehouses and aimed to give managers more flexibility. But executives told me that the Chino fulfillment center was not yet operating efficiently enough to handle such a dramatic alteration, and leadership didn't have great visibility into who was and wasn't present at work during a given shift. That could be a problem for both productivity and safety reasons. On top of that, worker schedules became less predictable as a result of the overhaul, leading many to feel that they had become a soulless cog in the "Amazonified" machine.

"A lot of Amazon folks know only one playbook," a former Walmart logistics manager told me.

The dynamic created an environment that felt much more transactional than employees were used to. Morale in Chino noticeably sagged, former employees say. Tensions reached a boiling point when the ex-Amazon GM addressed staff during a monthly business update. He had to deliver some bad news—Knight, the warehouse mechanic, can't quite remember whether it was about pay raises or something about overtime. Either way, it was not a good update. And when the warehouse boss delivered it in what many thought was an unsympathetic way, the response from the rank-and-file staff was instantaneous—and brutal.

"They booed him off the stage," Knight told me. "The fact that could happen to the biggest person in the building just shows . . . how crappy people felt. It was the perfect storm of people already being frustrated with management and feeling like none of them cared."

Within a few months of arriving, the general manager was out and headed back to the online retail giant and, according to the gossip among Walmart employees, to a giant new pay package as well. His quick about-face set off conspiracy theories among some Walmart staff, who imagined Jeff Bezos sending spies into Walmart to infiltrate their retail enemy's operations, cause chaos, and then report back. I didn't find a shred of information to back up the speculation, which would be especially surprising since many Amazon imports were doing their best to teach Walmart the Amazon way. But the speculation, however wild, spoke to the distrust between the underpaid and over-worked employees expected to execute one of the most critical parts of Walmart's e-commerce makeover and the newcomers in charge of leading them through it.

Some warehouse managers who'd come over from Amazon were also accused of fostering an all-boys-club, almost fratlike company culture. One former Amazon manager allegedly took subordinates with him to a strip club and asked staff members to charge alcohol on their corporate cards, saying he would approve it even though it was against company policy. These claims appeared in a gender discrimina-tion lawsuit filed against Walmart by a former warehouse automation engineer who alleged, after she was fired, that she had been passed over for a promotion because of her gender. Walmart settled the lawsuit out of court[3] and fired the former Amazon manager with a penchant for partying, according to Walmart spokesperson Erin Hulliberger.

Despite the chaos that some felt the Amazon takeover caused, several former Amazon employees hired by Walmart continued to take on more senior roles as warehouse performance improved. In late 2022, for example, Walmart tapped one of them, David Guggina, to oversee Walmart's entire US supply chain. Jet leaders had placed much of Walmart's e-commerce supply chain into the hands of those trained by the retailer's longtime nemesis. As the saying goes: If you can't beat 'em . . .

The Middle Mile

Remaking its fulfillment center operations in Amazon's image—for better or worse—was only one piece of how Jet leaders wanted to transform Walmart's execution of all things logistics, the deeply unsexy stuff that happens before and after an online customer clicks "Buy." Executives also wanted to rethink Walmart's reliance on large shipping and delivery carriers like FedEx, which at times had shown cracks in its reliability as online shopping grew both on Walmart.com and beyond.

Once again, they would look to former Amazon employees for help. After all, Amazon knew this problem well, and had spent years creating in-house solutions. It all started in late 2013, when many Amazon customers received Christmas deliveries later than promised, mainly because UPS was overwhelmed by the rise of last-minute holiday shopping online as well as by winter storms. Amazon cast blame on the shipping giant in notes to customers, saying that the online retailer had handed orders off to its shipping partner on time. To make amends for breaking its delivery promise, the online retailer also handed out a slew of $20 gift cards and refunded delivery fees.

Inside Amazon, executives were furious that they had disappointed their customers at the most crucial time of year. To make matters worse, they had little control over the fiasco. As a result, Amazon's then–logistics chief, Dave Clark, sought out one of his deputies, Mike Indresano, who had joined Amazon a year earlier after spending twenty-four years at FedEx. His experience at FedEx would be critical for Amazon, and there was no love lost between him and his former employer after he was unceremoniously escorted out by FedEx security upon giving notice that he was leaving the logistics titan for Amazon.[4]

According to Brad Stone's *Amazon Unbound*, Clark's question to Indresano was a burning one: How many sortation centers can you build by the end of 2014? The most Indresano had built at FedEx was four, but his answer to Clark was on an altogether different scale: he said he could build sixteen.

Indresano had experience overseeing this type of facility, called a sortation or "sort" center, at FedEx, but it was uncommon for these centers to be run by an individual retailer, even Amazon. At the time, the vast majority of Amazon's warehouses were so-called fulfillment centers—giant facilities—some as large as 1.2 million square feet, where warehouse staff would pluck merchandise off shelves and pack it into shipping boxes. Shipping partners like UPS and FedEx would then retrieve the orders from the warehouse and handle getting them to customers' homes, whether by plane or truck depending on the distance to the final destination.

Sortation centers, on the other hand, would be a new kind of warehouse for Amazon—maybe one-third or one-fourth the size of Amazon's largest fulfillment centers. At a high level, they would play a key role in allowing Amazon to eventually reduce its shipping costs per package and increase speed of delivery. On top of that, and maybe most importantly, sortation centers gave Amazon more control over customer orders once they left an Amazon fulfillment center, reducing the chance of ever disappointing as many customers as they did during the 2013 holiday season.

These "sort" centers would become part of the so-called middle mile of Amazon's supply chain. While customer orders would still be packed at the large fulfillment centers, their next step would now be different. Instead of UPS or FedEx picking up the packages from the FC, Amazon would transport the packages to one of its own sortation centers. At the sortation center, a combination of conveyor belts and workers would help organize customer packages into different groupings based on the zip codes of the delivery addresses. From there Amazon would drop off the customer orders at US Postal Service facilities or post offices throughout a given region, letting the USPS handle the most expensive piece of the supply chain: the "last mile" delivery to customers' homes. Postage per package would now cost Amazon a lot less, since a delivery partner was only taking the package a short distance from the post office to a nearby home or office.

This new process meant Amazon was handling extra steps of the supply chain itself rather than farming them out. But it came with an advantage that convinced company leaders that the extra work would be worth it. In regions where Amazon built sortation centers, Prime members had their order deadline for free two-day delivery extended by nine hours,[5] since orders were now remaining within the Amazon supply chain for longer and not being slowed down by all of the other packages, processes, and priorities of shipping partners like UPS and FedEx. The new partnership that the sortation centers created with the USPS also allowed Amazon to persuade the government logistics service to deliver packages on Sunday—a huge step in the evolution of e-commerce that the other shipping carriers had been unwilling to do. Now Prime members who needed merchandise before Monday could avoid weekend trips to stores like Walmart Supercenters, since placing a Prime order on Friday now meant it would arrive on Sunday. That was a huge development in the e-commerce and retail worlds, and another way that Amazon was making its service more convenient than competitors'.

Over time, as Amazon's sales volume increased, Amazon created its own "last mile" delivery operation, too. Called Amazon Logistics, the delivery network supplemented the work of UPS and the USPS, giving Amazon even more control over the customer experience postpurchase because it was now overseeing some orders all the way to a customer's front door. Of course, Amazon did it in a way that limited liability and the risk of unionization; it contracted with third-party delivery companies, even fronting as much as $10,000 so aspiring entrepreneurs could more easily create startup delivery operations from scratch. Amazon's growing logistics operation was creating a massive new moat between itself and Walmart, just as the creation of Amazon Prime had done more than a decade earlier.

While Indresano oversaw the massive sortation center buildout at Amazon—dubbed "the Sweet 16"—he eventually exited in 2017, burnt out and at odds with some of his counterparts who oversaw Amazon's network of fulfillment centers. The Amazon vice president of transportation left without another job lined up and was considering retirement after a combined thirty years of work between FedEx and Amazon.

But some months later, a friend recommended that Indresano

contact Walmart executives, knowing the company was undergoing a digital transformation and might be in the market for someone with his expertise. Indresano was admittedly skeptical of how serious Walmart was about investing in e-commerce, considering its historic struggles in the space. But the lunch recommendation triggered a memory of something one ex-Amazon colleague had told him when he was considering leaving the e-commerce titan: "Whatever you do, don't go to Walmart."

Indresano, however, was bitter about the way his Amazon career had ended, including feeling that this former colleague might have been happy to see him go. Maybe he should go work at Walmart after all, he thought. He quickly reached out to Nate Faust, the Jet executive in charge of Walmart's e-commerce supply chain. The two had spent some time together years earlier when Indresano was still at FedEx and Faust was working at Amazon after Bezos had acquired Diapers.com. And coincidentally, Faust already had Indresano atop the list of external candidates whom he planned to contact for the top e-commerce transportation role. So around six months after their first chat, in the summer of 2018, Indresano joined Walmart. There was much work to do. And Indresano wouldn't be alone. He was followed by several other senior Amazon employees as well.

Like Indresano, they would receive huge pay packages to make the move to the brick-and-mortar rival. As part of courting them, Jet leaders handed several of the Amazon defectors a VP title in the e-commerce division, despite that being a no-no in the brick-and-mortar division of Walmart. As a result, Indresano and a few others were advised not to use the job title in their email signatures because it would piss off long-timers who'd be furious over the supposed double standard.

"Some people said, 'Hell no,' and some people said 'Okay, if that makes life easier and helps my funding needs get approved to achieve my end goals, then fine,'" a former e-commerce executive told me.

"It was . . . a political battle royale," another former executive said.

Nonetheless, things were looking up for Walmart. At the time, its e-commerce sales were growing briskly thanks in large part to the expansion of the online grocery business. But Faust, Lore, and other former Jet executives knew they needed to drastically improve the customer experience for the types of merchandise that would be shipped from warehouses to customer doors in the future. They also knew that a big part of that process, as Amazon had realized many years earlier, was to take more control over what happened after packages left their warehouses. That often meant handing over control to FedEx, which handled at least 80 percent of Walmart's online orders in the US, according to former insiders.

In many ways, the FedEx relationship made sense for Walmart. Having one central national partner responsible for the majority of online orders meant, at least in theory, a more simplified end-to-end process for Walmart. And since e-commerce was still a tiny fraction of Walmart's overall sales—a significant portion of its growth was coming from those online orders for groceries that customers picked up at stores themselves—it made sense not to complicate something that was relatively immaterial to Walmart's current success.

Yet as the popularity of online shopping grew, both overall and on Walmart.com, some e-commerce leaders became concerned that FedEx was not investing enough to keep up with demand. During the 2018 holiday season, for example, FedEx only delivered 77.5 percent of its total packages on time, which meant around 1 out of every 4 packages shipped by FedEx would arrive later than promised. That same holiday season, UPS was at 86 percent reliability—about 1 out of every 7 packages. But Indresano knew firsthand that UPS could also fail, as the carrier did in spectacular fashion during the 2013 holiday season that convinced Amazon to start taking control of the "middle mile" and "last mile" of its supply chain, too.

As a result, Indresano set out to develop alternative options for Walmart to take more control over its e-commerce supply chain. One method, which Indresano knew well, was to replicate what he and his team had built over at Amazon. That was, to construct a network of regional sortation centers to cut per-package delivery costs and speed up delivery times, while taking more package volume away from FedEx and handing it over to the US Postal Service through local post offices.

But Indresano and his top associates had devised a more detailed plan than that. Few inside Walmart knew of it, and news of it never

leaked to the press. Under this secretive plan, Walmart would partner with a third-party logistics company called Newgistics, owned by
Pitney Bowes, which handles warehousing and the middle mile for
e-commerce brands before handing orders off to US post offices for
last-mile delivery, like Amazon started to do once it built its own sortation network.

The plan called for Walmart and Newgistics to set up a separate
company through a joint venture, in which both companies would
have an ownership stake. Newgistics would include its own sortation
centers in the new company, with Walmart promising to invest money
to potentially build dozens more. These sortation centers would then
handle both the packages of Newgistics e-commerce customers as well
as Walmart's e-commerce package volume. Since Newgistics already
partnered with the USPS for delivery to customers' doors, Walmart
would piggyback on that relationship to do the same. The new joint
company might also be called on to deliver customer orders to Walmart
stores, when a customer selected store pickup for an item that was only
stocked in a warehouse and not on a store shelf. Walmart's network of
thousands of in-house truck drivers and trucks might also play a role
in transporting goods between facilities under this plan.

To those involved in the negotiations, such an arrangement seemed
like a win-win. The additional package volume from Walmart could
reduce per-package cost for Newgistics, since the company's facilities would handle a greater volume of packages within the existing
warehouse infrastructure that it was already paying to operate. As a
result, productivity would increase, creating a more efficient operation.
Plus, the buildout of more sortation centers with Walmart's money
would also eventually translate into faster delivery speeds, and greater
geographic coverage, for Newgistics' other retailer partners and their
own customers as well.

For Walmart, the joint venture and network of new sortation
centers would play an important role in taking more control over its
delivery destiny. While it would require significant capital investment,
it promised to reduce per-package shipping costs in the long run—
something traditional Walmart execs could get behind. But, more
importantly for someone trained in the ways of Amazon customer

obsession, it would bring more reliability and speed to Walmart.com customer orders that couldn't be fulfilled out of a store.

"In e-commerce, the definition of success every year is around peak season," a former executive said. "And around peak, Amazon is the only retailer with few delivery issues because they own their own destiny."

But as months went by, members of Indresano's team found themselves questioning why Marc Lore, the chief executive of Walmart's US e-commerce operations, didn't seem to have the authority to unilaterally approve the plan. At each turn, the path to a yes—which at one point seemed to be a sure thing—was obstructed by some new delay or roadblock, which did little to build confidence among Walmart's e-commerce executives.

While the joint venture remained in corporate purgatory, Walmart looked for other ways to step up its delivery game and steal media and customer spotlight from Amazon. In the spring of 2019, Walmart was preparing to make a big announcement: free next-day delivery for hundreds of thousands of items, with no membership needed—just an online order that totaled at least $35.

Internally, the decision caused fierce debate. Faust, Lore, and other executives believed the next-day program would re-create some of the magic of Jet.com's Smart Cart. Walmart customers would receive their purchases faster, and Walmart would only qualify items for the program that could ship out of a single warehouse.

"It looked like it was a speed play," an executive in favor of the program told me, "but it was actually to incentivize consumers to build baskets that were all coming from a single building. One, it was a great experience. And two, it's a more profitable order."

Those in favor of the program also believed that the added restrictions of a next-day service would force the retailer to tighten up its logistics efforts throughout the company. Sink or swim. Still, Indresano was opposed to the decision, feeling the company was still disappointing customers too frequently with free two-day shipping—the first big service that launched under the Lore regime in early 2017—to start making promises on next-day deliveries. He also confided in colleagues that the launch seemed more designed to generate buzz among Walmart investors than to deliver an excellent feature to customers. But he was in no position to veto it, and the plan moved forward. The one compromise was that the next-day option would be turned off during the peak holiday season, when Walmart was already struggling to fulfill more conservative delivery promises.

Yet before Walmart could even announce the new offering, the executives would be in for a surprise: Amazon announced plans to shorten its flagship Amazon Prime delivery promise from two-day shipping to one-day. Walmart executives were stunned, suspecting Amazon had somehow learned of their plans in advance. In response, Walmart did something out of character: it sniped back with a tweet.

"One-day free shipping . . . without a membership fee," Walmart posted from its main Twitter account the day after Amazon's announcement. "Now THAT would be groundbreaking. Stay tuned."

A few weeks later, in May 2019, Walmart announced the next-day-delivery offer on a selection of around 200,000 items—a fraction of what Amazon was making available through its competing offer. The corporate sniping—however petty—returned to Twitter.

"Others are trying to up their fast shipping game," Amazon tweeted. "Fact is, Amazon customers in thousands of cities across 44 major metropolitan areas already have access to millions of items with free SAME DAY delivery. Customers are smart—they know the difference."

The Eleventh Hour

By the middle of 2019, almost a year after Indresano had joined Walmart to create and execute an e-commerce transportation strategy, some of his team were starting to lose hope that the joint venture would happen. But that July, Indresano and a few other e-commerce leaders finally presented to McMillon, the CFO, Brett Biggs, and other top Walmart execs in what they believed to be a final review. The feedback was good and they were pleased to hear what seemed to be full-on support pending the outcome of separate talks with Walmart's existing shipping partner, FedEx.

Indresano was also among the Walmart executives responsible for negotiating a new strategic deal with FedEx. The talks would seriously impact the futures of both companies, and so both McMillon and FedEx's founder and then-CEO Fred Smith were present in Bentonville at times. FedEx leaders knew that Walmart was considering taking more control over its e-commerce supply chain by building more sortation centers and handing off more of its e-commerce package volume to the US Postal Service. But the idea of a joint venture with Newgistics remained confidential.

When top FedEx and Walmart leaders met that same month, FedEx's Smith let McMillon and the rest of the room know what he thought of Walmart building its own sortation network and partnering more closely with the postal service. In short, he wasn't a fan. At the time, the USPS was experiencing brutal—and very public—financial challenges, and, thanks to its relationship with Amazon, found itself in then-president Donald Trump's crosshairs. Amazon itself was also a public punching bag for Trump, since Bezos owned the *Washington Post*, whose coverage of Trump the former president detested. Under these circumstances, some top Walmart officials were understandably nervous about turning their backs on FedEx for USPS, so one could imagine Smith's words resonating.

Indresano was also in the room and volleyed back at his former FedEx CEO with an opposing point of view. McMillon, all the while, did not let on all that he was thinking, leaving e-commerce executives wondering where the joint venture stood.

Soon after, Indresano would find out, as he was handed a new directive: get the deal done with FedEx. The joint venture with Newgistics wasn't happening, he was told, nor was any other plan for building out dozens of Walmart sortation centers and establishing a deeper relationship with the postal service.

"At the eleventh hour, it was 'No,'" someone familiar with the discussions told me.

It remained unclear how much Smith's words impacted McMillon's decision. But for Indresano, it didn't matter. Shortly after hearing that Walmart leadership was choosing to double down with FedEx rather than pursue his joint venture, Indresano resigned. He was still in disbelief that Walmart hired him with a monster pay package only to veto the plan he had architected. With Indresano out of the picture,

Nate Faust, the outgoing e-commerce supply chain boss, along with an Indresano deputy named Scott Ruffin, carried the FedEx negotiations across the finish line. Ruffin had worked for Indresano on his sortation center initiative at Amazon, and later led the development of Amazon's own cargo air service, Amazon Air. He would stay at Walmart another year before leaving in 2020 to launch his own startup. The new company, called Pandion, went to market with the goal of building a network of—what else—high-tech sortation center warehouses for e-commerce companies.

Years later, a former Walmart e-commerce executive pointed to the death of the joint venture idea as his biggest regret.

"That would be the one thing that I wish we had pushed harder for," the official said. "Without controlling the middle mile, you can never really control the last mile."

Without more control of the last mile, the questions became: Compared to Amazon, could Walmart ever truly satisfy consumers' insatiable hunger for rapid delivery? And were Walmart leaders even on the same page in wanting to do so?

THE GREATEST RETAILER
ON THE PLANET

Greg Foran was exasperated. He was seated in a conference room inside Walmart's Bentonville, Arkansas, home office on what must have felt like the millionth conference call with the retailer's supposed e-commerce savior, Marc Lore.

Foran was the CEO of Walmart's entire US operation—namely, its 4,700-plus stores—and he had been skeptical about the Jet.com acquisition from the start. He knew full well the history of turnover at the top of Walmart's e-commerce organization, as well as Lore's penchant for focusing on sales growth over profits. And he understood the impact that Lore's tactics might have on the overall Walmart US business he ran and the investments he could make in stores.

Now Foran was impatient as Lore babbled on about some pie-in-the-sky e-commerce initiative from the other end of the line. Foran pressed his finger against the mute button on his side of the line and lit into Lore to those assembled around the same Bentonville conference table. This guy doesn't know what the *hell* he's talking about, was the gist of Foran's diatribe.

The observer who relayed the account to me years later couldn't recall the specifics of the initiative Foran was disgusted with. But the more crucial point was that Foran, one of the most-respected retail leaders on the planet, was reaching his tipping point, and it seemed that Lore was the one pushing him closer to the edge.

The Retail King

There had been hope in the beginning. Foran and Lore had gotten together in 2016, back in the early days of the Walmart-Jet marriage, to try to make things work. They had been prodded by Walmart CEO Doug McMillon, who needed the two leaders to mesh for this grand experiment to pan out. The duo spent hours brainstorming ideas on a whiteboard before the deal was even consummated, sketching out ways that Walmart's four-thousand-plus stores could benefit from an e-commerce savant like Lore and how the company's performance in online retail might get a boost with insight and attention from the brick-and-mortar retail brilliance of Foran.

"When I first got to know Greg, and we're talking, and mapping stuff out, we got along really, really well," Lore told me. "And he was so happy that it was different than the regime before . . . we were communicating, we were talking; I guess they didn't really talk much before that."

Some of Foran's actions gave e-commerce leaders hope that he would buy into their vision. Case in point: at one point soon after the Jet acquisition, he gave tentative approval for a project that his own teams thought he never, ever would: combining the retailer's two separate shopping apps. One was the app that customers could use to order fresh groceries from a local Walmart store, and then have them ready curbside for pickup on the same day. Since the orders were packed by store employees, Foran's teams oversaw physical operations for the program and considered the initiative a point of pride. The other app was the general Walmart shopping app, through which shoppers could order all types of merchandise other than fresh groceries—from TVs to shampoo to crayons—and have them delivered to their home, mostly from warehouses. Lore's team was responsible for that.

Foran first joined Walmart in 2011, taking over the retailer's China business, where he reported to McMillon, who was then running the company's international operations. Once McMillon ascended to the chief executive role, he tapped Foran to take over Walmart's giant US stores operation. This stores division had struggled through nearly two years of flat or decreasing same-store sales and was plagued with issues ranging from poor in-stock rates to a subpar shopping experience compared to peers.

Foran was coming off a high-profile tenure at Woolworths, leading the supermarket division of Australia's largest retail chain, for which he first worked stocking shelves in his homeland of New Zealand (the company also has operations there). But his reign there ended disappointingly when the company passed him over for the CEO job.

"My father said, 'Well, that door shut; another's going to open, so get on with it,'" Foran told a New Zealand news channel in 2018.[1] "I love winning; I hate losing more. I learn more when I lose than what I ever do when I win."

Yet when Walmart announced Foran's promotion to run US stores, the move did not sit well with some.

"When they heard that we had appointed someone from New Zealand, [they] said, 'Are you out of your mind? You can't have a leader for the Walmart US business that's not American. He doesn't know our customers,'" McMillon said in the interview with the same New Zealand news network. "And I smiled and said, 'Just wait and see.'"

What critics may not have known was that even though the retail executive had never worked in the US, he came with intimate knowledge of the Walmart culture and model. He was mentored by Jack Shewmaker, one of Sam Walton's longtime No. 2 execs, who is credited as the creator of Walmart's Everyday Low Price promise.

"You've gotta remove yourself from the addiction to short-term sales and build long-term momentum," Shewmaker once said in extolling the benefits of an Everyday Low Price strategy.

After leaving Walmart, Shewmaker was a longtime consultant for Woolworths—or Woolies to locals—where, as Foran once told the *Harvard Business Review*,[2] he stressed to him the value of looking after both customers and associates alike.

Under Foran's watch, Walmart pulled back on store openings to improve the experience in existing stores for both customers and store workers. He widened shopping aisles from four feet to ten feet and decluttered them. He also invested nearly $3 billion early on into training and increased pay for associates—not only because it was "the right thing to do," as he told me, but also to try to reduce employee turnover and improve customer service. (The wage hike only moved the starting hourly wage to $9, with a promise of $10 the following year, but some Walmart employees previously only made the federal minimum of $7.25 an hour.) The investment crimped Walmart profits and was not well received by public market investors, even though critics would argue that the pay increases didn't go far enough. Walmart's market capitalization fell around $20 billion when the news was announced, but many rank-and-file store employees were more focused on how long overdue the pay raise was.

"You're making all this money off the backs of these workers, why not at least take care of them?" said Cynthia Murray, a Walmart store worker of twenty-two years who is a leader with the worker activist group United for Respect. "I mean, give them a decent wage to live off of."

Walmart wages had been so low for so long that even a significant percentage bump looked paltry to many outsiders. To leaders like Foran, though, the wage increase was nonetheless important. And Walmart colleagues acknowledge that, despite his outsider status, Foran's work ethic and frugality fit right in with Walmart leaders of generations past. Sam Walton drove a Ford pickup truck and started his days as early as 4:30 a.m. Foran aimed for five to six hours of sleep most nights, waking no later than 4 a.m., and was known to request meetings with colleagues as early as 6 a.m. He drove a Ford Explorer SUV despite total annual compensation of more than $11 million. On one important trip to Minnesota for a meeting with the always well-dressed leaders of the $500 billion health care giant UnitedHealth, who showed up in suits and ties and crisp white shirts, Foran removed the parka that had shielded him from the Minnesota winter and surprised everyone before him by revealing a decidedly dressed-down look: a short-sleeved Walmart polo.

"That was him," said Marcus Osborne, a longtime Walmart health care leader.

Like Walmart executives who came before him, Foran often hit the road on Saturdays to visit and inspect Walmart stores along with staff members. Store associates began tracking Foran's flights to prepare for his visits. But when the retail chief caught on to their efforts, his team began entering different flight details to throw his staff off.

By the time his second anniversary at Walmart rolled around, Foran had already visited nearly two hundred locations. "I get out to stores every single week," he said at a 2019 investor event. "About half the time I'm okay with it, and the other half I'm grumpy."[3]

When he was grumpy, those responsible for the source of his displeasure could expect Monday morning messages from the retail chief and their list of priorities to be blown up for the week. When he first arrived at Walmart in the US, he pushed grocery merchandise buyers to simplify the in-store assortment.

"I'm renowned as I walk stores of laying things like Ritz Crackers . . . out on the floor," he once told a room of investors. "I think we had nine different variants of Ritz Original Crackers, from a single pack to a double pack to a flat pack to a bonus pack, to a, to a, to a . . . What are we doing here?"

Colleagues say he paid special attention to the quality of fresh grocery items, from leafy greens to steak. On one occasion, he became so obsessed with improving the quality of Walmart's store brand of croissants—an odd choice to some, as it wasn't exactly a make-or-break item for the Supercenter chain—that he flew with a team to Canada to taste-test and source improved ones from a new supplier.

"Croissants and the in-store bakery offerings in general can drive people into the store in terms of aroma and quality," Foran said. "The point also isn't that it's 'croissants'—it's that we should strive to offer the best quality we can at a very favorable price point."

Some things about being a leader at Walmart, though, Foran had to get used to. Namely, what it was like to oversee a workforce with as many people as New Zealand's capital city of Auckland.

"Most major retailers—Costco, H-E-B, Food Lion—have four

hundred or five hundred stores," he once said. "We have almost five thousand. You can't underestimate what happens when you go up by a factor of ten. An awful lot of change management and communication is needed to do anything at Walmart. You've got to get the army to march."

As with an actual army leader, Foran's style—whether by necessity or personality—was at times unyielding. He favored a command-and-control style, where he liked to approve even the most mundane decisions. His expectations for everyone around him were sky-high and his dry wit was often accompanied by a sarcastic bite.

Foran defended his approach as one that was common among past company leaders, including Sam Walton himself. "You can't effect real change and real sustained fixes unless you get into the details," he told me.

McMillon once called Foran the "greatest retailer on the planet." But his style and priorities made him a polarizing figure. To many of his deputies, Foran was revered. Same-store sales at Walmart, an important metric for investors, had been disappointing before Foran's arrival, but under his guidance they grew for more than three years. In hindsight, e-commerce executives could appreciate the consistent, if unsexy, drumbeat of incremental improvements he rolled out at stores, which, at Walmart's scale, led to significant financial improvements.

Command and Control

But there was a downside to Foran's style. To a younger generation of Walmart employees, especially digitally savvy rank-and-file staff working on e-commerce operations, Foran came across as a relic of an era long past. His references to military battles or sailing competitions were viewed by some as outdated and out of touch. So were his remarks related to technology. It was not uncommon for him to refer to software engineering teams as "IT."

"I think we all gave him a pass because to run what he ran, you can see how someone could gravitate to a George Patton mentality," a former Jet leader said. "But he had a very rehearsed way of speaking that in the millennial tech world, just turned people off. It's from a different era. None of us gravitated to it."

Foran defended his approach—"Much of what happens in a business has parallels to other team-oriented pursuits regardless of the lingo used"—and maintained that there was "nothing unusual" in the cultural adjustment that both e-commerce and store employees experienced when the two organizations needed to work together.

Still, Foran's and Lore's management styles couldn't be more different. Lore excelled at crafting a crystal-clear vision for a product or consumer experience, but largely left the tactics and details to execute on that vision to his deputies. Some would argue that, at times, he could be too hands-off.

"I'm not a control person at all; I'm the opposite," Lore told me. "I'm just more of a social cohesion guy. I don't like confrontation and I don't like walls. And so, you know, I definitely tried to have a relationship with him. And he did, too."

But within a year or two of the Jet acquisition, the relationship between the top leaders had soured. What some viewed as Foran's years-long attack on e-commerce initiatives only fueled the divide. One of Foran's missions was to have Walmart return to the basics, which included refocusing on the company's Everyday Low Price promise, which Foran believed should be "so core to Walmart and what it stands for."

"I am cautious as I think about anything that could disrupt some key principles," he once said. "It doesn't mean that I wouldn't test some things and I wouldn't consider it, but I'm cautious."

This philosophy, coupled with his top-down approach to management, led to e-commerce casualties. Around the time Foran took over, more than one hundred employees were already six months into developing a new coupon feature that would allow in-store customers to earn coupon savings by simply scanning their phone at checkout and providing their phone number. Such a feature seemed like a win for customers. But in a world of everyday low prices, coupons shouldn't be a priority.

"One morning, after launching this in five stores as part of a beta launch, we got an email saying, 'Stop this project'—we didn't even get a call," a former Walmart employee said. "And that was it. We did not have a debrief; nobody from Bentonville ever cared to have a meeting with us; we just heard from other people about why they were [stopping] it."

There were also trickle-down effects that permeated several levels of management. At some point, if your bosses aren't getting along, it becomes clear. Then you and your counterparts on the other side of the business mirror the relationship. Eventually the whole environment degraded to the point that it was unclear whether Walmart store employees and e-commerce employees even worked for the same company. And that's simply bad for business.

"It was embarrassing at times," a former e-commerce employee told me. "There would be vendors we'd work with and I'd say something, and they'd respond with, 'I was down at a summit in Bentonville and heard something completely different.' So much of that happened."

One holiday season, Walmart's in-store team ran a huge discount on Roku TVs to drive foot traffic. The e-commerce TV department, however, refused to carry it. The doorbuster price made a ton of sense for in-store shopping, because the retailer knew that some customers who came in for a TV would go on to make other purchases that would help the retailer turn a profit. But online, most customers would order just that TV and be done. When you factor in the cost of shipping for the e-commerce division, it made zero sense to extend the in-store promotion to online customers.

On another occasion, the reverse happened: Walmart's e-commerce staff heavily discounted a basketball hoop that had been a top seller in stores for Black Friday weekend. As a result, the online sales began cannibalizing in-store sales and caused a major internal dustup. In an interview years later, Lore told me that such issues were expected at a company with two separate divisions whose goals were often misaligned.

"If you're telling each of us to optimize the [profit-and-loss statement] of our organization, and then e-commerce is discounting something that sells a ton in stores, stores can't make the same [profit] margin, they got to match it, or they sell less and it impacts their business," he said. "It's the innovator's dilemma . . . how do you cannibalize yourself?"

To e-commerce leaders, Foran and his deputies didn't always seem interested in finding out. But from Foran's point of view, the first priority had to be improving store operations and boosting profitability, which could ultimately help boost Walmart's omnichannel goals.

"My focus on the stores wasn't a function of my favoring traditional retail over e-commerce," he told me. "We needed to focus on both, but from the outset there was a very real sense of competitive pressure on the stores which we needed to respond to correctly."

Besides Amazon, Target was proving to be an increasingly dangerous competitor in general merchandise categories. And in the grocery sector, the European discount chains Aldi and Lidl were both targeting Walmart customers with their ultra-low prices and geographic expansions.

Store leaders also resented fawning press coverage of Walmart's e-commerce sales growth and the positive attention from Wall Street. They knew well the dirty little secret that at least half of Walmart e-commerce sales in the US came from the grocery curbside pickup business, which Foran's teams oversaw and which preceded Lore's arrival at Walmart.

"Online grocery fueled a huge amount of that growth and that was the worst-kept secret [inside Walmart]," Joe Gullo, a former Walmart and Jet logistics executive, told me. "If there was thirty percent growth, around twenty percent was online grocery that we had nothing to do with. Greg was justifiably upset."

Foran's disdain for some of the choices being made on the e-commerce side of the house also leaked out externally at times. In 2018, Walmart executives gathered inside Bentonville's home office for a clandestine meeting with senior leaders from Google. The technology giant and the retail behemoth shared a common foe in Amazon. Amazon was a threat to Google because, over time, more and more online shoppers began their product searches right on Amazon rather than on Google. This sucked potential search-advertising revenue away from Google. Then, by developing the voice assistant Alexa, Amazon saw potential in changing consumer behavior so that customers could voice their product searches out loud, rather than typing them into a search bar on an app or website. Inside Google, sirens were blaring.

"The thing Google fears the most is being irrelevant," a former insider told me. "There was a real fear that if voice was the future, Amazon would take over. Alexa would take over."

But during these meetings, Foran spoke so dismissively of e-commerce as a sector that some onlookers thought he must have been joking. He wasn't. The two sides did still partner on a feature that allowed customers to order groceries from Walmart by speaking orders out loud to Google's answer to Alexa, called Google Assistant. The feature never caught on. But years later, the disdain that Foran exhibited in those meetings for all things e-commerce was what some attendees remembered most.

"I don't know how Doug [McMillon] tolerated it," said one person who was present.

A Costly Joke

According to a variety of executives who worked inside Walmart at the time, Foran had issues with a number of Lore's moves and tactics as well. Store No. 8, the incubation arm, was one of them. It housed a variety of experimental startups not focused on the current Walmart customer and with time horizons for success that were many years down the road. Foran's job was to improve things inside Walmart stores today, not to fantasize about the store of the future.

"Greg tends to think in a two-year time horizon sometimes, and Marc thinks in a ten-year horizon," a former e-commerce executive said. "And so, navigating that balance was always quite tricky."

At first, senior leaders, including Foran, saw the incubator as a little side project designed to appease Lore. He couldn't do too much damage, but it also wouldn't cost too much. But over time, their opinion grew harsher. The first and most notable startup in the group was Jetblack, a text-message shopping concierge service run by one of the founders of Rent the Runway, Jenny Fleiss. When I broke the news about the startup, my headline read: "Walmart is developing a personal-shopper service for rich moms."[4] Many of the early customers were personal friends of Fleiss, upper-middle-class women, or wealthier, who lived in

New York City. A job listing at the time said the service was targeting a "high net worth urban consumer." Not exactly what Walmart lifers might expect from a Walmart initiative.

For Foran's leadership team, the startup was a sore spot almost from the beginning. It didn't seem to matter to this group that one of Jetblack's goals was to learn about new products that were attractive to a different clientele and might bring new revenue to Walmart.com if it stocked them. It didn't seem to matter that the venture might be a fruitful experiment in "conversational commerce"—or text-message-based shopping—which, if it took off, would set up Walmart to become a leader in this emerging space. Or that Jetblack customers did end up shopping with Amazon less frequently than they previously did.

"If you're in Bentonville and you've worked with Walmart for twelve or fifteen years, and without much context of Jetblack or Store No. 8's goals, I think it's natural to be skeptical of these initiatives," Fleiss told me.

Some longtime Walmart executives were flabbergasted when they learned that Jetblack had an annual budget of $60 million and was losing $15,000 *per* member—a drop in the bucket on Walmart's balance sheet, but an abomination to many leaders at a company who are proud to shave pennies off the cost of toilet paper packaging.[5] To them, all they saw in Jetblack was a costly way to go into the red.

Fleiss understood how store leaders and employees, whose business goals were closely tied to profitability, might chafe at a division that was given the freedom not to worry about the bottom line for a significant period of time. But she insisted that she and her team were well aware that a sustainable business model would be necessary over time.

Jetblack charged members $50 a month to order through text messaging just about any type of merchandise for fast delivery, except perishable food. Customers could also ask for recommendations, such as birthday gift ideas for a child of a certain age, and have returns picked up at their apartment buildings for free. While the long-term goal was to have computer algorithms respond to customers, field these requests, and automatically make recommendations, most of the work was done by members of the startup's human staff.

In the early days of the service, the Walmart-funded startup was so disconnected from the rest of the company that employees had to source CPG inventory from Amazon and Target, instead of Walmart, to get it to customers quickly. Of course, Jetblack lost considerable money on these orders. And with the average shopper purchasing more than ten items a week through the service, it's not surprising that those losses quickly mounted.

Later, employees finally got buy-in to tap into Jet.com's inventory to procure merchandise, or plucked goods off the shelves of an actual Walmart Supercenter in Secaucus, New Jersey, which sits less than ten miles from Manhattan. If Jetblack were an independent venture-capital-backed startup, such workarounds may have been viewed as ingenious hacks. After all, Marc Lore's Diapers.com got its start by backing up a truck to clean out local warehouse clubs before the big diaper brands were willing to sell merchandise directly to the startup. But inside Walmart, some Bentonville-based executives viewed the whole endeavor as a costly joke.

Jetblack employees also fielded requests for luxury goods such as Rolex watches, and once shipped a toy overnight to Saint-Tropez, France, after a delivery mishap resulted in a wealthy family leaving New York City for the posh locale without the children's gift in question, according to a former employee. It's not uncommon for Walmart execs to reference Sam Walton turning over in his grave when some type of drastic change is implemented or debated. And depending on who you ask, many of the examples include quite a touch of melodrama. But an anecdote such as the Saint-Tropez one might have very well sent Mr. Sam, as employees knew him, into a fury—even if he might appreciate the customer-centric goal behind it. Jetblack never grew to more than two thousand customers, partly because of the steep losses and partly because the service degraded as the customer count rose.

"Jenny built a great experience," a former Jetblack employee told me. "But it was not a business."

Fleiss, for her part, once told the *Wall Street Journal* that it would take five to seven years before the computer system would be ready to mostly replace the humans.[6] "This is a long journey," she said. "And I think we were aware of that going in."

But Walmart executives became antsy much sooner than that and, eventually, Lore saw the writing on the wall. He went out and secured agreements from outside investors, including FedEx, Microsoft, and Visa, to invest a total of $300 million to spin out Jetblack into an independent company. Under the terms of the deal, Walmart would retain a significant ownership stake, and former Jet and Walmart executive Nate Faust, who had already replaced Fleiss as CEO, would stay on to run the newly independent company as the chief executive.

Jetblack employees caught wind that something was up even if executives weren't filling them in on the potential spin-off—Faust seemed to always be holed up in a conference room working on something that was unclear to everyone else. Even though Jetblack had stopped accepting new customers, new customer accounts began showing up inside company systems. Sure enough, several of them were accounts linked to Microsoft corporate email addresses—one of the would-be new investors.

At the very last minute, though, McMillon, Walmart's CEO, told those involved that the deal was off. Lore and Faust were devastated and felt blindsided. At varying points during internal discussions, McMillon had told executives that he wasn't sure Jetblack would have a high probability of success. By the end of deliberations, though, his reasoning had flipped: if the new startup's idea did work, McMillon didn't want Walmart to be responsible for funding a competitor that could someday disrupt Walmart itself. The deal, however, was predicated on Walmart owning 50 percent of the new, independent business from the start—so in such a successful scenario, Walmart would reap robust rewards from the investment. Lore was so confused by McMillon's reasoning that he later told confidants that McMillon must have had another reason to squash the deal that he simply couldn't or wouldn't disclose. His guess was Greg Penner, the company chairman who worked closely with McMillon, but with whom Lore never built a close relationship.

"Marc was like, 'It was so illogical,'" someone who spoke to Lore told me. "'You don't want to own fifty percent of the next Amazon?'"

After McMillon's decision had been made, Faust called together the Jetblack staff for an announcement. Since news had leaked to the press that Jetblack may be spun off from Walmart into a separate company, many of the startup's employees were expecting that to be the news. Instead, Faust's news was much worse. Walmart was shutting down the startup and nearly three hundred employees would be losing their jobs.

Years later, McMillon told me he believed that Jetblack would have needed multiple rounds of large investments to survive as a standalone business. Even the CEO of the largest employer in the US had to pick and choose big investments, because of his board of directors and public market investors, as well as to maintain diplomacy internally among business chiefs with sometimes conflicting agendas. Plus, McMillon wanted to retain Jetblack's technical assets inside Walmart for potential use someday down the road.

"Voice and text are going to be part of what we do," McMillon told me. "That fruit hasn't shown up yet. But it will."

Exclusive Content

Foran and other brick-and-mortar leaders at the company also chafed over a series of acquisitions Lore and his team made during this time. One part of Lore's acquisition strategy was buying unsexy shopping sites like Shoes.com to help build better relationships with brands in certain product categories. The goals were to convince these brands to allow their merchandise to be sold on Walmart.com and to import their experienced staff to run these product categories on Walmart .com. Those acquisitions were viewed internally largely as successes, McMillon told me.

Yet at the same time, Walmart's e-commerce division also purchased several so-called digital-native brands—young companies that sell their own clothing lines, predominantly online, and predominantly to millennial shoppers. First there was ModCloth, the seller of vintage-style women's clothes, and then Bonobos, which had the unfortunate timing of being announced on the same day as Amazon's megapurchase of Whole Foods in June 2017.

The Bonobos deal was the subject of intense debate inside Walmart until it was finalized, leaving the startup's CEO, Andy Dunn, anxious, since he had passed on a separate deal to pursue the sale to Walmart.

In the end, Walmart did purchase Bonobos. And Dunn had a huge opportunity in front of him. Alongside the acquisition, Lore tasked the charismatic entrepreneur with a mission: build out a portfolio of digital-native consumer brands by acquiring popular startups. Lore told Dunn the goal was to acquire a new startup every three months.

"I was like, 'Holy shit! That sounds like fun,'" Dunn told me.

The first deal that Dunn and his team executed was a $100 million acquisition of Eloquii, a maker of plus-sized women's apparel mostly sold online, which was announced in the fall of 2018—more than a year after Walmart bought Bonobos. By inking the deal, Walmart was betting on a brand that was working to modernize a section of the apparel market worth more than $20 billion in the US alone. By some estimates, more than half of all American women are plus-sized.

"We got excited about this problem," Dunn told me in an interview at the time.[7] "[The plus-sized market] has been dramatically underserved and there's an amazing opportunity to go and bring delight to it."

Lore and team believed that deals like this one would give Walmart and its online stores exclusive merchandise that shoppers couldn't find on Amazon, which could help appeal to a new generation of consumers who typically wouldn't shop at Walmart. They referred to this merchandise as "proprietary content," and compared it to Netflix's foray into making its own shows to differentiate itself from other streaming services.

The hope was that bringing hipper, more premium brands into the Walmart fold might also make other product brands more amenable to selling on Jet.com or Walmart.com. They also believed that the Eloquii brand could eventually be successful in physical retail, if they were able to convince Walmart's stores division to carry the up-and-coming brand. Dunn thought it might make sense to get the store leadership on board before consummating the deal, but Lore advised him that it would be easier to do so once the startup was a Walmart property.

But soon after the Eloquii acquisition closed, Walmart executives discovered that the fashion startup's financials weren't as sound as Walmart thought. Dunn's staff had done due diligence on the startup, but apparently they weren't checking in on the financials frequently enough as the deal negotiations were approaching the finish line. That put the startup in a bad light from the beginning, and didn't look so good for Dunn, who was the internal champion for the acquisition.

Still, Dunn and his team believed they were brought in to acquire more young, exciting brands, and that's what they set out to do. If you gave any digital-native brand founder truth serum in 2018, there was a good chance they'd divulge that they had met with Dunn, Lore, or some other Walmart representative to talk about a sale.

The problem was that there was a huge disparity between the value of these digital-native companies according to the venture capitalists who had funded their growth and were betting on their future, and the more traditional leaders of Walmart who thought they were worth much less when looking at the businesses as they existed in the present. In many cases, venture capitalists were willing to value these startups at three, four, or five times their annual revenue because they believed they were the breakout consumer brands of the future and ones that would eventually turn a profit as more Americans discovered them. Walmart leaders like Foran, the store leader, and chief financial officer Brett Biggs focused heavily on the startups' money-losing ways, and thought those valuation multiples were absurd. Lore and Dunn loved the vision of Walmart owning a portfolio of the coolest new consumer brands that would help attract more affluent customers while keeping key merchandise off Amazon. But reality was proving a rather significant obstacle.

Nonetheless, Dunn came close to buying a second startup despite the Eloquii challenges: a sock brand called Bombas, which mostly sold its merchandise online and first gained attention after appearing on the business pitch competition *Shark Tank* in 2014. Bombas had great profit margins and had succeeded in building up brand loyalty in an apparel category known for little of it. Walmart eventually offered $125 million for the startup; Bombas wanted $175 million. If the talks had happened a year or two earlier, Lore may have been able to push through such a deal on his own. But Foran and his store leaders didn't have any interest in carrying Bombas socks in Walmart stores, and other executives were by now skeptical of Lore's acquisition strategy as well.

"I just wish we could have done, you know, three or five or seven other deals like that," Dunn said, referring to the Eloquii purchase. "That didn't happen. And at the time, I was really bummed about that. We pushed really hard to try to get stuff done, and I think the learning for me, with humility of looking back two years, is . . . a retailer that is mostly selling other brands is unlikely to go buy ten or twenty brands when it's more cost-effective to import the talent and figure out how to make those brands."

Dunn didn't do himself any favors by chatting with an outsider about his plans, either, even if it was a mentor of his. In the fall of 2018, the entrepreneur dined with Mickey Drexler, a legendary American retail executive who has held CEO roles at the Gap and J. Crew. The duo were meeting over lunch at Drexler's favorite haunt in New York's SoHo: the Italian café Sant Ambroeus. There, in what he thought was a private conversation, Dunn let a secret slip: Walmart had held discussions with the luggage startup Away about a possible acquisition.

When a reporter broke the news of the acquisition talks shortly thereafter,[8] rumors circulated inside Walmart that a journalist at the same restaurant had overheard the Dunn/Drexler chat. It's actually not clear who tipped the reporter off, but at Walmart, Bentonville-based executives, who were used to a company culture of discretion, wondered how news of e-commerce acquisitions or deal talks often seemed to leak to the press. Was someone intentionally leaking information to try to apply pressure on Foran, McMillon, or Biggs to support more ambitious—and expensive—acquisitions?

Eventually it was clear to all that the vision for acquiring a collection of digital-native brands was dead in the water. Lore was no longer aggressively advocating for such deals internally, and the focus had shifted to talking up the group's ability to create Walmart's own digital-native brands from scratch that could also be sold in Walmart stores. Under Dunn, the company in 2018 unveiled a mattress brand, Allswell, which was designed to compete against other bed-in-a-box mattress makers like Casper and Tuft & Needle. Dunn's team also worked on creating a new cosmetics brand, but it never saw the light of day.

By the middle of 2019, Dunn was informed that he was no longer reporting to Lore. His new boss, a Walmart and Sam's Club veteran named Ashley Buchanan, pressured Dunn and the execs running Bonobos and Eloquii to cut costs. The entrepreneur did not take well to the new arrangement.

"I was an extremely bad employee," Dunn admitted years later. "I'm just not good. I'm too rebellious to be good at that."

While Dunn's rebelliousness was tolerated by Lore, if not embraced, Buchanan did not find it amusing or endearing.

"Once I got moved into the mother ship reporting-wise, I was totally ineffective," Dunn said.

Within a few months, Dunn was out.[9]

10

OLD SCHOOL VS. NEW SCHOOL

While the brouhaha over Lore's acquisition strategy caused outsize turmoil, perhaps the most damning issue for Walmart leaders like Foran and the company's chief financial officer was that Lore and his deputies kept missing internal projections for the e-commerce division's business performance.

In Sam Walton's autobiography, he wrote, "I have occasionally heard myself compared to P. T. Barnum because of the way I love to get in front of a crowd and talk something up—an idea, a store, a product, the whole company—whatever I happen to be focused on right then. But underneath that personality, I have always had the soul of an operator, somebody who wants to make things work well, then better, then the best they possibly can."

Few who have spent considerable time around Lore can argue against his excellence at promotion, cheerleading, and vision-setting—some might even call it Walton-esque. The reason that so many talented people agreed to work for the entrepreneur, so many successful investors agreed to fund him, and so many consumers shopped from his companies is that he was outstanding in this role. He was a world-class vision-crafter and promoter.

But inside Walmart, more observers started questioning whether he or anyone else on his team had the operational skills to back up all that big talk. For a logical and disciplined leader like Foran, the e-commerce division's money-losing ways—as well as the leadership team's inability to hit internal projections—was inexcusable. Operational excellence was as core to Walmart's culture as anything. But to Lore and his deputies, it appeared to be a sideshow.

"It's one thing to miss your plan, but to not know you're missing a plan is a cardinal sin," a former Walmart logistics executive told me. "You're ceding credibility as a management team because at a certain point that says you don't understand your business."

The challenge for the e-commerce division at the time, according to leaders from that period, was multifaceted. For one, they said, top Walmart officials often took the internal goals that the digital leaders had set, and pushed them to unreasonable heights. The other issue was that they believed they were swimming in a much more volatile ocean than their counterparts running the physical stores, especially considering the dominance of their No. 1 rival, Amazon.

"We'd go and we'd say, 'Here's the number that we're confident with,'" a former e-commerce executive told me. "And I think any good manager would be like, let's do more than that. But Bentonville would come back with a number that we're just like, 'That's nothing that we think that we can achieve.'"

Repeatedly, Lore's division would not reach the goals set out for them, leading to tension that "permeated everything," the executive said.

The misses on the e-commerce side also affected bonuses for executives on the stores side. Foran's annual performance bonuses, for example, were heavily tied to the operating income of Walmart's US business, which included the e-commerce division that Lore ran. But that operating profit didn't factor into Lore's annual bonuses—the entrepreneur was mostly judged on sales growth, no matter the impact to the bottom line.[1]

Lore later admitted to me that the divergent incentive plans were a fundamental problem with the structure inside Walmart at the time. Sure, store leaders wanted to cut costs and hit profitability goals so they could provide Walmart customers with lower prices, or store employees with better wages. But you don't rise to that level at a company like Walmart without yearning to accumulate more wealth for yourself as well; in short, bonuses mattered—a lot. And if it wasn't bad enough that Lore's money-losing ways reduced the compensation that Foran took home, the accomplished retail operator also had to accept the extraordinary compensation package Lore secured before he even walked in the door.

During Walmart's 2017 fiscal year alone, Lore's compensation totaled more than $240 million, the majority of which came from the value of restricted stock units that the company granted the entrepreneur as part of the Jet acquisition. Walmart also agreed to pay Lore nearly $500 million in cash for his ownership stake in Jet.

Meanwhile, Foran earned around $11.5 million in total compensation for the same year, though he ran a much larger business in terms of both sales and profit. Colleagues say that Foran found the disparity galling. On several occasions, Foran referred to Lore as "the $3 billion man" when talking to colleagues. At other times, he wondered aloud half-jokingly whether the flashy entrepreneur's stock package was owing to him secretly being a long-lost cousin of the Walton family.

Innovator or Operator?

With this as a backdrop, panic would spread through senior e-commerce ranks as another quarter was ending and the results were looking much worse than company leaders were expecting. So, in the lead-up to the 2018 holiday season, e-commerce leaders under Lore instructed employees working on Walmart's marketplace business—the division that signs up small brands and merchants to sell directly to consumers through the Walmart.com website—to convert hundreds of millions of marketplace sales in just thirty days into drop-ship vendor (DSV) sales.

What this meant, in practice, was convincing merchants selling through Walmart's marketplace to relinquish control of the pricing of their products on Walmart.com, in exchange for a label that marked their products as "sold by Walmart" on Walmart.com—a label that increased the likelihood of a shopper buying a given product.

Those familiar with the directive said it seemed designed to boost revenue for Walmart since Walmart recorded an entire DSV product sale as revenue, while, for marketplace sales, just Walmart's commission of 8 to 15 percent of the purchase price was recorded as revenue. One person familiar with the initiative said it seemed "obvious" that it was a last-ditch effort to hit some type of big internal financial goal.

Even with this type of financial maneuvering, the e-commerce unit missed its goals that holiday season. Also, the unit lost more money than planned two years in a row under Lore, while the profits generated by Foran's US stores unit seemingly helped fund Lore's risky initiatives. At one point, the e-commerce division lost around $2 billion in a single calendar year.

"The internal narrative became that Marc couldn't hit both numbers at the same time," an insider told me. "It cost political capital. The honeymoon was over."

The idea that Lore couldn't run a profitable business also appeared to have been encouraged by his previous employer. In 2017, Amazon shut down Diapers.com and its parent company Quidsi, which Lore had sold to them six years earlier, and folded the website into the rest of Amazon.com. At the time, an Amazon spokesperson released a statement that read in part, "We have worked extremely hard for the past [six] years to get Quidsi to be profitable, and unfortunately we have not been able to do so."

It was extremely rare for a notoriously tight-lipped communications department to publicly discuss the finances of one of Amazon's smaller business units. It also was extremely odd, considering the fact that Quidsi was on track to generate significant free cash flow by the end of 2018, as sources later told me.[2]

Years later, I asked a former Amazon executive familiar with the decision about Amazon's public reasoning for shutting down Quidsi. The executive paused. He eventually managed an uncomfortable smile. "It was not very Amazonian," he said. "It was an unusual quote. For a lot of people, it stood out."

For former Quidsi executives, the motive seemed clear: to send a message to Wall Street investors and Walmart leadership that the executive they had just spent $3.3 billion on couldn't run or build profitable businesses. But amid the internal fallout following the 2018 holiday season at Walmart, e-commerce revenue chief Scott Hilton took the fall and was pushed out, while Lore, the $3 billion man, remained.

"At the end of the day, Marc had the public persona and access to people in Bentonville," an insider told me.

Still, by 2019, Lore was growing tired of the restraints being placed on his unit and what he saw as increased bureaucracy slowing down important initiatives. He was irked, perhaps most of all by the idea insinuated by McMillon and some board directors that he was only an innovator and not an operator with the chops to make the e-commerce business predictably profitable. Perhaps in an attempt to acknowledge his critics while also thumbing his nose at them, Lore took to wearing one of two hats around the office. One was inscribed with the word "Innovator" on the front and the other with the word "Operator."[3]

Some saw the hats as a way to innocently message to his own teams that they needed to take both types of roles seriously to be successful at Walmart, and for Walmart to be successful in this new age of Amazon. Either way, both hats were retired for good after the e-commerce leader wore one in a meeting with store employees and someone in attendance notified a superior that they thought the hat was insulting.

Years later, Lore was diplomatic in discussing any rift with Foran and assigned blame elsewhere.

"I think we did have a good relationship," Lore told me on one occasion. "It was a lot of stuff coming from people in the organization. Stuff would come up to Greg, like, 'Do you hear what Marc's doing?' And then Greg was like, 'Wait, what?' And a lot of the stuff wasn't true.

"But it just wears on you that you have to keep doing that," Lore added. "If every conversation we have is defensive like that . . . it just gets tiring. I think he was tired. I was tired."

The passage of time seemed to soften Foran's outlook as well, in a departure from what Walmart insiders observed years earlier.

"As to be expected in any organization during a phase of rapid transformation, naturally there are tensions and plenty of healthy debate," he wrote to me. "Quite often that is how meaningful progress is made."

Lore said the brick-and-mortar expert understood that the future of Walmart was one that, ideally, meshed the best of the stores business with the best of what online tools could offer. He said a bigger problem was the tribalism that had formed within the stores team, mostly based in Bentonville, and the e-commerce division, based in offices along the coasts.

Old School versus New School. Profit versus Growth. Huge compensation packages versus—well, extraordinary compensation packages. It was a culture clash as old as business itself. But it was threatening to eviscerate the momentum Walmart had been building while stepping out from Amazon's shadow.

"That's why I was always telling Doug, 'We've got to bring these orgs together,'" Lore said.

The plan was always to eventually unite the Walmart e-commerce and stores teams under one leader, and Foran wanted that role. But McMillon resisted.

With his path to more power and more control over the destiny of Walmart's US business blocked, Foran eventually opted to leave Walmart for a flight home and a new role to boot: CEO of Air New Zealand. He would finally occupy a chief executive role that oversaw an entire corporation, one that returned him to his home country— but also one far afield from the only industry he knew.

Three years later, he declined to address the desire he had expressed internally to run both the store and e-commerce divisions.

"I absolutely loved my time with Walmart," he told me, "and at the end of almost a decade felt like I'd done what I'd been brought in to do: reinvigorate both the Walmart China and Walmart US businesses, deliver significant tangible results, and position both businesses for continued growth."

In his place, McMillon and Walmart's board tapped John Furner, a younger executive who, like McMillon, all but grew up inside Walmart and was coming off a stint as the CEO of the Sam's Club division, like McMillon once did. Sam's Club often served as a testing ground for new technologies as well as experiments in organizational structure, which gave Furner some tech credibility. Furner's Walmart roots were also deep—his father had been a Walmart store manager himself. With his background, Furner was viewed as one of two or three potential successors to McMillon when the CEO decides to move on.

With Foran exiting, Lore and Furner quickly eliminated one of the past causes of friction: bonuses. Each of their bonuses entailed the performance of both digital and physical stores. Within a year, Lore's organization began reporting to Furner. With Furner's takeover, speculation ramped up about whether Lore would make it the full five years at Walmart that he had signed up for when he and McMillon struck the Jet deal in the second half of 2016. Such speculation had actually begun less than a year after the Jet acquisition was first consummated, but the rumors got louder in late 2018 into 2019. At one private social gathering attended by Lore, former Jet executives even placed bets on how long their friend and former boss would last.

The timing wasn't a coincidence. From late 2018 into early 2019—about halfway through Lore's five-year Walmart agreement—it became clear to some executives below Lore that his voice didn't carry the same weight it once did. E-commerce staff were shocked, for example, when Lore aggressively pitched an idea for a Jet.com physical store in New York City, yet was still rebuffed. Others couldn't believe that he couldn't get sign-off for the sortation warehouse expansion, championed by former Amazon exec Mike Indresano, when many had long thought it was a sure thing.

After e-commerce losses ballooned in 2018, McMillon delivered Lore a new, harsh reality: you need to stem the bleeding. Lore once reportedly quipped to reporters that Foran "makes the money; I lose it."[4] But Walmart's other leaders weren't laughing. With McMillon and the board tightening his leash, Lore began pulling back on many of his most aggressive plans, including the acquisition strategy around digital-native brands run by Bonobos's Andy Dunn. Some insiders say part of this was a strategic move by Lore—that he chose to partially disconnect and stop challenging some disappointing decisions on expensive investments so the stores and e-commerce divisions could quickly unite under Furner. He also hoped that Walmart might let him out of his five-year agreement early to get back to his startup ways if he stopped rabble-rousing.

But it wasn't only Lore's free-spending ways in business that ruffled feathers in Bentonville. His flashy city lifestyle didn't help, either, considering the modesty with which most longtime Walmart executives carried themselves back at the home office. Lore, at times, recognized this.

When the news broke that he had purchased a nearly $44 million Manhattan penthouse apartment,[5] making him a neighbor to celebrities like Jennifer Lawrence, Lore was furious. He had tried, but failed, to conceal himself as the buyer, and he knew what the perception would be back in Bentonville. After all, Sam Walton himself had made his opinion on the matter abundantly clear:

"We're not ashamed of having money, but I just don't believe a big showy lifestyle is appropriate for anywhere, least of all here in Bentonville where folks work hard for their money and where we all know that everyone puts on their trousers one leg at a time," the Walmart founder wrote in his memoir. The ethos of frugality ran deep inside the company.

On another occasion, Lore showed up at Teterboro Airport for a flight to Bentonville on one of Walmart's private jets. He pulled up to the airport in a Bentley car, which typically costs at least $150,000 on the *low* end. He was also accompanied by his then-girlfriend—Lore and his wife had recently divorced—and the pair, each sporting designer shades, looked like a Hollywood power couple.

One of Lore's fellow passengers apparently didn't like what they saw, and the anecdote made its way all the way up to McMillon, the CEO. In a subsequent meeting, McMillon requested that Lore act more low-key—the Bentley came up in the conversation. It wasn't clear what the specific problem was, but Lore later told confidants that he thought the fact that he was divorced and traveling with his girlfriend was not a welcome turn of life events at a company like Walmart, where some newcomers believed religion and the sanctity of marriage were held up on a pedestal as much as the Everyday Low Price guarantee.

It probably didn't help Lore's cause that, on another occasion, he was spotted being a little too affectionate with his girlfriend in public at one of Walmart's annual shareholder meetings. For all of his entrepreneurial brilliance and empathetic leadership qualities, Lore at times baffled longtime friends and Walmart executives alike with actions or commentary that appeared naïve or out of touch. He was proud of the fact, for example, that he didn't read much outside of what was directly necessary for his job.

"Reading takes time away from thinking . . . you get a little brainwashed," he once told a group of Harvard business students. "I like to talk to people, take in the world, think about stuff, and think about a better way."

The Lore Goodbye

Finally, in early 2021, a Walmart spokesperson reached out to me with a message: Lore was departing the company—a little less than a year ahead of schedule—and wanted to talk to me about it before the news went public. In our discussion, Lore spoke positively of Walmart, and encouraged its leaders "to continue to be bold and not be a follower."[6]

"The fast-follower strategy is not going to get it done," he said.

He acknowledged that the failed acquisition program he had once heralded was his biggest disappointment. But he added that he had hoped "people think about Walmart a bit differently than they did four and a half years ago."

Months later, I asked Lore in a phone call whether he ever got complete buy-in for his vision of what the Walmart of the future could, even should, become. The short answer: not completely.

"There were just so many voices, and key people with different opinions . . . and I wasn't the CEO of the overall company where I could sit people down and say, 'Okay, we're gonna keep banging on this vision,'" he told me.

But he said he believed that most top executives still at the company believed that the e-commerce division was on a path to become quite profitable in the future—something that Foran wasn't shy about proclaiming would never happen when he was at the helm of Walmart stores.

"That's half the battle," Lore said.

In many ways, McMillon's bet on Lore and Jet was a success. Under Lore, Walmart.com grew into the clear No. 2 online shopping site in the US after Amazon, having doubled its market share for online sales during Lore's tenure. The merchandise selection on Walmart.com, thanks in part to some of Lore's less sexy acquisitions, also grew to eight times the size of the product catalogue he had inherited. Walmart's delivery speeds also improved.

Even store leaders cheered the impact on Walmart's stock price. It increased more than 80 percent from the time of Lore's arrival, and the company's price-to-earnings ratio—which compares the stock price to company earnings per share—doubled, signaling that investors believed the company had a positive growth outlook still in front of it.

The company's industry reputation also improved. Technology executives who never would have considered joining the retail giant stopped viewing Walmart as the digital dinosaur it once was. Lore and his team had indeed succeeded in changing the Walmart narrative, both in the press and on Wall Street, where many leaders still thought it mattered most.

But that glass-half-full view of Lore's Walmart tenure is only part of the picture. Walmart's e-commerce sales, though second only to Amazon's, still were around six to seven times smaller than the tech giant's at the time that Lore announced he was leaving. What's more, if you were grading some of Lore's most ambitious bets, including the digital-brand acquisition strategy and the startup incubator, you could make a case for handing Lore a C or D. Perhaps an Incomplete if you were being generous. Jet.com also shut down and the once-heralded Smart Cart innovation never surfaced on Walmart.com in a meaningful way.

Across the board, Walmart leaders told me that the culture clash between Lore and Foran was understandable, if not expected. They made the case that if either of the executives had controlled the other's division, Walmart would be in a much worse place than it is today. But did Walmart really get its money's worth by spending $3.3 billion on Jet and billions more on new e-commerce leaders and the programs they led? From a stock price and narrative perspective, the answer is clearly yes. And in the world of megacorporations and megacapitalism, maybe that's enough.

But there are other perspectives that are worthy to consider, and those are where the what-ifs lie. What if Doug McMillon had intervened more often between Lore and Foran to unlock stalemates that slowed down decision-making and, thus, progress? What if Lore had leaned more aggressively into new ideas that took advantage of Walmart's biggest differentiator from Amazon—its stores? And what if McMillon didn't wait more than three years to unify the two divisions and cultures under a single leader who could bridge the gap and execute on a single vision of reinvention?

"I get questions about, 'Did you leave that separate too long or just the right amount?'" McMillon said in early 2022, seated across from me inside the CEO's office that Sam Walton once inhabited. "You guys can figure that out over time; I don't know. But I'm convinced keeping it independent and separate for a period of time was necessary."

Perhaps in the end, what mattered most for Walmart is that a single leader was responsible for the entire US business—stores and websites alike—by the time a global pandemic upended Walmart's business, and all of our lives, in the year 2020.

11
RETAIL DOCTORS

Doug McMillon sounded determined. It was Thursday, June 28, 2018, and the biggest business news story of the day was very bad news for Walmart and its CEO.

That same morning, Amazon had announced that it had signed an agreement to purchase a young company called PillPack, a five-year-old online pharmacy backed by venture capitalists. PillPack sold prescription drugs specifically to Americans who take multiple medications every day, and had licenses in forty-nine states to ship those drugs—packaged in organized daily packs—to customers' doors. Not only would the acquisition give Amazon the pharmacy licenses and expertise to finally enter the highly regulated but ripe-for-disruption $350 billion prescription drug market, but it also landed another blow on Walmart, which had been extremely close to buying PillPack itself.

Just a few months earlier, PillPack and Walmart were so close to securing a deal that staff on both sides had already discussed the possibility of announcing the news to the American public through an appearance on a national morning show. But in the final days of a nearly two-month period of due diligence, Walmart suddenly hit the brakes on the deal, stunning just about everyone involved on the PillPack side. Walmart offered little explanation, other than that they needed to pause the talks and would be back in touch in about a month or so.

Several years later, when the US Department of Justice sued Walmart for its pharmacy division's alleged role in the opioid epidemic,[1] it became clear that the DOJ had been investigating Walmart during the time of the PillPack talks in the first half of 2018.[2] It didn't take much for people close to the deal to start wondering whether the DOJ probe might have been a reason for the pause.

Either way, when news broke that PillPack was selling to Amazon instead, McMillon, one of the most powerful businessmen in the world, phoned PillPack's thirty-two-year-old CEO, TJ Parker, and pleaded with him to reconsider the Amazon deal.

"I think you made the wrong decision," McMillon told him, according to someone familiar with the conversation. "We were the right buyer."

McMillon was apologetic about his company's mismanagement of the acquisition process and vowed to work one-on-one with Parker to push a sale to Walmart across the finish line if the entrepreneur backed out of the Amazon deal. Of course, it was already far too late. Like with the battle for Marc Lore's Diapers.com years earlier, Amazon had ripped a promising company right out of Walmart's grasp. And this time it happened in the $4 trillion health care industry, which each company had big hopes of disrupting, just as they had each first done with retail decades ago.

Pill-Oh! Fight

In 1978, when Doug McMillon was still just a middle schooler growing up in Jonesboro, Arkansas, Walmart opened its first pharmacy location, along with auto parts and jewelry departments, as it started to inch toward an all-in-one shopping experience format that it eventually formalized with the introduction of the Supercenter a decade later. By the time McMillon took over as CEO, his company had opened thousands of pharmacy locations and had grown to become the third-largest pharmacy player in the country, only surpassed in size by Walgreens and CVS. Pharmacies offered customers another reason to visit Walmart stores, and roam a Supercenter's maze of merchandise-packed aisles before or after picking up a prescription in the back or corner of the store.

At the same time, mail-order pharmacies, which had been in existence for decades, were being reinvented. Amazon had once owned a large piece of an online pharmacy called Drugstore.com, which rose and fell during the Web 1.0 era. But now new players began entering the space in a renewed effort to make buying and receiving prescription drugs much easier to do online. One of these young companies was PillPack, founded in 2013 and launched publicly the following year. TJ Parker, the son of a New Hampshire pharmacist, had teamed up with a technical cofounder named Elliot Cohen, whom he met at an MIT hackathon.

Together, their vision for the company was fairly straightforward: to make it as easy as possible for the tens of millions of Americans who take multiple medications for chronic conditions on a daily basis to purchase their prescriptions online and have help keeping track of what to take when. PillPack presorted the medications into small packs organized by the time and day that the customer needs to take them, eliminating one stressful piece of care for those taking several pills a day. By 2017, PillPack had ripped out all the off-the-shelf software and computer systems it had previously used to run its operation and began using a homegrown system that made running an online pharmacy much less complicated than running traditional pharmacies in the brick-and-mortar world.

Walmart took notice. PillPack's core business was interesting, but the *way* it ran its business was even more attractive. PillPack's software, and other technology chops, were especially attractive to those who were plain-faced about how bad Walmart Pharmacy's IT systems were.

"Nothing they had was rocket science," a former Walmart Health division executive told me. "Nothing they had was something that Walmart couldn't have done. It's just that Walmart *wasn't* going to do it."

By 2017, PillPack's leaders were meeting with potential partners to talk about large commercial agreements. One of them was Walmart. After months of on-and-off conversations, Walmart executive Lori Flees posed a question to PillPack's founders: How about we just buy you outright? While the entrepreneurs believed they had a clear path to building a long-term, sustainable, independent company, they knew it was going to be capital-intensive, and the funds they currently had in the bank definitely weren't going to cut it. They still weren't convinced that selling was the right path—they felt confident they could attain more venture capital when necessary—but they let Flees and team know that they were certainly open to the idea of selling.

Late that summer, Parker traveled to New Jersey to meet with Marc Lore, Walmart's e-commerce chief, who had floated in and out of the discussion for months. After rebuffing some lower offers, Parker told him that anything less than $500 million wouldn't even be worth discussing with the startup's board of directors. (PillPack had been valued at around $300 million in its most recent round of venture funding.) Soon after, Flees notified Parker that the two sides were too far apart on a fair purchase price, but they should stay close and still consider a commercial arrangement if it made sense. Right before the end of that year, though, Flees got back in touch and said she thought the two sides could make a deal work after all.

Parker was indeed interested. But first, the banker the company had hired to help run a potential sale process felt it necessary to get other bidders involved. Top of mind was a certain Seattle-based tech giant that finally seemed ready to enter the online pharmacy space.[3] In late 2017, Parker and his cofounder Cohen flew to Seattle to pitch a large contingent of Amazon officials on a potential acquisition. The assorted staff included Doug Herrington, the onetime head of Amazon's consumables and grocery business, who had since been elevated to run Amazon's entire North American retail business. Amazon had also been toying with building an online pharmacy, and members of that fledgling team also packed into the conference room to hear from the entrepreneurs.

Unfortunately for Parker and Cohen, their pitch didn't land, and

Herrington and company hinted that they might be able to build an online pharmacy on their own. Amazon, like many new entrants attempting to penetrate the prescription space, felt that they had to target customers who paid for medications in cash, because powerful industry middlemen, called pharmacy benefit managers (PBMs), had a stranglehold over whose customers could and couldn't use insurance for prescription drugs. The rise of high-deductible plans also played in the company's favor.

"Let's just get out of the insurance quandary altogether and let's build something customers love for the twenty percent that need to, or can, pay in cash," was how Greg Greeley, the former head of Amazon Prime, recalled the internal discussions. "Then it was just a matter of when do we prioritize this. We were going to build it."

With one big suitor seemingly off the table, Parker and Cohen continued to go deeper into conversation with Walmart in a series of visits to the home office in Bentonville. Walmart leaders also traveled to PillPack's headquarters in New Hampshire for an up-close look at their operations. Things seemed on track.

Then, after a conversation with Marc Lore, Parker felt confident that a final offer would value his company at at least $600 million, with added compensation on top for both founders and their staff. They were about to become generationally wealthy.

By late winter of 2018, the two sides had entered an exclusive forty-five-day negotiation window, during which Walmart could complete due diligence and secure a deal. Within that time frame, which eventually was extended by a week or two, PillPack was not permitted to discuss an acquisition with any other companies. By then PillPack's founders were probably most excited about envisioning a world in which Walmart.com customers would be able to purchase prescriptions for delivery alongside toys, or toiletries, or maybe even groceries.

"The core thesis," according to someone familiar with the deal talks, "was that if you could give consumers the same tools to shop pharmacy as they shop for other categories in their life, you could fix a bunch of the knock-on supply chain [and] drug pricing issues."

Some Walmart executives, however, had a much less sexy idea. They wanted to use PillPack and its software to make Walmart's existing pharmacies operate more efficiently and economically.

"We coveted their systems," said Marcus Osborne, a fourteen-year veteran of Walmart who served as the head of the Walmart Health division before departing in 2021.

At the time, Walmart was staring down a necessary investment of hundreds of millions of dollars to upgrade its own pharmacy technology system. For maybe $100 million more, some inside Walmart thought the retailer could get that from PillPack with the added bonus of continuing to grow the startup's existing core business.

The Walmart executive who delivered the message about what Walmart really wanted from PillPack was Flees, the same company leader who was initially hired in 2014 to serve as Doug McMillon's corporate strategy lead. And just like she had done when counseling Marc Lore on how to pitch some of his initiatives to Walmart's more traditional store leaders, Flees was now counseling PillPack's founders on the right way to win over the Walmart execs who needed to sign off on the deal. The Walmart corporate translator was at it again.

Walmart's pharmacies did indeed need a lot of help, even if they had at one time been innovative in their own right. In 2006, for example, Walmart introduced a plan to charge customers only $4 per prescription for the generic version of around three hundred of the most commonly prescribed medications.

"There was no certainty that they weren't going to lose their shirt on that deal," Osborne, the longtime Walmart health care executive, said.

But for the tens of millions of Americans without insurance, or with high-deductible plans, the initiative was a true game changer.

"It was a spectacular success," he said.

But that had been one of Walmart's few innovations in the pharmacy space. (In the summer of 2021, Walmart's announcement that it would begin selling an affordable private-label version of analog insulin had the potential to become another.)[4] McMillon believed that Walmart had an opportunity to be even more disruptive in the health care industry and needed to keep trying to make its own imprint on the sector. In 2015, CVS's acquisition of Target's pharmacies prompted McMillon to ask Flees to evaluate what Walmart could and should be doing in health care. The chance to buy PillPack, along with its technological prowess and talent, represented a potential new era for pharmacy innovation at Walmart.

Once Walmart paused on the talks, though, PillPack reengaged Amazon. This time Parker was confident he had nailed his pitch in a new meeting with a longtime Amazon executive named Nader Kabbani, who had been put in charge of Amazon's internal pharmacy plans. After the meeting, Parker stretched out across the lawn in Seattle's Olympic Sculpture Park, pulled out his phone, and shot off a text to his executive team.

It was the best pitch of his life, he said, and he was confident the deal was going to happen.

That meant Walmart's chances were all but dead. Not even a call from the CEO of the world's largest retailer could change that.

Meanwhile, Amazon's acquisition of PillPack, for a little over $750 million up front (two sources said the total all-in value eventually reached $1 billion), paved the way for the tech giant to launch its own pharmacy online, with innovative industry entrepreneurs leading the way. It had been a long time coming, though some close to the deal found it odd that Jeff Bezos never met with PillPack's founders during the acquisition process. After all, Bezos had been burned once before.

All the way back in early 1999, Amazon had bought a 46 percent stake in an upstart website called Drugstore.com, with Bezos joining its board of directors as a result. As its name indicated, Drugstore.com aimed to sell the types of products commonly found in local drugstores, and that included prescription drugs. Among the challenges Drugstore.com faced was the cold shoulder it was getting from some of the powerful middlemen of the prescription drug industry—PBMs. Years later, these same middlemen would spar with PillPack as its service gained more traction, at one point costing the startup one-third of its customers.[5] Dawn Lepore, one of Drugstore.com's former CEOs, said a major turning point was when a large PBM called Medco shut Drugstore.com out of its insurance network, which included tens of millions of US customers.

"For 1 out of 5 people who came to the site, we would have to tell them we didn't take their insurance," Lepore said in a 2018 interview.[6]

Amazon eventually sold its stake in Drugstore.com as the business foundered. The idea of building an online pharmacy inside Amazon, however, percolated for years, with multiple teams coming up with ideas on how the tech giant might enter the space. Eventually, leadership aligned on the PillPack acquisition as the best path to accomplish their goals. Then, in November 2020, Amazon introduced Amazon Pharmacy, separate from the PillPack business, and of course with free two-day delivery for Prime members. The company said at the time that Prime members without prescription drug coverage, or with a high-deductible plan, could save up to 80 percent on generic drugs and 40 percent on brand-name drugs when paying in cash. Amazon Pharmacy also developed a tool for shoppers to compare drug prices in-cash versus with-insurance before checking out.

"Our goal is to make accessing prescription medications as simple as any other purchase: saving customers time, giving them more control over their purchases, and helping them stay healthy," Amazon spokesperson Jacqui Miller told me in an email at the time.

It sounded a lot like the vision the PillPack founders were excited to build at Walmart, before the deal ultimately fell apart. Even with the introduction of Amazon Pharmacy, Amazon continued to encourage PillPack customers to use that service since it was designed for those who regularly take multiple medications. On the other hand, Amazon Pharmacy might appeal to those with less regular or pressing medication needs. Someone who might only need blood pressure medication or prescription pills for anxiety. The logistics behind the service, however, wouldn't be able to serve customers who needed a prescription filled the same day, such as an antibiotic to treat an infection.

Eventually PillPack's founders hoped that the pharmacy would evolve to a place where customers could use it to compare the prices of different medications designed to treat the same ailment. That would require a format similar to what Amazon had pioneered years before with the Amazon Marketplace, through which merchants big and small vie with each other and, many times, Amazon itself. In this case, prescription drug makers and third-party pharmacies would not only be competing with each other for a sale but possibly with PillPack or Amazon Pharmacy as well.

"It's supercomplicated," a source said.

But, over time, Parker recognized that even with Amazon's reputation for experimentation and innovation, it was difficult to get big initiatives off the ground at the company. Bureaucracy had finally crept in, as it had done at Walmart many years ago, and it was difficult to build healthcare technology inside the systems of a retail organization. Parker, just like Marc Lore at Walmart, began feeling stifled.

By the time the entrepreneur left Amazon in 2022, his full vision for Amazon's potential in the pharmacy world was not yet realized, but he remained hopeful that someday down the road it would be. Meanwhile, elsewhere in the company, another health-related initiative was receiving strong public backing from Amazon's new CEO, Andy Jassy, despite being a much tinier business than Amazon's pharmacy initiatives.

Amazon Care

As the coronavirus pandemic whipsawed around the world in early 2020, and variants catalyzed new waves of the Covid-19 virus every few months, an Amazon executive named Kristen Helton could only grimace at the missed opportunity—both for Amazon and for people all over the US desperate for medical consultation. Telemedicine— the practice of consulting with a health care provider by phone or videoconference—was suddenly becoming a necessity rather than a nice-to-have, and Helton's team inside Amazon was working on a service that they felt was even better.

"We got . . . so many requests, and I would have loved to have served those customers," Helton told me in an interview in 2022. "We just weren't quite ready to do it."

It might have been especially disappointing to Helton, as the former entrepreneur and technologist had been working for years toward a big moment like this one. In 2015, she and two other entrepreneurs were building a startup based on an implantable body sensor smaller than a grain of rice that would continuously monitor a person's body chemistry. One early use case was for wound-healing specialists to track the oxygen levels in the legs of patients, in an attempt to avoid amputation.[7]

Then an investor introduced her to a technologist named Babak Parviz.

Parviz was well-known in the technology industry for leading the team that created the "smart" glasses known as Google Glass. But a year before Helton's meeting with Parviz, he had left Google for Amazon, where he was overseeing an experimental research lab dubbed Grand Challenge, where some of Amazon's most prized employees were tasked with thinking big and super long-term on new moonshot ventures.[8]

Upon meeting Parviz, Helton posed a question: Could you imagine doing something in health care?

"Come think of something good and put it to paper," Helton recalled Parviz responding, "and if you can get it funded, then we'll do something in health care."

Though captivated by inventing technologies that might represent the future a decade down the road, Helton also knew that the health care industry was in need of immediate innovation, especially when it came to addressing more foundational problems with shorter timelines for improvement. And because of Amazon's track record of innovation, coupled with its gargantuan customer base, Helton believed the tech giant could be a legitimate player in health care if company leaders had the will. She took the job.

By the end of 2016, Helton had come up with a promising idea for a new health care service and, with the help of Parviz, had crafted the seminal document that just about every new initiative at Amazon emanates from: a PRFAQ memo, which aims to imagine how the company would market the service in a press release upon launch, and how it would answer the most common questions the general public might have.

With the dateline of June 1, 2018, the imaginary press release introduced "Amazon Care"—"Comprehensive, high-quality healthcare, anytime, anywhere, available in minutes."

"Care enables direct access to a medical professional in minutes from nearly any internet-enabled device via a video link," the document read, "enables collection of medical data from an at-home device, and provides access to Mobile Medics for at-home procedures such as blood draws and vaccinations."

Not only would Amazon Care patients be able to video-chat or message with medical professionals, but they'd also be able to request in-person care from registered nurses when needed. In the retail world, such an approach would be dubbed "omnichannel"—reaching customers in all sales channels, whether via e-commerce or brick-and-mortar stores. And as with many of Amazon's past innovations, from Amazon Prime to Amazon Fresh, adding a convenience layer for customers was paramount. In the case of Amazon Care, that meant that registered nurses would visit Amazon Care patients if necessary, rather than customers trekking out to a doctor's office while ill.

The service's first customers would be Amazon's own employees and their immediate families—a sizable endeavor on its own for the country's second-largest private-sector employer. But the ambition was always bigger—to offer at some point down the road an innovative Amazon health care service to Americans unaffiliated with Amazon, as well.

Amazon executives often say that they will only enter crowded sectors if they feel they have a highly differentiated product or service, so simply competing head-on with telemedicine companies that had been building their service and customer bases for years seemed like a nonstarter. But Helton and team also had conducted research into what was missing in the space.

With the help of several physicians, they identified nearly fifty thousand different reasons why a patient might visit a primary care physician over the course of a year. What they found posed a hard truth about the limitations of telemedicine: less than 6 percent of those visits could be completely handled via a video call with a health care provider.

Helton envisioned Amazon sending patients an at-home testing device that could act as a camera, thermometer, and stethoscope all in one. When this device was combined with the videoconferencing feature, Amazon Care could suddenly address about 20 percent, or one in five, traditional primary care visits, for conditions like ear infections and rashes. Finally, with the third leg of the Amazon Care stool—at-home visits by a medical professional—the service would be able to handle medical events that make up more than two in three traditional primary care visits.

By September 2016, Jeff Bezos had reviewed the document with Helton. By early the following the year, the Amazon CEO gave her the green light to move forward. Over the course of 2017 and 2018, Helton and her team modified the Amazon Care service from the original one envisioned in the PRFAQ memo. One of the most prominent changes involved moving away from sending the at-home diagnostic devices to patients' homes. The company would eventually provide them instead to the nurses who would be dispatched to patients' homes, though that took some time.

In 2018, Amazon began recruiting nurses and doctors with emergency room experience in the lead-up to a planned 2019 launch. Helton and others were interested in that kind of experience because they envisioned the service initially serving as a replacement for urgent care visits, not the longer-term vision of acting as primary care physicians. To some of these new hires, the opportunity seemed almost too good to be true. Many received raises over what they previously were earning, and an important role on the ground floor of an initiative that recruiters promised would "change the face of health care."

"When hospitals are like, 'You need to focus on the patient experience,' I'm like, 'I'm just trying to keep this person from dying,'" an Amazon Care nurse who previously worked in emergency rooms told me. "This was the first time I got to be customer-obsessed."

They eventually realized they would technically be working for a separate company, called Oasis—which would later be renamed Care Medical—but the only client was Amazon Care. That year, Amazon began a pilot test of the service for a subset of Amazon employees and their families living in Seattle. During those early days, the same startup atmosphere that was attractive to the former hospital workers was also shocking in some respects. Some early medical staff, for example, were surprised to find that Amazon Care execs were intent on having company engineers create key software—an electronic medical record (EMR) system—from scratch, rather than using commonly used systems that already had a good reputation in the health care industry. That created some safety gaps that Care team professionals found problematic. For example, nurses had to inform tech staff that each page on a patient's medical chart should include their allergies. There was also frustration that Amazon's tech platform made it difficult to share records with other medical providers, a feature that is used frequently in common EMR systems.

"They don't look at something and say what is right about health care," a former nurse said. "They only focus on what is wrong."

The equipment that medical staff carried with them to patient visits was also lacking, some former employees said. The blood pressure cuff and pulse oximeter were ones you could pull off the shelf at a Walgreens, and the equipment used to transmit images of a patient's throat or ear to a doctor on the other end of a computer felt like it was hacked together. Seeing images from a child's throat or ear was especially challenging.

"It never really worked, and the quality wasn't good," a former Care Medical nurse told me.

On a visit to meet with the Amazon Care team, Dr. Atul Gawande, the celebrated surgeon and author, seemed bewildered by the quality of equipment—or lack thereof.

"This is bad," Gawande said, according to someone who was present.

(From 2018 to 2020, Gawande was CEO of Haven, a joint venture between Amazon, JPMorgan Chase, and Berkshire Hathaway, aimed at reducing health care costs at the companies while improving care for their employees and, eventually, sharing their innovations with the outside world. The venture was later dissolved after leaders recognized that a main goal, to serve as a central health benefits office for three companies with vastly different geographies and cultures, was going to be too complicated. "Once that became clear," Gawande explained, "it threatened to become a very expensive think tank."[9] The *Wall Street Journal* also reported that concerns from the three companies over how they were being asked to share data with the consortium, along with pushback from insurance companies, "stymied Haven's efforts to determine how much the companies paid for medical care and why."[10])

Amazon's self-proclaimed customer obsession also led to some decisions early on that might have appealed to employees who were the service's patients, but made some medical staff uneasy. Commonly prescribed antibiotics like Z-Pak pills were stored in locked cabinets inside one of Amazon's downtown Seattle office towers, and nurses were expected to deliver them themselves to patient doors. There was no pharmacist supervision.

"It was a convenience thing," a former nurse told me. "They were trying to be a really white-glove, all-inclusive, concierge medicine service."

Eventually there was enough pushback that Amazon contracted out with a local pharmacy chain that filled patient orders. The medical staff also found themselves having to shoot down what they saw as ill-advised ideas. One, for example, would have allowed patients to order whatever blood work they wanted without a doctor's supervision or direction.

"They hired physicians and nurse practitioners trained to look for disease process but wanted to bypass them and just go with Dr. Google," one nurse said.

Over time, Care Medical nurses began seeing more kids and infants—the children of Amazon employees. But some basic equipment for pediatric care had not been purchased, such as infant scales, or had to be fought for to procure, such as pulse oximeters designed specifically for infants. Early on, there was also no protocol or process for following up with significantly ill patients. In one instance, a nurse paid a visit to a man who was violently ill with the flu. He refused to go to the emergency room as the nurse advised, so she requested that her bosses let her drop by for a follow-up visit later in the day. Her request was denied. She instead settled for a phone check-in later that evening.

"I didn't have anything to back me up—no protocol."

The work environment for the clinical team did seem to improve, however, after Kristi Henderson, an executive with extensive experience in telehealth, joined Amazon Care in 2019. Over a year-plus at the company, she successfully pushed for nurses to get new equipment—an existing device called TytoCare, designed specifically for medical staff conducting in-home visits with a doctor looking on remotely. She also oversaw the creation of a "command center" that allowed staff to monitor the whereabouts of nurses in the field at all times.

But a little over a year after joining, Henderson left the company, frustrated, former colleagues say, by internal roadblocks she faced on both the business and clinical sides of the operation. All the time, though, customer satisfaction scores among Amazon's employees remained strong. Patients—or customers, as Amazon Care's leadership team insisted on calling them—could message or videoconference with a nurse or doctor 24/7, and receive medicine deliveries quickly.

"My son had an ear infection during the early days of Covid when Seattle felt like a scene from *Outbreak*," Chance Kelch, a former Amazon executive, said. "He was fully scream-crying."

Kelch used the video-calling feature of Amazon Care to receive a diagnosis, and had a prescription delivered to his home within an hour.

"It was magic," he said.

The pandemic provided other opportunities, and challenges, for the service. Management decided to pause in-person nurse visits in the early days of the pandemic but set up a drive-through Covid-19 testing site for Amazon employees. The first day on the job, one medical assistant who was now being asked to administer Covid tests was trailed by a superior who timed each interaction with a patient. The medical assistant wasn't going fast enough, she was told, in what might not be a surprise to Amazon warehouse workers, who must hit quotas and have their performance monitored in real time.

"In my clinical eyes, I was taking the time to properly explain the process to the patient and provide them with the adequate instructions for isolation and test results," the former employee said.

As Amazon Care pulled back from in-home visits, which had been seen as a key differentiator of their service, competing telehealth services were receiving an influx of new patients while Amazon was still just testing its service out on its own staff. Prior to the pandemic, less than 1 percent of total outpatient visits to a health care provider were conducted via telemedicine. But in the first six months of the Covid pandemic, that number shot up to 13 percent.[11] For Amazon, there was never going to be a better time. But the Amazon Care service was nowhere near ready for prime time.

In an interview, Kristen Helton, the Amazon Care boss, called that wasted opportunity her "biggest regret." At times Helton questioned whether the pursuit was worth it. Should Amazon really be in this space? But then she would look at the high customer satisfaction scores or get a pep talk from longtime Amazon employees, and put her head back down to keep building.

While the service was still restricted to just Amazon employees, nurses were rarely overwhelmed with work but were often asked to pick up extra shifts or days anyway. They assumed that Amazon, with its obsession with customer satisfaction, just wanted to make sure it could live up to its promise that patients, especially its own employees, wouldn't have to wait long for a virtual appointment.

In the spring of 2021, Amazon announced a big milestone: they were opening up Amazon Care to employees of outside companies also located in Washington State. Precor, a maker of workout equipment and a subsidiary of Peloton, was the first to sign up. By the summer, Amazon opened up the telemedicine portion of the service to its employees in all fifty states, and said its in-person service would expand that year to a handful of other cities, including Boston, Austin, and Washington, DC. By February 2022, Amazon had added a few more employers to its service, and promised to expand in-person services to twenty more metro areas.[12] That same year, Amazon began permitting Amazon Care patients to use the service for more than just urgent care needs; the service began offering primary care services, replacing the typical in-office annual physical with a convenient nurse visit at home.

But there were signs that the service still didn't have full company support. In the same month of the expansion announcement, Amazon's Alexa division announced a partnership with a virtual health care rival called Teladoc, in a surprise to industry insiders who questioned what that partnership said about the future of Amazon Care. Why would Amazon, after all, boost the visibility of a one-day competitor of Amazon Care if it had faith in Amazon Care?

"It's . . . about when do we feel like we've really nailed a compelling customer experience," Helton, the Amazon Care leader, told me. "When we think we've done that, then you'll see the next [revision] of Care and Alexa."

What went unsaid was that Amazon had not yet been able to cut deals with many of the big insurance companies that would sign off on adding Amazon Care as a covered medical service in their networks. As a result, Amazon Care had to pitch each employer individually to get them to cover much of the costs of the service for their own employees—an approach that threatened to eventually doom the service.

Even so, the most powerful full-time employee at Amazon—CEO Andy Jassy—appeared publicly to have a soft spot for the service. In late 2021, he labeled Amazon Care one of the company innovations he was most excited about while speaking at an employee town hall meeting.[13]

"What we're trying to do with Amazon Care and telemedicine . . . radically changes [the] game," he said.

The game, however, had many players. Over in Bentonville, another dominant player in the retail industry was investing significant resources and time into building its own health care service. In doing so, it hoped to take advantage of the thousands of assets it possessed that its Seattle-based rival didn't: all those giant brick-and-mortar stores.

Dr. Walmart

When McMillon took over his dream job in 2014, his company was already well on its way to taking another crack at creating a doctor's-office-type experience within some of its stores. During the previous decade, Walmart had worked through several iterations of partnerships that resulted in other companies operating urgent-care-like facilities within its Supercenters.

But that strategy largely flopped, as even a corporate titan like Walmart ran into the realities of an entrenched and unwelcoming industry to would-be disrupters. In some instances, Walmart leased space to entities with ulterior motives: hospital networks. One hospital network, for example, ran a shuttle bus from their Walmart clinic to the hospital, seemingly attempting to turn low-profit clinic patients into high-profit hospital patients.

"I understand why the hospitals do it, because they build the Taj Mahal to health care," Osborne said, "but like, that's not what people need."

But those hospital networks understood what Walmart would soon find out. The economics of urgent-care-type facilities can be brutal.

"The money is in chronic illness," Osborne added. "A diabetic who comes back every month makes you more money than somebody who has a strep throat once a year."

So the world's biggest retailer would eventually try its hand at creating and running its own medical facilities. One main goal, reminiscent of Amazon with Amazon Care, was to serve its own employees, and hopefully offer superior care. Another was to bring down the company's own health care costs along the way. Reducing health care costs was something that even Sam Walton felt passionately about. Way back in 1991, while Walton was undergoing treatments for the blood cancer that he would succumb to a year later, he made an impassioned case for Walmart to use its might in a new way. His plea came shortly after he discovered how much a hospital was marking up the cost of an MRI he underwent.

"We've got to get the hospitals and doctors in line," he told a room full of employees during one of the company's regular Saturday morning leadership meetings.[14] "We've got to get those charges under control.

"These people are skinning us alive," he added.

Years later, Walmart's benefits division introduced an innovative program called Centers of Excellence (COEs) in partnership with a handful of top hospitals across the US. Under the initiative, Walmart covered the cost of travel to these partner hospitals for company employees in need of certain major surgeries and transplants, while facilitating second opinions and remote reviews of cancer treatment plans, too. The company was trying to reduce the number of unnecessary or inappropriate procedures or surgeries performed on their employees by local doctors or hospitals. The idea was that these COE relationships would improve the health and care of employees while eventually reducing Walmart's health care payments.

"I heard from Walmart a righteous indignation about inappropriate care," Dr. Jonathan Slotkin, a spine surgeon with one of the COEs, told me. "There's a throughline there to the Sam indignation in that video."

On the retail side of the business, leaders would take a different approach. Starting in 2014, Walmart began rolling out what would end up being nineteen facilities dubbed "Care Clinics" inside Supercenter stores in Texas, South Carolina, and Georgia. They were run by nurse practitioners and designed to make access to a health facility more convenient in small communities. By doing so, Walmart could encourage its employees to visit a nurse or doctor more frequently, rather than let medical issues fester to the point that an expensive emergency room visit was eventually needed. If Walmart could exchange an ER visit for even a couple of clinic visits, the hope was that its employees would be healthier and Walmart's health care costs would decrease. Reducing these costs could have a drastic impact on the retailer's bottom line.

At launch, Walmart employees and families enrolled in the company's health plans paid just $4 for a visit, in what seemed like a nod to the $4 cost of generic drugs at Walmart pharmacies that had served as a major disruption a decade earlier. Nonemployees would pay $40 a visit. The large insurance carriers were not brought on board in the early days, so the pilot test was really aimed at gaining traction first with employees before courting other customers.

Some critics viewed the initiative as a way to drive mom-and-pop doctor's offices off the map. But leaders of the program saw it very differently.

"That wasn't it at all," a former Walmart health executive told me. "It was that we actually had a utilization problem amongst our own associates in the wrong direction, meaning they never used health care until they had a big problem. And then they used the emergency room and got admitted to the hospital."

In locales where Walmart opened Care Clinics, emergency room visits among Walmart workers did in fact decrease, this former exec said. In turn, Walmart's benefits division experienced cost savings. That was important because Care Clinic leaders thought these savings should be taken into account when calculating the profitability of the initiative. The savings were also why the company was willing to subsidize the cost of a visit and only charge employees $4.

But things were never quite that simple for leaders of nonretail businesses operating within the retail kingdom of Walmart. They reported into the US stores division of the company, run by Greg Foran, Walmart's longtime US CEO—the no-BS retail operator who had at times sparred with Marc Lore over the e-commerce division's spending and money-losing ways. Foran was supportive of the *idea* of Walmart playing a bigger role in health care but did not see things the same way as the Clinic Care leaders. He ultimately disregarded the cost savings from reduced employee ER visits and mandated that the facilities run profitably on their own without accounting for those savings.

"He wanted to be supportive of health care in every way possible, but it couldn't get in the way of him doing his job," the former health care executive told me. "His number one job was to fix US stores and he couldn't allow capital or focus to cause any distraction from that."

"In his mind, it was like, 'I've got a first-things-first problem,'" said Osborne, the longtime health executive at Walmart. "You can't do nineteen things in parallel."

Without that accounting allowance, a clinic's march to profitability was much longer, and looked especially bad in light of shorter ROI timelines for a Supercenter store. Of course, they were remarkably different businesses—a fact that seemed to get lost on some of the company's brick-and-mortar retail leaders. As a result, the Care Clinic original business plan had to be scrapped, too. Those $4 visits for employees no longer made much sense. Walmart had been subsidizing the price of visits for associates so that they would use the clinics more and take trips to the hospital less.

But if the Care Clinic team wasn't getting financial credit for that trade-off, the original economics of the business model just couldn't work. In turn, Walmart needed to pursue deals with the large insurance players in the industry so that the service was more attractive to nonemployees as well. It was a death blow.

"That basically just made the clinic less affordable to the general public," the former executive said, "and started to mimic something that looked more like the status quo of health care."

After Flees came on board as McMillon's lead strategy executive, he tasked her with digging deep into health care opportunities and how Walmart should play in the sector. They weren't convinced that Care Clinics were the answer, and fixing the company's e-commerce business was a much bigger priority for Walmart given the direction in which the retail world was heading. As it happened, on the same spring day in 2016 that McMillon met with an intriguing entrepreneur named Marc Lore, who was still running an independent Jet, Flees was meeting with representatives from Aetna to discuss a potential health care partnership. When both returned, the CEO had a message for his strategy chief.

"I need you to slow down what you're doing in health care because I want you to focus on Jet and help do the diligence," McMillon told Flees.

Eventually the Care Clinic initiative fizzled out while Walmart leaders agreed to elevate health and wellness into its own division of the company—in part to attract what they hoped would be better talent—and rethink the best way to make an impact. In 2019, the company conducted a survey of its customers, across all demographics, to get a better feel for their health care priorities. More than 40 percent of those surveyed revealed that cost was the biggest impediment to getting health care. The company also focused on the finding that 80 percent of their US store locations are in communities that the government labels as medically underserved. Around 150 million people visit a Walmart store in the US every week, so leaders remained convinced that there was a role for the company to play.

McMillon's health care pursuits also seemed to be influenced by external and internal conversations alike.

"I think he was partially influenced by the [Walton] family, who had started to get more interested and focused and believe there was opportunity," Osborne said, "but I also think he was being influenced by his peers. He would say, 'I go to Davos [Switzerland, home of the World Economic Forum] and every conversation ends up being a health care conversation.'"

By the fall of 2019, Walmart introduced a new type of health facility, called Walmart Health. The company pitched the new health care format as "the first to put primary and urgent care, labs, x-ray and diagnostics, counseling, dental, optical and hearing services all in one facility." It was a mini-supercenter of medical care, alongside a real Supercenter. The retailer promised affordable prices, and transparency on what visits cost, with or without insurance.

If Walmart Care Clinics, run by nurse practitioners, were a first step toward Walmart serving as a primary physician, Walmart Health facilities were a two-footed leap forward. These facilities would have their own entrances from Walmart parking lots, rather than being buried deep inside a store like Care Clinics were. Walmart chose the first two locations, both in Georgia, because of high rates of chronic disease and a below-average number of primary care physicians in the area.[15]

"For them to try to make a dent here, and do something about skyrocketing health care costs, is in the interest of their own bottom line as well as the right thing to do," said Christina Farr, a former top healthtech journalist who now invests in the field as a venture capitalist.

But stability was hard to come by at the top ranks of Walmart's health unit. Less than a year after he oversaw the launch of the new Walmart Health facilities, and only two years into his tenure at Walmart, a top executive named Sean Slovenski left the company to take a CEO role at a small health-tech startup. Shortly after the first Walmart Health clinic launched, John Furner, the CEO of Sam's Club, had replaced Foran as the Walmart US CEO. Insiders told me that Furner and other top leaders came away unimpressed with Slovenski's vision for Walmart Health and how it was going to make money. Slovenski, on the other hand, did not appreciate that his plans for a massive rollout of thousands of Walmart Health clinics, which had been approved under Foran, now seemed at risk.[16] Walmart's bigness was also a problem.

"I'm not a big company animal," Slovenski said after his departure.[17] "As soon as I get to the point where bureaucracy is the rule of the day . . . I stop doing well in that environment. And Walmart is the biggest company in the world so of course it's got bureaucracy and it wasn't my cup of tea."

Osborne, the former leader of the Walmart Health clinics, understood how the bureaucracy of the organization, and the structure that had someone like Slovenski reporting up to a CEO mostly focused on the core retail business, could be disillusioning.

"Walmart US . . . is now a holding company, but they don't manage it like a holding company; it's like a retail business that happens to have this little health care thing on the side," Osborne said. "And so I think that Sean rightfully chafed against that. It's like, 'I'm trying to run this business, and you're making me spend twenty-eight hours a week in these [meetings] that don't have any meaning to what I'm doing. I don't care about whether mac-and-cheese is out of stock.'

"No disrespect," Osborne added, "[these meetings] are ninety-eight percent a waste of time when it comes to the management and leadership of your health care business."

Months after Slovenski's departure, Walmart hired Dr. Cheryl Pegus, a former cardiologist who once worked at Pfizer and as Walgreens' first chief medical officer, to replace Slovenski and lead the company's health and wellness efforts. Prior to Walmart, she was the chief medical officer for Cambia Health Solutions, a health insurance company. While the US CEO, John Furner, was intrigued by the idea of hiring a health technology executive to fill the role—specifically, the top health executive from Facebook parent company Meta—McMillon felt the company needed a doctor with health insurance industry experience, like Pegus.

Under Pegus, the rollout of new Walmart Health centers slowed. In the three years following the first center opening its doors, only twenty-six more locations, across four states, followed. Of course, the yearslong pandemic likely played a role in the deliberate pace. In October 2022, Pegus's organization announced that sixteen new Walmart Health facilities would open in Florida alone over the course of the following year. While that seemed like a positive sign, it was still not clear that the retailer had yet landed on a slam-dunk successful model for a health care offering. In reviews on Google, the majority of the

Walmart Health clinics had ratings of fewer than four out of five stars. Insider also reported in the fall of 2021 that "prices aren't as low or clear-cut as they appear, thanks in part to hidden fees, and problems with billing patients and insurers have gotten in the way of Walmart Health's ability to improve healthcare for patients."

That same year, Walmart made a move to add telehealth services to its Walmart Health division by acquiring a decade-old company called MeMD. MeMD was later rebranded to Walmart Health Virtual Care and became an option for patients who visit one of the company's Walmart Health locations in Florida. The expansion marked a first step toward offering an approach to health care that Walmart is already intimately familiar with from the retail world: an omnichannel experience.

"It's the same thing in grocery—sometimes people just want to go online and have it delivered and they don't want to go into a store. And other times, people want to go pick out their avocados, because they know exactly when they're going to eat them," Flees told me in 2022. "Health care is not so different—sometimes they want to physically see someone. And sometimes they just need to get the advice as quickly as they can get it. Our strategy is the same."

Obviously, Walmart had deep expertise in the retail industry before it expanded into e-commerce. The same can't be said for either its physical health care facilities or its virtual ones. But at the very top of the company, the most important voice at Walmart was preaching patience—at least outwardly. Inside Doug McMillon's office on Walmart's Bentonville campus in 2022, I asked the company's chief decision-maker how serious the company's commitment is amid some of the challenges encountered thus far.

"If this is a nine-inning game, we're somewhere in the top of the second," McMillon told me. "We're just really still getting started."

With the hiring of Pegus, McMillon said, Walmart finally had the right talent on board.

"She's able to articulate a plan in a way that feels more understandable and complete to us," the CEO told me.

For Walmart Health long-timers, though, it's hard not to feel like it's Groundhog Day. The company has cycled through nine leaders of the health and wellness division in just ten years, creating a revolving door of missed opportunity.

"Every time somebody new comes in, you take a step back, because they think they need to redo the strategy," Osborne said.

In that interview with McMillon in early 2022, the CEO said he was confident the unit would show more progress over the next two years. He also let on that while he believed the health care division could become a slightly profitable addition to the company at some point, its role in the "strengthening of the Supercenters" was perhaps more important.

According to Osborne, the CEO also was candid internally about the financial role that a large health care business could play in defending against an Amazon encroachment. Namely, that a large-scale, multifaceted health care division could generate $10 billion a year in new cash flow for Walmart. With that additional cash on hand, Walmart could close the cash flow gap between itself and Amazon, and have the financial might to defend itself against a business assault on its core grocery business—so the thinking went.

In Osborne's mind, that $10 billion figure was certainly attainable with long-term commitment and heavy investment. But the motivation itself was troublesome.

"Walmart is strangely at its best when it almost isn't focused on economics," Osborne said, with a nod to the $4 generics initiative of the mid-2000s. "When it's just saying, 'I'm going to do something that dramatically improves the lives of people.'"

Either way, for those who've worked on pieces of the company's health care initiatives in the early days, any long-term success would be a long time coming.

"I believe and hope that Walmart will be one of the country's most profound health care companies," a former Walmart health executive told me, "but I am frustrated with the pace at which they have moved."

After a pause, the executive reconsidered his stance a bit.

"But if you look at their history, it's not actually abnormal," he said.

It took a couple of decades for Walmart to perfect what would end up becoming the Supercenter model, he went on. The same could be said for the company's move into grocery sales. So only about a decade into the company's foray into operating its own health facilities, maybe there is hope that Walmart would eventually find a successful model.

"I'm hopeful that they'll still be on the twenty-year plan and they'll get it right and nail it and scale it," he told me. "And the question will then be, 'Are they too late?' Because Amazon works in cycles much shorter than twenty years."

Sure enough, in July 2022, Amazon announced another chess move even bolder than the PillPack acquisition. The company reported it had agreed to pay $3.9 billion to acquire One Medical, a company that runs a network of doctor's offices and guarantees same-day or next-day appointments for a $200 annual fee. The company also provides 24/7 virtual care. Between PillPack, Amazon Pharmacy, Amazon Care, and One Medical, the tech giant that got its start selling physical books over the internet was now amassing the pieces to build a game changer in health care.

"We think health care is high on the list of experiences that need reinvention," Amazon Health Services senior vice president Neil Lindsay said in a statement at the time. "Booking an appointment, waiting weeks or even months to be seen, taking time off work, driving to a clinic, finding a parking spot, waiting in the waiting room then the exam room for what is too often a rushed few minutes with a doctor, then making another trip to a pharmacy—we see lots of opportunity to both improve the quality of the experience *and* give people back valuable time in their days."

In the aftermath of the One Medical announcement, though, the company would make a less celebrated one: Amazon blindsided its Amazon Care employees and medical staff alike by revealing that it was shutting down the telehealth and in-home service at the end of 2022. CEO Andy Jassy said shortly after the announcement that the Amazon Care shutdown decision was made before the One Medical deal,[18] and a former Amazon health care leader confirmed to me that the viability of Amazon Care was in question long before the One Medical talks began. In retrospect, there had been some hints that the business line might be bleeding money. In the months preceding the shutdown announcement, Amazon Care nurses were told that they needed to fit in more home visits per day to improve their productivity. Jassy would later call the in-home-visit component of the service "unique and differentiated," but the CEO also admitted that the company could not figure out the right economic model to support it.

Still, the news was especially difficult for those nurses who had fled the despair of emergency room work during the pandemic for better work-life balance and the promise of a lofty, well-intentioned mission.

"It felt like I was a part of something big—part of what health care was going to turn into," an Amazon Care nurse told me a few days after receiving the bad news. "I'm devastated; I've literally just cried every day since because I don't want to go back to the hospital. I found this holy grail of a job and I don't want to go back to the hospital."

While nurses like this one dealt with a post-Amazon reality, Amazon's other healthcare plans slowly moved forward. In early September of 2022, One Medical revealed that it and Amazon had received requests from the Federal Trade Commission for more information about the proposed acquisition, signaling a longer government review before the deal could be approved. But many in the industry still expected the acquisition to eventually get the green light, catapulting Amazon deep into the health care industry as Walmart tried to build its presence with a more organic approach.[19]

Osborne, the former Walmart Health leader, believes Amazon's One Medical acquisition could "absolutely" spell trouble for Walmart's health care ambitions in the long run. But as has often been the case during the titan's decades-long attempts at reinvention in areas from e-commerce to health care, the biggest barrier may be the one staring back through the mirror. All of the Walmart Health division's leadership changes and "wildly inconsistent commitment" from the company's top executives will be a lot to overcome, Osborne said.

Sure enough, in November 2022, news broke that Pegus, Walmart's health care leader in whom McMillon preached confidence during our interview just seven months earlier, was departing the company to join a JPMorgan Chase health care unit.

"Walmart Health's biggest threat," Osborne said, "is Walmart."

12
PANDEMIC POWER STRUGGLE

On Sunday, February 23, 2020, I boarded a United Airlines flight at New Jersey's Newark Liberty International Airport that was destined for Seattle, Washington. A month earlier, the first case of Covid-19 had been confirmed in Washington State. But to me, and to most of the rest of the world that was continuing to live life normally, the novel coronavirus was not yet a cause for major concern—and it mostly remained barred from my mind during my five-hour plane ride until a fellow passenger began to sneeze into his open hand, over and over again, seemingly ignorant of the fact that this was unacceptable behavior, even during normal times.

Still, most of my mental focus was on preparing for something that Amazon representatives had tipped me off to just a few days earlier. I was one of a select group of journalists invited to take a sneak peek at a new retail concept the tech giant had developed and would unveil to the public later that week: a grocery store.

Of course, it wasn't just any grocery store. It was, according to the Gospel of Amazon, the grocery store of the future: outfitted with cameras, sensors, and computer vision, this Amazon grocery store eliminated the need for shoppers to fork over cash or payment cards before walking out the door with their groceries. Amazon called it Just Walk

Out Technology—or JWOT to industry geeks. No cashiers needed. Convenience reincarnated at the altar of Jeff Bezos.

While Walmart's No. 1 customer priority has long been to save people money, Amazon's has long been a prioritization of convenience. This store was the manifestation of what Amazon thought convenience could look like if someone had to step out from behind a computer to shop for groceries in person.

Two years earlier, Amazon had first introduced the idea of high-tech cashierless shopping with a store that I had described as "a cross between a 7-Eleven and a Pret A Manger sandwich shop."[1] Now, with the new grocery concept, Amazon was bringing the concept to a 10,000-square-foot supermarket that was more reminiscent of a Trader's Joe's than a Kroger, Walmart, or even Whole Foods. There was no deli counter, butcher, or bakery—the computer vision couldn't accurately track those items yet. Produce items were sold by the unit or bundle rather than by weight, so that the cameras and computer could handle the price computations.

Nonetheless, the new store concept highlighted Amazon's unsated appetite for gobbling up market share in the $900 billion US grocery industry, despite having spent nearly $14 billion in 2017 to acquire Whole Foods[2] and making same-day grocery delivery a free perk for Prime members in 2019.[3] Even with the acquisition of Whole Foods, even with the popularity of delivery startups like Instacart, and Shipt, which Target purchased, Amazon executives knew that only a small percentage of Americans were regularly ordering their groceries online. Amazon was taking another giant step toward infiltrating the world of physical retail it had long shunned—the one Walmart had long owned. The testing and learning had just begun. Little did the Amazon officials I met with that day know, though, how daunting the internal and external hurdles to come would be.

Walmart Plus

Around the same time, in conference rooms at Walmart's home office in northwest Arkansas and the retailer's e-commerce digs in Hoboken,

New Jersey, and the San Francisco Bay area, company executives were planning their own secretive launch. Until I caught wind of it. Just a few days after returning from the Seattle trip, I broke the news that Walmart was finally gearing up to unveil its own innovation: a competitor to Amazon Prime.

Walmart Plus (stylized as Walmart+)[4] was expected to launch as a rebrand of Walmart's existing Delivery Unlimited service, which was already charging customers $98 a year for unlimited, same-day delivery of fresh groceries from one of the 1,600-plus Walmart stores in the US where the program was available. But the Delivery Unlimited service didn't have a real internal champion behind it or, as a result, any significant marketing muscle. Walmart's US CEO, Greg Foran, despite the urgency created by Amazon's Whole Foods acquisition, still preferred that Walmart's focus be placed on the grocery pickup business, a much more profitable service, rather than delivery. Delivery Unlimited also never felt like a membership, something that several executives, including Doug McMillon, believed Walmart could benefit from.

As internal conversations about if and how the service might transform into a membership ensued, Marc Lore stressed to his senior counterparts that Walmart should consider pricing the membership below cost. His theory was that if the price remained at $98 a year, that would lead to comparisons with Amazon Prime, which, at the time, cost only a bit more at $119 a year. Lore doubted how many Americans would pay for two subscriptions, especially when, in areas such as same-day delivery and video streaming, Amazon's membership offered more value. In his view, most Americans would pick one or the other, and he wasn't confident Walmart+ had enough going for it to win out.

If, on the other hand, Walmart priced its membership low enough, he reasoned, a large pool of Amazon Prime customers might be willing to simply purchase a Walmart+ membership in addition to their Prime subscription, utilizing Walmart+ mainly for grocery delivery while continuing to rely on Amazon, at least in the short term, for fast delivery of general merchandise and its entertainment perks. Then, little by little, as Walmart added more value to the Walmart+ program, the retailer might have a better shot at convincing Amazon Prime customers to drop the more expensive program altogether.

The move would require short-term losses by charging just $49 a year for unlimited grocery deliveries, but in exchange for the long-term prospect of chipping away at Amazon's biggest retail strength. And, the truth was, Walmart was never going to turn much of a profit from the membership fee alone and would, either way, need to eventually convince Walmart+ shoppers to order more items that had higher profit margins than groceries, such as household décor or apparel.

Lore knew that making this case would be an uphill battle, and it probably didn't help that his own strategy team had pushed a $98 membership years earlier in a 2018 strategy white paper crafted for the company's board of directors. Also, by the time talk of Walmart+ picked up steam, Lore's voice didn't carry as much weight as it once did. Despite this, Lore tried to make a compelling case that the lower membership price and resulting lower membership revenue might be offset by Walmart needing to spend less on marketing to attract new members. A better deal, Lore knew, would lead to more free, word-of-mouth marketing, which could reduce how much paid advertising the retailer might need to boost sign-ups.

Lore believed that his boss, McMillon, understood the thinking, but it didn't fly with others, like the company's chief financial officer, Brett Biggs. Even some e-commerce leaders working for Lore believed that the $98 price point was more than fair considering how much lower Walmart's prices were on individual grocery items than competitors like Target, or Kroger, or Amazon, for that matter. If a Walmart+ customer placed a large grocery order on a weekly basis, the thinking went, they could expect that they would save at least $10 a week on actual grocery prices compared to other competitors with delivery offerings. If you added those savings up over the course of the year, that amounted to more than $500 in grocery savings, in exchange for just the $98 membership fee to have those savings delivered to your door.

From that point of view, some wanted to make the case publicly that the $98 price point was a steal. But when the service did eventually launch in September 2020, the corporate messaging didn't focus on that. A top Walmart executive, instead, referred to it as "the ultimate life hack."[5]

"It was always about convenience," one of these people said, disapprovingly. "Convenience? Amazon's convenient. Instacart's convenient. Saying that we're convenient is not something new."

The membership also included discounts of 5 cents per gallon at Walmart gas stations, as well as access to a service, called Scan & Go, that allowed shoppers to check out in Walmart stores without waiting in line—a tool Walmart had briefly tested but discontinued several years earlier. But the long-term vision for Walmart+ was for the program to add more perks, like discounts on prescription drugs at Walmart pharmacies, which it eventually did. In 2022, Walmart also added an entertainment perk to the membership: a free subscription to Paramount+, which included TV shows from networks such as CBS and Nickelodeon, as well as movies from Paramount and Miramax.

But back in February 2020, when I broke the news of Walmart+, the program was still a month or two from its scheduled public launch. Before it could get out the door, though, the entire world was turned upside down by a pandemic, the scale of which the world hadn't experienced in over a hundred years. Walmart executives would find themselves firefighting on myriad fronts, including trying to keep up with demand for a volume of online grocery orders that they could have only dreamed of in preceding years. Amazon, too, was about to face a string of disruptive crises, some outside its control—and some self-inflicted.

Prime Pandemic

Ever since Amazon launched an online marketplace in 2002 to allow outside merchants to sell merchandise through its website, the massive product catalogue that it helped create proved crucial to propelling the Amazon flywheel. But as online shopping exploded during the pandemic, that same strength transformed into a major complication. While urgent necessities like soap, toilet paper, hand sanitizer, and masks were in high demand on Amazon.com, Amazon warehouses were also stocked with merchandise that seemed less important: everything from dress clothes to video game consoles. And space was running low.

In mid-March of 2020, Amazon instituted sweeping changes in which products it would store and ship from its warehouses, in a move it said was aimed at keeping essential items in stock and speeding up orders. At the time, Amazon said it would be "temporarily prioritizing household staples, medical supplies, and other high-demand products coming into our fulfillment centers so that we can more quickly receive, restock and deliver these products to customers."

By "prioritizing," Amazon meant it would no longer accept new shipments to its warehouses for discretionary items from marketplace sellers, or bigger vendors, through early April of 2020. During that time, Amazon would still sell all types of products, including nonessential ones, through its website, but outside sellers offering discretionary goods would have to store and ship this merchandise on their own, rather than having Amazon handle those tasks, as it did through its ultrapopular Fulfillment by Amazon (FBA) service.

Even with the changes, Amazon's website and shipping services practically ground to a halt. Not only was top merchandise in short supply, but the company's warehouse workers were calling out, either because they or their loved ones were falling ill, or for fear of contracting the virus in Amazon facilities that employed thousands of workers each. Worker attendance fell by as much as 30 percent.[6] While Amazon did lead many of its competitors in rolling out safety measures like social distancing, mandatory masking, and temperature checks, some workers said at the time that they still often had to hit their quotas, making social distancing difficult or impossible. Another common complaint in the pandemic's earliest days was that Amazon leadership was not being transparent enough about the spread of the virus inside their facilities.

"It affects your nerves, your mental state, your way of thinking—because you have to be cautious in everything you do now," a worker at a Staten Island, New York, Amazon facility said at the time.[7] "It's like I'm risking my life for a dollar."

Amazon workers weren't alone. At Walmart, workers were agitating for better health precautions, too. In early April of 2020, Walmart had to temporarily close a Pennsylvania warehouse after a rapid rise in Covid-19 cases. Covid-19 outbreaks also hit several Supercenter stores, including a Massachusetts location that Walmart temporarily closed after about a dozen employees there tested positive. A dozen US state attorneys general wrote to Walmart in early June of that year to denounce what they said were unsatisfactory precautions to protect both Walmart employees and customers.

A few days after Amazon's announcement about prioritizing essential merchandise, some goods, even though in stock in Amazon's warehouses, were showing delivery times of more than a month—even for Prime members.[8] For several weeks, such delivery delays prevailed, as the ripple effects of the pathogen seemed to be the only external force capable of bringing Amazon's services to their knees. On social media, Prime members wondered whether Amazon might refund them a portion of their membership fee, since Prime's core perk of express shipping was essentially nonexistent. Yes, there were once-in-a-generation extenuating circumstances, but would Amazon reduce the price of Prime for a customer if the situation was reversed? Unlikely. Yet no Prime refund was coming. Despite the fact that Prime's main benefit was essentially unavailable at the most crucial time in the company's history, company executives chose to basically look the other way.

I asked Jamil Ghani, the head of Prime, if there were internal debates over the right move to make for a company that boasts about its "customer obsession" to, at times, a nauseating degree.

"I'm not going to comment on internal conversations and meetings," he said. "But what I can say is that [Prime member] engagement levels, and [customer] acquisition and retention performance, and then also anecdotes from members around the world, just substantiates that Prime was doing an essential service for members, regardless of the state of supply chain disruptions globally for everybody."

Translation: People were still using Prime benefits, sticking with the service, or signing up for the service if they weren't already members, so why would we refund anyone? Customers voted with their wallets and actions, the reasoning went. Still, the decision seemed

unbecoming of a corporation with the self-proclaimed mission of being "Earth's most customer-centric company."

The move, or lack thereof, was another proof point of how crucial
Prime was to Amazon's domination, and how much Walmart suffered
from lacking a counterattack. Over time, as Covid-19 variants and
resulting lockdowns whipsawed across the country, sending retail,
hospitality, and restaurant workers into unemployment lines en masse,
millions of Americans found themselves worse off financially than
they had been just a few months earlier. With e-commerce surging in
popularity—necessity, even—something counterintuitive happened.
Even among those low-income households struggling to make ends
meet, Prime membership surged during the crisis.

"The pandemic has been, unfortunately, a real accelerant there, as
the overall population of households on some form of government
assistance has increased significantly," Ghani told me.

Yet, thanks to the disruption caused by the pandemic, Walmart's
counterattack would be delayed from a possible launch in February or
March 2020 to a new launch date in July. But July came and went, and
the launch was pushed back once again. This time to September.

In the meantime, each company had a lot more to worry about than
just new initiatives, or customer demand and whether they could fulfill
it during the first few months of the pandemic. Store and warehouse
employees started to speak out, accusing company leaders of not taking enough precautions to protect them from contracting the novel
coronavirus and not being transparent enough about how many co-
workers were getting infected. For Amazon specifically, the resulting
internal showdown would have the potential to alter the company in
myriad ways for years to come.

Union Avoidance

For the first decade and a half of Amazon's existence, working conditions inside the company's warehouse network were not a hot topic of
media or governmental scrutiny. Amazon was not yet hugely popular
and had fewer than ten US warehouses for more than a decade. Labor

activists and union supporters also were busy attacking their Public Enemy No. 1: the much bigger, and more powerful, small business killer, Walmart. Plus, in its early days, Amazon wasn't always so intensely preoccupied with quotas and performance metrics that would later draw scrutiny from both within and outside its warehouse walls.

A former longtime corporate employee, who worked as an HR manager for the warehouse division, told me they saw a major shift in that direction at Amazon around 2010. "When I joined, it was very apparent to me that the leaders in the facility really cared about the people," they said.[9] "The Amazon that I left in fulfillment was . . . not that way."

This former manager attributed part of the change to an increased reliance on performance data, as well as the implementation of so-called standard operating procedures. "We almost overindexed on processes," she told me, while also acknowledging the business upsides to adding more structure to warehouse work. But another key factor was the type of warehouse leaders the company recruited as Amazon expanded to meet exploding customer demand. "It was all about just drive, drive, drive."

This timeline also aligns with the internal rise of a pull-no-punches leader named Dave Clark. The former HR manager noticed warehouse culture shifting around 2010, which was the same year Clark was appointed to run the company's North American operations, chief among them its warehouse network. Under Clark's leadership, Amazon's logistics prowess increased, but some say the harshness of conditions did too. Early in his career, as a warehouse general manager, Clark was known to lurk in the shadows so he could catch, and terminate, frontline workers he considered to be slacking on the job. The tactic earned him the nickname the Sniper.

"He's a driver to the point that he leaves bodies in his wake," the former HR manager told me, while at the same time acknowledging Clark's high intelligence.

In Amazon's earliest days as a startup, the company was also especially frugal and only wanted to pay the market rate for warehouse work in its first few locations. But over time, as the company matured, executives in its operations division began to see the benefit of paying more than rivals for warehouse associates, especially when hiring in a new state for the first time.

"There's an existential threat to not paying above market," was how the company started thinking about it, according to a longtime former senior leader in Amazon's human resources department. "We certainly don't want the most talented folks to go down the street to Target or Walmart."

What came with the pay—and better-than-average benefits—was taxing labor. A dozen miles or more of walking across the hard warehouse floor all day. Strict quotas, punishing performance rules, and a grueling climate, literally. An investigation in 2011 by the *Morning Call*, a Pennsylvania newspaper, revealed that one local Amazon warehouse kept an ambulance parked outside during the summer because so many workers were falling ill from high temperatures in the facility.[10]

In the wake of the exposé, Bezos quickly announced a plan to spend more than $50 million retrofitting its large warehouses with air-conditioning. But it was a huge black eye for the company and served to galvanize activists and labor groups who, along with online shoppers of the time, had long saved their major labor criticisms for the Bentonville behemoth.

"Walmart was evil among particular urban, Democratic kinds of customers that Amazon was going after," says Stacy Mitchell, codirector of the nonprofit Institute for Local Self-Reliance and a longtime critic of both Walmart's and Amazon's business practices. "And that's interesting because they sort of got away with having horrible labor practices and a bunch of other stuff that Walmart got a lot more PR blowback on because [Walmart was] red-state and country music, and culturally different."

A couple of years after the warehouse heat exposé, in 2013, a union in Germany sparred with Amazon over bonuses and other issues. The next year Amazon faced its first real threat of unionization in the US when a small group of equipment technicians and mechanics—not rank-and-file pickers and packers—chose to go forward with a union vote at a warehouse in Delaware. In the end, a majority of the twenty-seven workers voted against unionization in the face of a fierce union-busting campaign by Amazon.

A few years later, Amazon defeated another unionization drive of similar workers at a warehouse in Virginia before it even reached a vote, the *New York Times* reported in 2021.[11] But Amazon later agreed to a settlement with federal regulators after the union accused it of breaking labor laws during its fight against the union drive. On the break room walls, Amazon had to post a notice in which it agreed not to engage in certain union-busting behavior. "'We will not threaten you with the loss of your job' if you are a union supporter, Amazon wrote," according to the *Times*.[12] "'We will not interrogate you' about the union or 'engage in surveillance of you' while you participate in union activities. 'We will not threaten you with unspecified reprisals' because you are a union supporter. 'We will not threaten to "get" union supporters.'"

This was not especially surprising behavior for Amazon. Amazon's anti-union efforts went way back, just like Walmart's. Over the years, Sam Walton's company was fierce in its opposition to labor organizers, pulling out stop after stop to disrupt any sliver of momentum. In 2000, a small group of meatcutters voted in favor of unionizing at a Texas Walmart. Shortly thereafter, Walmart said it was going to begin carrying only prepackaged meat, eliminating the work of butchers, in a decision supposedly made prior to the union vote. The company also shut down a Supercenter in Canada after a majority of workers voted to unionize.

"It has struggled from the beginning," a Walmart spokesman said of the store's supposed financial troubles at the time.[13] "The situation has continued to deteriorate since the union. The store environment became very fractured because there were some people who were part of the union and some who were not."

Union-busting behavior has been so common throughout Walmart's history that a former top executive, named Tom Coughlin, who was caught misappropriating company funds, had tried to cover up his misdeeds by telling underlings the moneys were being used to pay off union members for intel.

"Sam always fought the union; we all have," said Burt Stacy, the retired executive once hired by Sam Walton to run the Bank of Bentonville, and the best friend of Walmart's second CEO, David Glass.

"Because we can't see how anything the union could do would be good for Walmart."

Amazon leaders felt the same way. In the 2000s, Amazon began tracking the threat of unionization at each of its warehouses, according to the former senior human resources manager, building a heat map in Excel to identify unionization "hot spots." These danger zones were calculated based on dozens of metrics, including the frequency of worker pay raises and the safety record of the warehouse.

The thinking was, if management could identify discontent at a warehouse early enough, the company could intervene before workers began considering unionization. "If my workforce has to band together and go into collective bargaining, I have failed as an employer," the former senior HR manager said of the company's thinking.[14] Walmart executives had long said a similar thing. Eventually, though, Amazon would find itself facing the prospect of that very failure.

Not Smart or Articulate

In the earliest days of the pandemic, many employers were failing to adequately protect their workers from the virus, and some Amazon workers felt like their company was one of them. At the time, a long-time Amazon warehouse worker named Chris Smalls was growing concerned. Several of his colleagues were sick, possibly with Covid, but the facility remained open, and he didn't believe that managers were being transparent. So, in late March of 2020, Smalls led a small walk-out at his Amazon facility in Staten Island, New York, to protest and call on Amazon to temporarily shut the warehouse down. He briefed some media on the plan, and outlets like CNBC and Vice covered the walkout, which involved about fifty workers.

"Amazon is a breeding ground for the coronavirus," Smalls told Vice at the time.[15] "We're going to be the second wave. Right now, I'm trying to prevent that."

Shortly thereafter, Amazon made a grave error: the company fired Smalls. The company's official line was that Smalls was fired for violating quarantine by showing up on property for the walkout when Amazon had sent him home because he had been exposed to a coworker diagnosed with Covid-19. But to many, including an HR manager at the warehouse, the termination wasn't warranted and reeked of retaliation. Sure enough, New York State attorney general Letitia James later ruled that Amazon's firing of Smalls was illegal.

Things only snowballed from there. Shortly after Smalls's firing, the company's top lawyer, David Zapolsky, a white man, referred to Smalls, a Black man, as "not smart or articulate" in notes summarizing a meeting with top Amazon leaders, including Jeff Bezos. Zapolsky also encouraged colleagues to make Smalls the focal point of unionizing efforts when communicating with the press. Zapolsky's notes from this meeting leaked to the press after he mistakenly emailed them to Amazon's entire legal division.[16] Outraged, Amazon corporate employees began to question the company's actions and what some saw as racist comments from Zapolsky. The tech workers fumed on an internal Listserv that included thousands of employees, and later in smaller groups on Chime, the company's workplace messaging system, after a Listserv moderator squashed one of the email threads.[17]

Smalls told a reporter that the leaked notes "exposed who Jeff Bezos is as a person, who's around him, who's giving him counsel—the types of conversations that they have about their employees, and their focus on smearing me.

"That tells you right there they don't care about us," Smalls continued. "It's never going to be Amazon v. Chris Smalls. It's Amazon v. the people."[18]

After the leak, Amazon issued a statement on Zapolsky's behalf, but it did not include any of the words typically associated with a sincere apology, such as *sorry, apologize,* or *regret,* for the comments made about Smalls.

The statement read, "My comments were personal and emotional. I was frustrated and upset that an Amazon employee would endanger the health and safety of other Amazonians by repeatedly returning to the premises after having been warned to quarantine himself after exposure to virus Covid-19. I let my emotions draft my words and get the better of me."

An Amazon spokesperson, Dan Perlet, told reporters that Zapolsky did not know that Smalls was Black when he wrote up the meeting notes, even though photos of Smalls protesting outside the warehouse were commonly included in media coverage of the event.

Despite the internal and media firestorm that Zapolsky's comments incited, Amazon officials kept a target on Smalls's back. Less than two months after Smalls's firing, I interviewed Dave Clark and came away stunned. During the interview, Clark twice brought up Smalls—unprompted—to use him as an example of wrongdoing among dissenting workers. Clark insisted that Smalls was fired for his breaking of quarantine and no other reason.

"I've been here twenty-one years, and I have never seen anybody punished or terminated or anything for speaking out or having a contrary opinion or debating something," he told me back then. "And that continues to be the case."

Clark may have believed that, but the facts suggested the truth was more complicated. Just in the first few months of the pandemic alone, Amazon fired or reprimanded at least a dozen employees who were involved in worker protests or who spoke out about warehouse working conditions. Smalls, though, was not going away. In early 2021, Smalls, along with friend and coworker Derrick Palmer, traveled to Bessemer, Alabama, where the Retail, Wholesale and Department Store Union was gearing up for a union vote at a giant Amazon warehouse that employed six thousand workers. Smalls came back to the Northeast invigorated by the workers' efforts in the notoriously anti-union South, vowing to "bring it back up here to New York, and try to organize even my former facility."[19]

Within a few months, Smalls and Palmer decided to do just that, but not with the help of the RWDSU, which they "found less than welcoming to them and thought the professionals seemed like outsiders who had descended on the community," according to the New York Times.[20] Instead they founded their own union, called the Amazon Labor Union, which would eventually, against all odds, make labor history.

While all of this was going on in the early spring of 2021, tensions were rising inside Amazon's executive ranks. While the mail-in voting for the Bessemer union election was happening, Amazon's leadership created an unnecessary media storm of their own. It started with a tweet from Clark, who had since been promoted to CEO of Amazon's worldwide consumer business. Senator Bernie Sanders, a longtime critic of Amazon, had announced that he would be visiting Alabama to attend a pro-union rally in Birmingham and meet with Amazon workers attempting to organize the nearby warehouse.

I welcome @SenSanders to Birmingham and appreciate his push for a progressive workplace, Clark posted, before unleashing a snarky punch line. I often say we are the Bernie Sanders of employers, but that's not quite right because we actually deliver a progressive workplace.

Clark went on to compare Amazon's minimum hourly pay at the time—$15—to that of Sanders's home state of Vermont—which was less than $12. But the insults didn't stop there. In fact, that's when things went haywire. A few hours after Clark's ill-advised thread, the "Amazon News" media relations Twitter account, with more than 170,000 followers at the time, went after Congressman Mark Pocan, who had called Clark's "progressive workplace" assertion into question.

Paying workers $15/hr doesn't make you a 'progressive workplace' when you union-bust & make workers urinate in water bottles, Pocan wrote.

You don't really believe the peeing in bottles thing, do you? the official Amazon News account replied. If that were true, nobody would work for us.

As it turned out, peeing in bottles wasn't common among Amazon *warehouse* employees other than on very rare occasions. But it's a different story for Amazon delivery drivers. No, these drivers are not technically Amazon's direct employees, but they deliver out of Amazon-branded vans, wear Amazon-branded attire, and are managed by Amazon technology and quotas. These quotas can be grinding, pushing drivers to blow past potential bathroom breaks for fear of being reprimanded or losing their jobs. Amazon has said that the average delivery route includes 250 packages during a ten-hour shift and that 90 percent of drivers complete their routes on time; that's in contrast to reports by some drivers that routes can total as many as 375 packages, not even counting the busiest shopping weeks. To much of the outside world, they are rightfully viewed as a key part of the Amazon machine and are essentially Amazon workers.

Amazon ended up apologizing for the specific blunder after an investigative news site published internal Amazon documents showing that it was common knowledge inside the company's logistics division that their delivery drivers often left behind bottles and bags full of human waste.[21]

Later, the Amazon News account also targeted Senator Elizabeth Warren after she posted a tweet and video that called out Amazon for its tax-avoidance strategy. After Warren's response, Amazon's Twitter account twisted Warren's counterattack and claimed Warren just said she's going to break up an American company so that they can't criticize her anymore.

Inside Amazon, alarm bells were ringing both within the communications division and across the rest of the company. Suddenly, some Amazon officials who had never been willing to take my calls before seemed eager to talk. To them this behavior crossed a line, counterproductive at best and supremely embarrassing and damaging at worst. No one I spoke to could believe what they were witnessing: one of the most powerful companies in the world, a model for so many others, engaging in a virtual pissing match with top government officials, including two senators, both of whom were onetime presidential hopefuls.

The tweets were so out of character that a security engineer at the company filed an internal support ticket that was either trying to alert others or perhaps simply pointing out the absurdity of what was taking place.

"Suspicious activity on @amazonnews Twitter account," the alert read.

"The tweets in question do not match the usual content posted by this account . . . [and] are unnecessarily antagonistic (risking Amazon's brand) and may be a result of unauthorized access."

The only thing that made sense to many insiders and outsiders was that, at a minimum, Jeff Bezos must have been okay with the approach. But within a few days, I had discovered that it was more than that— the Twitter outbursts were a direct result of the CEO expressing his frustration to his deputies that they weren't more aggressive in combating allegations and criticisms that he and other Amazon leaders found misleading or false.[22] As it was later revealed, Bezos and his spokesman at the time—former Obama White House press secretary Jay Carney—actually penned some of these tweets themselves.[23]

While the company's top leaders might have been celebrating their sophomoric tit-for-tats, some members of Amazon's public policy team—those responsible for the company's relationship with lawmakers—were beside themselves. Amazon was already a target of powerful Democrat and Republican politicians in an antitrust probe into the company's power and business practices. Amazon staff members in Washington, DC, already knew that the company's standing inside the nation's capital had deteriorated in recent years. Now Bezos and team were seen as unnecessarily antagonizing powerful senators with large followings on another high-profile topic. This lack of self-awareness was painfully obvious to everyone except the company leaders who should have known better.

Within a few weeks, though, the labor tide seemed to be moving back in Amazon's favor—Amazon came out victorious in the Bessemer union election by a significant margin. But inside the company, the feeling of victory was muted. The company's main spokesperson during the Bessemer union campaign exited Amazon shortly after the vote. And despite the win, there were signs Amazon's reputation had suffered during the pandemic. In May 2020, the share of people who said they had a positive impression of Amazon dropped to 58 percent from 74 percent in January, according to two separate polls of more than one thousand people conducted by Survey Monkey for the media outlets *Fortune* and Recode.[24] Jeff Bezos seemed to recognize as much in his final shareholder letter as CEO, which was published in the same month as the Bessemer victory.

"I think we need to do a better job for our employees," he wrote, in a paragraph sandwiched between otherwise strong defenses of the company's labor practices. "While the voting results were lopsided and our direct relationship with employees is strong, it's clear to me that we need a better *vision* for how we create value for employees—a vision for their success."

Later in the letter, he added a new mission for the company he had shepherded for so long as CEO, but was now handing over to a long-time protégé named Andy Jassy.

"We have always wanted to be Earth's Most Customer-Centric Company," he wrote. "We won't change that. It's what got us here. But I am committing us to an addition. We are going to be Earth's Best Employer and Earth's Safest Place to Work."

As it turned out, though, the Earth's Best Employer mission was going to soon face another roadblock: a National Labor Relations Board (NLRB) official called for a redo of the union vote after ruling that Amazon's placement of a USPS mailbox in the parking lot of the Bessemer warehouse, and its encouragement for workers to use it to submit their mail-in ballots, had unfairly influenced the election. Amazon's retail CEO, Dave Clark, among other leaders, had pushed for the installation of the mailbox, thinking it would encourage apathetic workers, who would likely favor the company, to vote. But the move instead resulted in union organizers in Bessemer getting another shot at a vote.[25]

Back on Staten Island, Chris Smalls and the Amazon Labor Union accumulated enough support among workers to qualify for a union election to take place in the first half of 2022. All the while, Amazon's self-inflicted blunders continued. A month before the Staten Island union vote, Amazon officials called the police on Smalls when he showed up to deliver lunch to warehouse workers. The New York City Police Department arrested him and charged him with trespassing, saying Smalls had ignored several requests to leave the property.[26] More media coverage soon followed. Smalls said that he and other organizers still working at Amazon often brought food to feed workers when their budget allowed, and that Amazon was well aware.

"I drop off the food, I pick up the food. I drop off literature," he said. "I should have been treated like any other visitor leaving the parking lot. But on this day," he added, "Amazon decided to escalate things and, unfortunately, that kind of backfired on them as well."[27]

Finally, in March 2022, the tallying for both the second Bessemer election and the first Staten Island election began on the same day. The general public, including reporters, could watch the ballot counting via livestream. Based on Amazon's history of defeating unionization attempts, a union win seemed like a long shot.

To many following along with these events, including me, the Staten Island vote seemed like an even longer shot than a union win in Bessemer. Yes, it was taking place in a borough of New York City, where unions are far more popular than in the South. But the employees who formed the Amazon Labor Union seemingly had little to no experience organizing workers. Their track record was nonexistent, and Amazon management and anti-union consultants made sure to hammer that message home in mandatory worker meetings.

But on the day of the simultaneous elections, as I switched between livestreams, something quickly caught my attention: "Yes" votes for the Amazon Labor Union in Staten Island were significantly outpacing "No" votes, and the trend would continue all the way to the end of the counting the following day. Amazingly, the underfunded, inexperienced Amazon Labor Union won their election, 2,654 to 2,131.

Results for the redo election at the warehouse in Bessemer, however, were still undecided six months after the vote; the Retail, Wholesale and Department Store Union was trailing by a little more than 100 votes, but the two sides contested more than 400 ballots that needed to be scrutinized and potentially recounted before a winner could be determined.

Back on Staten Island, Amazon quickly announced it was contesting the results there, accusing both the Amazon Labor Union and the NLRB, which oversees US union elections, of more than two dozen infractions combined.[28] But that summer, an NLRB official who oversaw the objection hearing recommended that all of Amazon's objections be thrown out and that the Amazon Labor Union win be certified. Amazon CEO Andy Jassy later indicated at a tech conference that he was still not ready to accept defeat, and would continue to challenge the results.

"I think [it's] going to take a long time to play out because I think it's unlikely the NLRB is going to [rule] against themselves," Bezos's successor said.[29]

The Amazon Labor Union's landmark victory, the first ever at an Amazon warehouse in the US, would have to wait to be finalized. But on the day that the election results were first announced, Chris Smalls took a Twitter victory lap. Everyone, including Amazon's leaders, had vastly underestimated him.

@amazon wanted to make me the face of the whole unionizing efforts against them, Smalls tweeted. welp there you go! @JeffBezos @David-Zapolsky CONGRATULATIONS.

13
WALMART 2040

While Chris Smalls's union win on Staten Island placed Amazon in an unprecedented position, the company was facing other major transitions amid the daily turbulence of a world besieged by an ongoing pandemic and supply chain woes. In February 2021, a year before the union win, Amazon had announced that Jeff Bezos, the only CEO the company had ever known, would be passing on his role that July to a longtime executive named Andy Jassy.

Early in his career, Jassy had served as Bezos's first technical adviser—also known as a "shadow"—a role similar to a chief of staff that would become one of the most sought-after positions at the company for those with grand ambition. Jassy then spent fifteen years launching and running Amazon Web Services, Amazon's unsexy but innovative and highly profitable cloud-computing business that powers websites big and small and generated $62 billion in revenue in 2021 alone.

"The hallmark of most great leaders at Amazon is they combine passion and customer obsession with the ability to dive deep into the details, the metrics, the [profits and losses]," Bill Carr, the former head of Amazon Prime's video offering, told me after the CEO transition was announced.[1] "But a great leader at Amazon can operate at fifty thousand feet above sea level as well, and Andy is one of those people."

Jassy inherited serious challenges on several fronts. One was to attempt to balance the seesaw of customer shopping habits as Covid waves crashed and then receded. For the first year or so of the global crisis, for example, online ordering exploded as a world of customers was locked in their homes either by government mandate, illness, or precaution. Pundits were predicting that online shopping was going to take over much sooner than previously understood—making up five to ten years of ground in a single twelve months.

But a funny thing happened in 2021 and 2022: brick-and-mortar shopping made a comeback.

For Amazon, its past moves toward a more balanced portfolio of sales channels now looked prescient. In addition to the acquisition of Whole Foods, Amazon was creating a new grocery store chain called Amazon Fresh—the same name that accompanied its ship-from-warehouse grocery home delivery service. The stores were designed to sell at lower price points with more mainstream brands—think Doritos and Oreos—than its upscale corporate sibling, Whole Foods. The first location, a 35,000-square-foot store in Los Angeles, opened in September 2020 and was outfitted with tech-infused shopping carts called "Dash Carts," which used cameras and sensors to calculate a customer's order as they placed items into them. The stores would also double as mini-warehouses to help fulfill Amazon Fresh delivery orders.

By the fall of 2022, there were forty-three Fresh locations, more than half of which were located in California and Illinois. A year earlier, Amazon had added a $9.95 delivery fee for Whole Foods orders for Prime members to account for rising operational costs, the company said. It was a very un-Amazonian, and arguably anticonsumer, move to begin charging money for a service that had previously been included in a Prime membership. Lawsuits followed.[2]

"We had a decision: we could think about raising prices broadly on products, or we could isolate it into a fee for the service itself," Stephenie Landry, then the Amazon VP in charge of grocery delivery services, told me in late 2021. "We decided to do the latter . . . because we wanted to keep product prices low."

The move angered a vocal subset of Prime customers but also gave an opening to Walmart, which used the opportunity to market its grocery-centric delivery membership Walmart+ to existing Amazon Prime customers. Meanwhile, Amazon Fresh deliveries remained free for Prime members for orders over $35, which meant that either the service's costs were not rising like Whole Foods' were or that Amazon was okay raising the price of individual food prices at Amazon Fresh behind the scenes.

Amazon never announced this intent but, sure enough, Amazon Fresh prices began to rise between 2021 and 2022, and it wasn't just inflation. For example, one month after a new Amazon Fresh store opened in the Chicago area in early 2021, a random sampling of groceries at the store cost about 4 percent more than a comparative sample at Walmart. At that point, Amazon Fresh could be confused for a Walmart Supercenter competitor.

But a year later, the cost disparity between the two grocers had widened to more than 25 percent, according to an analysis by the grocery research firm Brick Meets Click. Whether by design or not, it sure looked like Amazon was launching in certain areas with incredibly low prices that almost matched Walmart's, giving shoppers the impression of being a discount food chain, before gradually increasing them to compete more directly with regional full-price grocers like Jewel Osco in Chicago and H-E-B in Texas.

Either way, Amazon executives believed that the fact that customers were returning to stores to shop bolstered one of their key defenses against antitrust hawks: that the physical retail world was far from dead, and the future lay in the intersection of digital and physical.

"In the retail world, customers are voting that all of these hybrid models that combine physical locations and online tools are very valuable to them," Jeff Wilke, the former CEO of Amazon's worldwide consumer business and Bezos's longtime No. 2, told me in early 2021. "I continue to struggle to find a customer who . . . wakes up and says, 'What do I want to buy online today?' They wake up and say, 'What do I need?'"

This argument—that Amazon competes in all of retail and not just in a separate online market where it controls more than half of sales in some product categories—would be repeated over and over again as the company faced a barrage of antitrust scrutiny in the early 2020s.

Amazon's main argument was that whatever its market share was in US e-commerce—around 40 percent, according to a common estimate, but higher in several core online retail categories—it only accounted for a single-digit percentage of the overall US retail market, including brick-and-mortar shopping.

Still, Amazon seemed intent on building the Everything Retailer, and the flip-flop of where consumers were shopping made it seem crucial to its long-term ambition. Store sales were rebounding. E-commerce growth plateaued. That's why, at least on the surface, it was curious when Amazon announced in March 2022 a major retrenchment in physical retail: the closure of sixty-eight of their physical stores that sold books, electronics, and other general merchandise in the US and UK and had been built as part of a seven-year experiment.

Among them were bookstores, under the name Amazon Books, which first opened to the public in 2015. The stores were designed to bring some of the benefits of shopping for books on Amazon.com into the real world, such as a book's customer rating. They were also about— even more so, according to some former store employees—selling customers on Amazon gadgets such as Kindles and Alexa-powered Echo smart speakers and tablets. On top of that, the stores were also used as a way to sign up customers to trials for subscription services, such as Amazon Prime and the audiobook service Audible.

Once the pandemic hit, and the bookstores reopened after a months-long shutdown, some store leaders urged store managers to increase the percentage of customers who agreed to sign up at checkout for a free trial of one of these services. But this prodding took a shady turn in some cases. Prior to the pandemic, store customers could view one of the free trial offers on a screen in front of them. But to reduce customers potentially spreading germs once the pandemic hit, bookstore cashiers were also given the ability to sign the customer up for a trial from their side, after explaining the offering and asking for permission from the customer. However, employees who worked at some Amazon Books stores on the East Coast told me that their managers often automatically signed customers up for free subscription trials, such as the audio service Audible, without giving them the choice.

"They would tell them, 'This is your subscription. You can cancel it anytime,' instead of giving them the choice to hit 'No thank you,'" a former bookstore employee told me. "I don't think customers even realized it."

Many didn't, not until months later, when they would return to the store, befuddled or irate, to inquire why they were being charged for a subscription they didn't remember registering for. In October 2020, Chris Garlock, an assistant manager in one of the Amazon Books stores, emailed a regional manager explaining that a former colleague had observed store employees accepting the free trial on behalf of a customer without getting their prior consent. Garlock had also looked up internal data that showed that some colleagues were signing up store customers for free trials at abnormally high rates compared to their previous performance and that of employees at other stores.

"A consistent pattern like this does real damage to a brand's reputation and business," he wrote. "But more to the point, it is unethical; to trick or defraud a person into receiving something they didn't choose is wrong and shouldn't be something we allow or condone at Amazon."

For several more months, though, internal data indicated that managers and sales staff at several stores were still signing up customers for free trials at abnormally high rates. Finally, in early 2021, store managers received a stern reminder of the right way to offer the free trials to customers.

"Good on them to do that," Garlock told me, "but this is something they should have done months prior."

Amazon spokesperson Jordan Deagle told me that there was no corporate mandate to increase sign-ups for free trials of Amazon subscriptions. In early 2019, after some Amazon Books customers complained about being signed up for free trials, division leaders reviewed training and explained to associates how to more clearly explain the terms and conditions of the subscription trials to customers, the spokesperson said. But Deagle declined to comment on how or why such behavior was occurring well into the following year.

Managers were also known to offer on-the-spot discounts to unload Amazon devices to help hit internal goals for units sold. Rumors spread among staff in some stores that some managers even occasionally bought store merchandise themselves to boost sales, only to later return it.

"Digital subscriptions and device sales were much more important than any of the book sales," another former store associate said. "That's what our manager made sure we knew."

The e-commerce giant just couldn't break away from its digital DNA, even in a physical store setting.

Before Amazon announced the closures publicly, store leaders received a message instructing them to shutter their storefront at 1 p.m. local time that day. As soon as the store was shuttered, they received a follow-up message with the bad news: all Amazon Books stores were closing at the end of April.

The announcement was made shortly after Amazon had hired a longtime retail executive, Tony Hoggett of UK supermarket giant Tesco, to take over the physical store operations. Though the decision to cut the Books stores, as well as a smaller chain called 4-star that sold general merchandise, was made before the new executive joined, there was little surprise inside some corners of Amazon that it happened nonetheless.

"It had very little clear direction of purpose, and no real differentiating factor," one corporate employee who worked in the store division told me. From a financial perspective, the meager revenue generated from the stores served as a sore spot to those leading the much more crucial e-commerce business. In a way, the resentment was not all that different from what fueled the Walmart battles between e-commerce and store leaders, but reversed.

Amazon's drive to building the Everything Retailer had hit a pothole. A big one.

The Store Advantage

A few days after news of the closures broke, I found myself at Walmart's home office in Bentonville, seated across from Doug McMillon himself. I told him I was curious for his thoughts on the physical retail about-face of his chief internet rival. Would McMillon offer up any version of a chiding or I-told-ya-so? Before the question finished tumbling from my mouth, McMillon let out a little chuckle, leading me to believe he might.

"Both are hard; e-commerce is hard, stores are hard," McMillon said instead, matter-of-factly. "And when something's not working, cut bait and move on. Try something else."

After all, McMillon could have been giving himself a pep talk, especially as the company endured the challenges of unifying its store and e-commerce operations under one leader in John Furner, the former Sam's Club CEO who replaced Greg Foran as Walmart US CEO in late 2019—a few months before the Covid-19 pandemic erupted.

Under Furner, the company forced a large swath of its e-commerce workforce to relocate to Bentonville from offices on the coasts, or give up their job altogether, though with a generous severance package. The move was pitched as a necessity to running a unified retail operation where some divisions such as merchandising were now responsible for both Walmart's websites and stores. Walmart management also felt pressure to bring more of the workforce back to Arkansas because the Walton family was spending heavily on a new 350-acre corporate campus scheduled to open in phases through 2025.

Publicly, Walmart confirmed the layoffs of 1,200 corporate workers as the e-commerce and retail divisions combined. But a source familiar with the move said the real number was upward of 3,000 people. While power was centralizing under Furner, the hope was that the unified organization would actually help Walmart move faster. Amazon had taken the opposite approach over the years. The organization became famous in the business world for its so-called two-pizza teams—a group of employees given the autonomy to pursue a new idea for a product or service and which was small enough to be fed by two pizzas. With his move to Walmart from Sam's Club, Furner brought with him a different approach, known as "four in a box."

Like the two-pizza team, it was designed to increase the speed at which the company could test out new ideas, products, and services or solve thorny problems, whether for store workers or for customers.

The organizational structure called for one member in the team to be from the appropriate business division, one employee to represent the customer or user experience, one from the engineering group, and a final one who's from the product design organization. The alternative, legacy approach is someone in the center coming up with a cool idea and then handing it over to a team to start to build.

"What ends up happening, in my opinion, if you're not careful is people find really cool solutions and then they go try to find a problem to attach it to," Furner said.

Furner's arrival also caused a variety of other changes. The company's long-questioned separation of its e-commerce ordering systems into two separate shopping apps finally ended. While there had once been technical, philosophical, and business reasons to run the two separately, those days were long gone. To Furner, who tended to lean into the digital world more willingly than his predecessor Foran, the confusion that arose from competing corporate interests had gone on too long.

"If a customer was in the orange app, which is really the grocery app, and they typed in Legos, it would say nothing available," Furner said. "What I was always worried about then was the swipe of the app—does that lead them to go to the blue app or does it lead them to go to a competitive app where you just know [the Legos are] going to be?"

In many cases, the answer was clear and would not favor Walmart. Furner knew it. Orange and blue finally came together in 2021, with the hope that it would create an e-commerce future brighter than any brown that a mixture of those two colors might produce in the real world.

Having taken over shortly before the start of the pandemic, Furner oversaw a host of other initiatives to help Walmart satisfy changing consumer habits. For far too long, Walmart had neglected the advantage that its Supercenters posed as potential mini-warehouses to serve online customers in their area. Amazon executives long knew that if Walmart could figure out how to unlock deliveries out of their stores, the retailer could potentially beat Amazon in the convenience game with same-day delivery or faster.

But it was difficult for a giant retailer like Walmart to get an accurate enough reading on in-store inventory to ensure that online customers weren't disappointed by out-of-stock messages after placing an order. That's one of the reasons Walmart invested heavily in a startup called Bossa Nova Robotics, whose robots roamed Supercenters and reported back on inventory information, before Furner blindsided the startup company and its leaders by ending the partnership right in the middle of a nationwide rollout in late 2020.[3] Even still, other retailers, including Target, used in-store inventory to fulfill online orders well enough to prove it was possible.

With the onset of the pandemic, Walmart no longer had a choice. At the center of heightened consumer demand was a rise in online grocery ordering—both from customers looking for delivery and ones seeking curbside pickup. While the company struggled to keep up there—Walmart actually ceded 10 percentage points of market share to Instacart in the US online grocery market during the first year of the pandemic, according to an internal memo I viewed[4]—it began utilizing its four-thousand-plus store footprint, and the inventory within, in other ways.

"Literally over a period of like, three or four weeks, we started being able to ship out of 2,500 stores, because we had to," said Greg Smith, Walmart's supply chain chief from 2017 until early 2021. "And then all of a sudden, we got more bold about connecting it all."

Walmart also made conversions to about three dozen of its distribution centers—warehouses typically used to ship products to stores—to allow them to serve as fulfillment centers, too, shipping merchandise to customers' doors. Eventually Walmart also got more aggressive in rerouting online orders from the fulfillment centers that historically filled e-commerce orders to local stores that had the merchandise in stock. The result was a customer experience that at some points felt like magic—order an item online, expect it to show up in two to four days, and instead end up finding it on your porch that same day, in a Walmart shopping bag instead of a box or plastic mailer.

"I'm pretty biased to get the customer what they want, when they want, and how they want it," Furner told me. "Our job is to figure out how you do that in a way that your costs are low enough that you can have a winning value. Because there's a phrase I think about a lot that goes something like, 'Loyalty in retail is the absence of something better.'"

That fear is also a key reason Walmart introduced an even faster delivery option in 2020 with Express Delivery, which promised grocery or merchandise orders at your door within two hours. At a weekly Monday meeting Furner hosts with staff, the CEO tests the service, which costs $10 per delivery for Walmart+ members and a steep $17.95 for nonmembers. During this period, Walmart also began testing a new mode for fast delivery: drones. Another area where Amazon first attracted attention.

All the way back in 2013, on the eve of the Cyber Monday shopping holiday, Jeff Bezos, in a made-for-TV spectacle, announced that Amazon had started testing drone delivery. He predicted that the service would be available to customers in four or five years. But by 2021, Amazon's tests were still limited to a handful of employees and a few others. One reason is that Amazon was building its own drones, rather than farming out the work. It was not smooth. The tech giant caught the ire of the Federal Aviation Administration during testing, including one crash that ignited a twenty-five-acre brushfire in Oregon.[5] The company reportedly spent more than $2 billion on the initiative in the first eight years, with little to show for it to the outside world.

Walmart, on the other hand, got some tests off the ground in its home state of Arkansas in the fall of 2021, via partnership tests with two companies, DroneUp and Zipline. On a visit to Bentonville in early 2022, I made my way out to Pea Ridge, Arkansas, population 6,559, to witness a drone delivery up close. At first I was pitched on watching a live customer delivery, but ultimately I was shown a demo flight instead; the change of plans went unexplained.

The fifty-pound Zipline drone launched out of a catapult-like device at its cruising speed of 60 miles per hour. It then traveled in a half-circle direction while navigating 25 mile-per-hour wind gusts, before dropping a blue Walmart box, affixed to a small white paper parachute, over an open field owned by Walmart. After the drop was made, the drone automatically calculated wind speeds and directions to decide on the best path back to base. It then returned at 40 miles per hour, catching its tail on a zipline stretched between two metal poles, or "recovery arms," in the company's lingo, to end the flight.

By the spring of 2022, Walmart had announced that its other partner, DroneUp, was helping it launch drone deliveries in a total of thirty-four locations with the ability to reach 4 million households across six states. In these areas, customers could pay $3.99 for a drone delivery order, from a selection of more than 10,000 items, that weighs less than ten pounds in total. Zipline got its start by making humanitarian drops in conflict zones. But here, in the great consumerist country, the drone missions were solely focused on first-world convenience.

"[W]hile we initially thought customers would use the service for emergency items, we're finding they use it for its sheer convenience, like a quick fix for a weeknight meal," David Guggina, a former Amazon employee turned Walmart exec, said in the Walmart press release announcing the move. "Case in point: The top-selling item at one of our current hubs is Hamburger Helper."

While Walmart sped ahead of Amazon, at least on the surface, in testing the next generation of speedy delivery, Amazon was still trying to get a different express delivery service back on track. Back in the spring of 2019, before the Covid pandemic, Amazon had stunned Walmart by announcing that the core Prime membership expectation of two-day shipping was moving to a one-day norm over the course of the year. At that exact time, Walmart was also readying for its own announcement regarding a next-day-delivery offering. But once the pandemic hit, Amazon had enough trouble getting packages to customers even in a week. One-day Prime was mostly a pipe dream. Two years later, in 2022, the one-day service still seemed to be nowhere near standard, even as Amazon hiked the price of Prime from $119 to $139 a year. As late as the second half of 2022, many Prime deliveries didn't even guarantee two-day shipping; rather, just "free shipping." In fact, in the summer of 2022, a former Amazon logistics analyst, named Peter Freese, conducted an experiment in the company's home state of Washington, after being flabbergasted that two-day shipping seemed to no longer be available in his hometown, a few hours from Seattle. He found that in one-third of all counties in the state, top-selling Amazon products labeled as Prime-eligible would take a minimum of four to five business days to arrive. Other Prime members in communities across the country talked of a similar disappearance of Prime two-day shipping. Something seemed up.[6]

Issues like these have long been John Felton's job to obsess over. Felton was Amazon's head of worldwide delivery services throughout the first two years of the pandemic. In an interview in early 2022, he would not accept that Prime was far off the performance of pre-pandemic days. But he did admit that there was still much work to do to deliver on the one-day-shipping promise that was by this point mostly a three-year-old mirage.

"My job is to wake up paranoid about we are not being convenient enough for customers," he told be.

In the middle of 2022, Felton was named the head of all of Amazon's operations divisions, after Amazon's consumer and operations leader Dave Clark—the former warehouse leader once known as the Sniper—stunned the business world by leaving Amazon for a CEO role at an up-and-coming supply chain startup. With Clark's departure, Felton was promoted and added the warehouse and transportation networks to his existing purview of delivery offerings. Amid the shuffle, the two executives who had been running warehousing and transportation divisions as his peers exited the company, much to the disappointment of rank-and-file employees. They were two of the most senior Black executives at the company, including the only one at the time to ever serve on the CEO's senior leadership team, known as the S team: a longtime GM executive named Alicia Boler Davis, or ABD as she was known internally.

For a few years, Jassy had been the executive sponsor of Amazon's Black Employee Network, an affinity group for rank-and-file employees. When he took over for Jeff Bezos as CEO, some employees hoped that the company would do a better job attracting, promoting, and retaining top Black talent, especially given promises the company made after George Floyd's murder in 2020. As I exposed in a series of stories in 2021,[7] Black corporate employees at Amazon I spoke to said they often faced bias and discrimination at the company.

"I think the 'accomplishment' of getting a corporate role at Amazon—the best-paying role of my life—and the opportunity to do something at a scale I never imagined, ended up with pain and trauma I could not have anticipated," a Black female PhD who worked at Amazon for several years told me for Recode in 2021.[8] "I've never felt more used and disposable in my life."

Amazon staff who worked on diversity and inclusion initiatives at the time told me that internal data showed that Amazon's review and promotion systems created an uneven playing field where Black employees received "least effective" marks more often than all other colleagues and were promoted at a lower rate than non-Black peers. Recode reviewed some of this data for the Amazon Web Services division of the company, where Jassy was CEO until succeeding Bezos, and it showed large disparities in performance review ratings between Black and white employees. At the time, Amazon disputed the specifics of the data but declined to provide alternative data.

Over the next few months, a half-dozen women who worked in corporate roles at Amazon sued the company, with most alleging race discrimination. Watching two of the most senior Black leaders leave the company when a white male peer was promoted over them did nothing to boost the mood. Around the same time, two other Black executives also departed from senior roles at Amazon. The average tenure of the four corporate leaders was less than three years.

"In my mind I'm thinking, 'What do they know that I don't know?'" a Black midlevel manager in Amazon corporate told me at the time.

Amazon and Antitrust

As Amazon continued to attract scrutiny over its treatment of both warehouse and corporate employees during the first two years of the pandemic, the company also drew unwanted attention from politicians and regulators alike that had been years in the making.

In the late 2010s, the power and valuations that Amazon and other titans of the technology industry were accumulating incited a new movement in antitrust circles, catalyzed by a law school paper written by a then-unknown law student named Lina Khan. In her seminal paper, "Amazon's Antitrust Paradox," published in the *Yale Law Journal*, Khan argued that our interpretation of antitrust laws was outdated in light of a new digital economy, and there was a need to return to the days when merely having low prices or providing free services wasn't enough to avoid scrutiny for anticompetitive behavior. At the core of her argument, and of those Big Tech critics who promoted her view, was that the tech giants like Amazon had built the new railroads of the web and were the gatekeepers to all sorts of crucial interconnected parts.

"Amazon doesn't just want to dominate markets; it wants to own the infrastructure that underpins those markets," said Stacy Mitchell, the longtime critic of both Amazon and Walmart who runs a left-leaning think tank called the Institute for Local Self-Reliance (ILSR). "And that's an order of magnitude difference of a monopoly ambition than Walmart's."

Mitchell had spent many years agitating for the government to step in to slow down Walmart during its go-go Supercenter growth years and she is still clear today that she finds the company's power over some sectors problematic. "They dictate across the entire food chain," she said. But in her view, and that of many Big Tech critics in her circles, Amazon poses an altogether different threat to business competition.

"It's not just the retail platform, but it's AWS [Amazon Web Services], it's the logistics piece, it's [Alexa] and being the interface for how we interact with the web, and all the devices and everything that are connected to the smart home," she said. "It enables Amazon to favor its own goods and services in those markets, to levy a kind of tax on all the businesses that rely on that infrastructure, and to surveil all of that activity and use that intelligence to its own advantage."

As the pressure from Washington, DC, increased, Amazon leaders were becoming heated. In one key annual meeting of Bezos's senior leaders in early 2020, Jassy, the then-CEO of AWS, digested the content of a memo sitting in front of him. It laid out Amazon's plans for messaging in response to accusations that it was too big or too powerful and engaged in anticompetitive behavior. As Bezos listened in by phone, Jassy pointedly asked those before him why the messaging didn't argue that Walmart, and AWS rival Microsoft, should be investigated. Other top company officials tried to explain that each of those companies had already been scrutinized years ago and their time had passed. But Jassy's reaction left a lasting impression on those in attendance.

"It was very clear from his comments that we shouldn't let our foot off the gas," someone in attendance told me years later.

In subsequent years, especially in the part of the company that focused on so-called competition issues, "there wasn't a day that Walmart didn't come up." The fact that Walmart, with more annual revenue than Amazon, was not being scrutinized by policy makers drove executives like Jassy crazy. It didn't help when Amazon executives discovered that Walmart was indirectly funding a nonprofit front group called Free and Fair Markets, which was bombarding reporters and social media with anti-Amazon accusations. For some time, Amazon leaders suspected that a competitor, or group of competitors, was funding the operation but couldn't prove it. One of Amazon's longtime spokesmen, Drew Herdener, grew frustrated every time the group placed an op-ed or social media message that got traction.

"How does the press not know this is a front group?" he would lament.

As a result, an Amazon communications staffer named Doug Stone spent upward of a year trying to help reporters uncover the group's funders. Finally, in the fall of 2019, the *Wall Street Journal* pulled back the veil in an exposé titled "A 'Grass Roots' Campaign to Take Down Amazon Is Funded by Amazon's Biggest Rivals."[9] A Walmart spokesperson denied funding the group to the newspaper—the article had stated that Walmart used an intermediary to pass along funds to FFM, so the company's defense might have been a matter of semantics—but said that Walmart "share[s] concerns about issues" that the group was publicizing.

That same year, lawmakers on the House of Representatives' Subcommittee on Antitrust, Commercial and Administrative Law announced a congressional investigation into alleged anticompetitive practices of Amazon, as well as Google, Facebook, and Apple. Lina Khan, the former law student who wrote "Amazon's Antitrust Paradox," was hired as a legal counsel to help research and write the report, though she did not craft the section on Amazon. The investigation was highlighted by a CEO hearing in 2020 in which all the chief executives, including Jeff Bezos, testified in front of the lawmakers. The theatrics, however, were muted by the business leaders testifying virtually via videoconference, instead of in-person, because of the Covid-19 pandemic. It would be Bezos's first time testifying in front of Congress and, initially, some top Amazon company officials without experience working with or in the government wanted to politely decline the congressional invitation and offer up another company executive instead.

"There was some magical thinking going on," a person familiar with the deliberations told me.

Eventually, they relented and Bezos agreed to testify.

Months later, the congressional investigations staff delivered a four-hundred-page report outlining each company's alleged misdeeds and policy recommendations to help rein them in. The report argued that Amazon unfairly gleans data and information from its third-party sellers that it uses to strengthen the retail side of its business, including favoring its own product brands over those of competitors, giving this merchandise exclusive space on its virtual shelves, and prioritizing it in search results. Another criticism was that Amazon can charge sellers ever-increasing fees for everything from advertising to warehousing because of its dominant position, and that most sellers and brands have practically no negotiating power. Amazon also was known to penalize sellers if they sold their merchandise for lower prices on other retail sites—even their own—a practice that some sellers argued artificially inflates consumer prices across the web.[10]

During the congressional probe, some close to the investigation who had initially thought the practices of Google and Facebook were much more problematic than Amazon's ended up being blown away by many facets of Amazon's business practices. One finding that stood out was just how many huge Fortune 500 brands felt bullied by the tech giant and unable to negotiate fair deals. On the other end of the business spectrum, staff members were stunned by how easily the tech giant could kill small businesses overnight through many means, including a simple change to the search engine algorithm on Amazon.com, cloning a seller's product under an Amazon brand, or accidentally booting a seller off the platform because of an unwieldly algorithm. The power disparity was not all that different from the one Walmart had enjoyed for so many years.

To make matters worse, those investigating Amazon also discovered how impossible it can be for merchants selling on Amazon to get clear answers for why the company has punished them, or even get a helpful human on the phone. In one of the most moving moments of the hearing, a congresswoman played a recording of an interview with a woman who owned a textbook-selling business on Amazon with her husband. This small business owner told the story of how their family business was suddenly kicked off the platform without notice or explanation, instantaneously wiping out their livelihood and that of more than a dozen employees.

That same year, the love-hate relationship between Amazon and some of its top sellers seemed to reach a boiling point when merchants began consistently airing their grievances on Twitter, where some had developed strong industry followings. One of them, Shinghi Detlefsen, also possessed another trait that caught the attention of Amazon higher-ups: he had previously worked for six years in technology-related roles inside Amazon before leaving to help run a retail business on Amazon that his wife had started. After continuously tweeting complaints and suggestions at Dave Clark, Amazon's then CEO for its global consumer business, he finally got a response in March 2021. Soon after, Amazon's VP of seller support, Dharmesh Mehta, became active on Twitter, responding to some of Detlefsen's tweets and telling the seller community to keep the feedback coming. All was not suddenly right in the world of Amazon's treatment of its small merchant partners, but someone was finally listening, and to some top sellers, that felt at least like a start of better, fairer days selling on the platform.

As for the congressional investigation, it was not the end of Amazon's troubles. The report, and its policy recommendations, led to companion bills being brought forward in both the House and the Senate in 2022 that, if passed, had the power to seriously upend the way Amazon does business. They would prevent the tech giant from favoring some of its own products and services, whether its own brands of products such as Amazon Basics batteries, or its Fulfillment by Amazon warehousing service for merchants. Publicly, Amazon fought the bills aggressively, in some cases partnering with Google to fund front groups that ran TV ad blitzes alleging the legislation would potentially kill Amazon Prime. Behind the scenes, however, Amazon executives stressed to lawmakers all the warehouse jobs they had created in a given congressional district—"good jobs," as they would repeat over and over again.

As scrutiny ramped up in previous years, Amazon executives had discussed internally what significant business changes they might be willing to make if push came to shove, as an olive branch of sorts to regulators or legislators. One that sources said some executives agreed on was to give up their so-called private-label business—essentially the practice of selling merchandise under Amazon's own brand names. As of early 2023, though, they were still in the private-label business.

Still, the Federal Trade Commission continued to probe Amazon's business practices behind the scenes. A year earlier, the odds of the antitrust enforcement agency taking some action against Amazon seemed to jump when President Joe Biden nominated the thirty-two-year-old Khan to fill one of the five FTC commissioner roles and to lead the agency as its chair. It was a remarkable ascent for the former counsel on the congressional Big Tech investigation who was a complete unknown in Washington prior to publishing "Amazon's Antitrust Paradox" just four years earlier. In Europe in late 2022, Amazon agreed to a series of changes to its website and business practices to settle charges by regulators that the company engaged in anticompetitive behavior.

Taken together, the combination of significant turnover at the top of Amazon and scrutiny from all sides should have provided vast openings for rivals, chief among them Walmart. The question, as always, was how committed Walmart was to continuing to reinvent itself, and how quickly Doug McMillon could turn the ship around.

Walmart 2040

Before Marc Lore, the e-commerce impresario, left Walmart for good in 2021, he and a strategy executive named Sloan Eddleston crafted a memo, dubbed "Walmart 2040," to document the changes they advised the retailer to pursue if it wanted to still be thriving in two decades. Many longtime executives still believed that Walmart would eventually beat Amazon by offering lower prices—both on the internet and in stores, especially if new legislation or antitrust enforcement forced the company to split into parts. Lore dismissed this thinking as wishful and antiquated.

In his assessment, there were three crucial facets of retail wars over time: price, selection, and convenience. Walmart, Lore believed, would have a very difficult time beating Amazon on price because Amazon has a much larger product catalogue powered by hundreds of thousands of independent merchants. Those merchants boost Amazon's profits through the various fees they pay to sell through the site. He also believed Amazon would be tough to overtake in convenience because of the broad adoption of Amazon Prime, its massive warehouse network blanketing the country, and the buildout of its own giant delivery network.

The only answer, in Lore's view, was to pursue leadership in the buzzy, but still nascent, retail area called conversational commerce. Essentially, selling goods via voice interactions with smart speakers or text message conversations, like his first internal startup, Jetblack, had tried to do. Lore and Eddleston envisioned a one-on-one personalized shopping experience at massive scale. Text your desired product—or type of product—or describe the recipient of a gift you need to buy—and let Walmart do what it has done well since Sam Walton dreamed up the crazy retail innovation sixty years earlier. Merchandise. Curate.

Walmart could stop chasing the idea of matching Amazon in the breadth of its product listings if it could push the best product for every customer interaction in front of a person rather than have them search through the increasingly messy bazaar of Amazon or Walmart's websites. Amazon, in Lore's view, has weaknesses, and curation is absolutely one of them. Hyperpersonalization would beat unlimited selection. If there was one thing Walmart proved with the expensive experiment of Jetblack, it was that the service weakened a customer's reliance on Amazon.

McMillon seemed to grasp the idea, and the promise. But enough to invest what it would take? A billion or maybe multiple? Lore doubted it.

To be fair, McMillon still had other big investments that took priority in the short run, both in the US and abroad. In India, in 2018, Walmart made the biggest acquisition in its history, spending $16 billion for a 77 percent stake in a fast-growing e-commerce company called Flipkart. Flipkart's chief rival in India? Amazon, which Walmart had to outmaneuver to keep Flipkart out of its hands.

With both companies never making the progress they wanted in the biggest international e-commerce market of China, India was seen as the next online shopping battleground, thanks to its huge population, growing middle class, and cheap mobile data, which saw many Indians logging onto the internet for the first time with their mobile phones. Walmart chairman, and Sam Walton grandson-in-law, Greg Penner, was a huge proponent of the deal.[11]

"Let's go for the kill," Penner reportedly told Walmart's fellow board directors when the group was considering whether to make a minority investment in the young company or buy total control.

Outside India, the company was also investing big in new initiatives. Health care was one. Spending billions on robotics and automation additions to fulfillment centers and its old-school distribution centers was another. But many were extensions of the retail business that looked very similar to Amazon's ecosystem. While Marc Lore drove some of those decisions—one of his former senior leaders told me that Lore was adamant that Walmart expand its product marketplace from other sellers as wide and fast as possible despite arguments for restraint— Doug McMillon had also grown extremely attracted to the idea of "making money while we sleep," according to a former company insider.

In an interview in his office in early 2022, McMillon stressed the importance of these new business lines and more, including the membership program Walmart+, an online advertising business called Walmart Connect, and a new business that sells access to sales trend data from Walmart.com transactions. All three business lines come with inspiration, in one way or another, from Amazon. Walmart even hired one of Amazon's former top advertising executives in 2021 to oversee them. Years earlier, Walmart hired a different former Amazon leader to run Walmart Fulfillment Services, the retailer's version of Fulfillment by Amazon—both services that charge online merchants fees to store and ship their orders for them.

"It's sort of ironic," a former Jet executive told me. "We ended up going down more of an Amazon-type route."

Of the portfolio of new business lines just getting off the ground in the early 2020s, McMillon said the goal is to "end up with a more diversified and resilient business over time because you're making money in different ways." While much of the media's focus remained on just one area of this business line expansion—the Amazon Prime competitor called Walmart+—the CEO said he was going to do his best to divert investors' and journalists' attention away from the service.

"I'm glad we have it, and it'll grow," he said, "but I'm going to try to keep the world from focusing on that more than they should. Think about what we've talked about for almost an hour and we haven't gotten to this subject. It is not the most important thing in the company. It's a thing in the company."

That may have been the whole story, but it also could have spoken to early struggles to build a customer base. A year earlier, I had reported that an internal company memo revealed that the membership team needed to improve renewal rates as well as the percentage of free-trial participants who went on to become full paying members.[12]

Walmart also was aggressive in pressuring its employees to register for a membership,[13] which the company provided to them for free. But by the fall of 2022, two years after launch, Walmart+ still only had an estimated 11 million members in the US, compared to nearly 170 million for Amazon Prime. That November, Walmart offered the membership at half price for two days. As Marc Lore once told me, Walmart would eventually need to convince Amazon customers to cancel their Prime membership and defect to Walmart+ if it was going to do more than simply tread water.

Either way, it was clear in our conversation that McMillon wanted to set conservative expectations for the Walmart membership program. It would be an uphill battle to even come close to competing with the Amazon Prime wrecking ball. After all, corporate conservatism had spread like a weed inside the onetime retail innovator in the two decades between Amazon's birth and McMillon's Walmart take-over. Could McMillon, finally, against his own makeup, break that trend once and for all?

"I'm not naturally a risk taker," he told me. "I don't gamble. I don't jump off bridges with a bungee cord. I don't. I'm not a risk taker."

"But this company," he added, "to be here in the next generation, *has* to take risks."

14
WINNER SELLS ALL

A s McMillon and Walmart had learned the hard way, it's one thing to be willing to take risks, but another to execute successfully on them. After all, Walmart had occasionally been willing to make big digital-focused bets since the 2010s, but they were few and far between, and just playing the game was not always enough. In 2011, Walmart paid $300 million for a Silicon Valley startup called Kosmix[1]— a sizable sum at the time—but the deal did little to alter the arc of the company's digital future. In the acquisition pursuits of both Diapers .com's parent company, Quidsi, as well as PillPack, the retail titan had dragged its feet, enabling Amazon to beat it to the punch.

But Walmart kept at it. Eighteen months before I sat down with McMillon, in the fall of 2020, Walmart was on the verge of taking another risky stab: a multibillion-dollar investment in TikTok, the blockbuster app that had tens of millions of people scrolling through videos on their smartphone for hours upon hours each day. At the direction of then-president Donald Trump, TikTok's China-based parent company was being forced to sell off its US operations. Walmart and the database software company Oracle were prepared to purchase a combined 20 percent of the company; the retailer was to provide "ecommerce, fulfillment, payments and other omnichannel services" to the video-sharing service.

To some, the idea of a match between the trendiest app of the time with an old-school retailer that was anything but trendy sounded preposterous. But to me, even with the possibility of it becoming a costly distraction, it signaled something more interesting: that Walmart was finally trying to invent a digital future where it would lead, not follow, Amazon. Even when Walmart had paid $16 billion two years earlier for a majority stake in Flipkart, Amazon's top competitor in India, the Bentonville behemoth was chasing from behind. But with the TikTok alignment, no longer were McMillon and Walmart simply aiming at Jeff Bezos's back; they were attempting to sprint ahead. With it, the deal could have set Walmart up to become a leader in the emerging sector of the commerce industry focused on selling goods via social media platforms, as well as livestream shopping—an area of video commerce that was already booming in Asia, but still nascent in the US.

It also seemed noteworthy that the company was pursuing the deal even without the support of its onetime e-commerce savior, Marc Lore, who had expressed misgivings about it internally and was then promptly shut out of the discussions. Lore was already on the way out of the company at the time and a more powerful voice was championing it: Walmart chairman Greg Penner. (Despite Penner's support of the Jet acquisition, he and Lore never developed a close rapport. "That was the one thing I was disappointed about," Lore told me, "that I didn't have enough time with Penner.") Walmart's major digital pursuits weren't going to die with Lore's departure.

Once again, though, someone would snatch away the opportunity even before McMillon and company could take the leap. Months after Walmart announced its intent to make the investment, and Trump lost his 2020 reelection bid, the Biden administration ended up shelving the idea of forcing the TikTok sale altogether. While that same administration reversed course two years later, in 2023, and threatened to ban the app if its Chinese owners did not sell it, a renewed Walmart/TikTok deal was no guarantee. Walmart would likely have to look elsewhere for its next digital moonshot, and it was not clear that any of its current internal initiatives would get them there, though they were numerous.

Walmart was continuing to expand an in-home delivery business, as an add-on fee to Walmart+, which some executives believed had the potential to eventually beat out Amazon on convenience. This service grew out of the initial tests that happened back in 2017 when Doug McMillon reportedly heard about Amazon testing a similar service, and instructed his e-commerce team to beat them to the punch. As it evolved out of Walmart's Store No. 8 incubation arm, it grew to consist of a Walmart delivery driver actually bringing the groceries inside a customer's home, packing them away in the customer's refrigerator if desired, and grabbing return orders if instructed to do so—all the while recording the interaction via a camera on their vest as the security layer. As of 2022, the waiting list for the service was long, but it still wasn't clear whether millions of customers would desire it, or whether Walmart could even operate it effectively at that scale.

Walmart also acquired, in late 2022, a robotics company called Alert Innovation, which makes one of the automation systems Walmart is utilizing to handle the picking and sorting of online grocery store orders in mini-warehouses attached to Walmart stores. In logistics, Walmart introduced a service called GoLocal, allowing local businesses, big and small, to contract out their deliveries to the traditional retailer. The move seemed smart, though aggressive, considering Walmart still had much work to do to perfect home delivery of its own merchandise. And like Amazon, Walmart was also starting to build out a legitimate advertising business on its websites and apps, but was way behind its rival, which had already been investing big in that department for years. Amazon generated $31 billion in revenue from ads on its shopping site and apps in 2021, compared to just $2 billion for Walmart.

Of course, Walmart was also investing in its online marketplace to make it more attractive for e-commerce merchants to sell through, and in its warehouse services to attract more merchants to ship through. But online sellers weren't signing up to sell or advertise on Walmart .com because the company was offering much better selling and advertising tools for them, or a larger customer base; many were simply doing so because they wanted someone—anyone—to provide a viable alternative to selling on Amazon. While it was true that thanks to Amazon's open platform, millions of micro merchants from Cedar Springs, Michigan, to Shenzhen, China, were suddenly capable of selling a piece of merchandise to millions of customers essentially overnight, the relationship between corporate behemoth and tiny merchant was often complicated. Yes, many sellers were grateful that, armed with nothing more than a supplier connection, a warehouse storage agreement with the Fulfillment by Amazon service, and a couple of hundred dollars to throw at Amazon ads, they could start a business on Amazon without ever personally touching or shipping a single unit of merchandise themselves. But these same sellers often had to sustain sometimes sudden and arbitrary account suspensions; seemingly ever-increasing fees; and the fear of having their product listings hijacked by nefarious rivals or, worse, their merchandise cloned by Amazon itself. The relationship, was, to say the least, tenuous. Walmart offered a chance to make some money in a less nerve-racking way. Just maybe.

But again, many of Walmart's new strategies and tactics—from its ads business to its marketplace for small merchants—had already become table stakes just to keep up with Amazon's advancements. Yes, McMillon and team were diversifying Walmart and, at least theoretically, strengthening its foundation. But would that be enough to do anything more than delay Amazon's inevitable victory? Was the competition with Amazon truly making Walmart a threat or just no longer a laughingstock?

Don Harris, the onetime boss and major fan of Doug McMillon whose own father was once a Sam Walton deputy, remembered fondly the days when competition forced Walmart to execute at its highest level, and the best-performing stores were the ones located nearest to rivals.

"They had to be, because I knew that person could walk right down the street," he said.

But as an online shopper and Walmart+ member in his personal life, he'd been frustrated in recent years—especially as a lifelong Walmart champion—by how long it was taking for the company to fully harness its advantages over Amazon to offer customers what they want, when they want, and where they want, both for buying and returning merchandise. Walmart had, Harris told me, the assets, influence, and money to make faster progress in becoming the go-to everything retailer that seamlessly integrates its websites, stores, and warehouses for the benefit of the customer above all. And with the Waltons still controlling a majority of the company's shares, McMillon should get whatever financial runway he needed to transform the retailer more quickly, without fear of an activist investor causing a ruckus.

"I just don't know what's taking so long," Harris told me over Zoom in early 2022 from his home in northwest Arkansas. "I think competition should be making us better. And my concern is, are we letting bureaucracy slow us down? No one is in a position to do this, with a better CEO, than us. Get on with it!"

When I met with McMillon a couple of months later, he was fully aware that bureaucracy was a long-term hurdle. The organization was still in the midst of a transition away from a centralized, top-down entity to a more agile, faster-mover structure. Walmart was also trying to do a lot of different important things at the same time, he said, and didn't always have enough manpower to execute quickly on those ideas. So while McMillon said he was encouraged by the pace of progress in some parts of the organization, overall, "I'm still dissatisfied with the lack of speed," he said.

That's what made Amazon's continued rise for so many years so astonishing. Over in Seattle, the company maintained a rapid pace of progress even as it grew into the second-largest private-sector employer in the US, only after Walmart, with more than one million employees. One key was a decentralized structure that empowered autonomous teams. With no centralized technology team, for example, engineers and other technical talent are spread out across various business units, meaning there's not the same type of internal competition for technical resources that you might find in a centralized organization. New product development went something like this: idea, memo, small investment, small team, development sprint, launch, kill, or scale. Repeat. Quite the legacy for the two-pizza teams that former Walmart IT boss Rick Dalzell helped create as Amazon's first chief information officer, with some inspiration from what he had learned from his former employer in Arkansas. Amazon's secret sauce, perhaps as much as anything else, was its speed.

That was true for a very long time. But in the late 2010s, as Jeff Bezos's attention was diverted in new directions, from his rocket company, Blue Origin, to his new love interest, employees and former executives started whispering about a new reality they felt creeping into Amazon. True innovations seemed scarce. Decision-making was slowing. Amazon was still a dangerous competitor to all, and an existential threat to Walmart, but the organization seemed to be grinding in maintenance mode. Some feared they were witnessing the early stages of what Bezos had once labeled in a 2017 all-hands meeting as "Day 2"—the successor to "Day 1," where he hoped Amazon would always remain, experimenting and moving fast.

"Day Two is stasis," Bezos had said. "Followed by irrelevance. Followed by excruciating, painful decline. Followed by death."

This corporate purgatory wouldn't occur overnight. It might even last decades. But it was, as most companies including Walmart had experienced, nearly inevitable. Yet the customer demand for Amazon's shopping, entertainment, and cloud-computing services during the first year of the Covid-19 pandemic provided a brief reprieve from this debate. There was no time for complacency or slow decision-making with customers demanding so much.

But new risks emerged, for both Amazon and Walmart. Pandemic-driven supply chain woes, flip-flopping consumer shopping habits causing inventory gluts, and the worst US inflation rate since the early 1980s made business more unpredictable than ever, even for these two goliaths. By the middle of 2022, amid an economy showing signs of slipping into a recession, Amazon posted its slowest revenue growth rate in two decades.[2] Around the same time, Walmart warned Wall Street of shrinking profits. That fall, Walmart's US CEO, John Furner, visited the giant cargo container port in Long Beach, California, and watched as merchandise that the retailer had ordered in advance of the 2021 holiday season was just making its way onto US shores a whole year later. Things were certainly not back to normal. At Amazon, the company was also navigating the first CEO transition in its history, with Andy Jassy replacing Jeff Bezos as chief executive. From late 2022 into 2023, Jassy oversaw the largest layoff process in the company's history, with more than twenty-seven thousand corporate employees losing their jobs.

On the labor front, serious challenges remained for both giants as well. In mid-2021, as the pandemic was still fueling high online shopping rates, a research team inside Amazon flagged a major concern: at the company's current warehouse growth trajectory, and sky-high worker turnover rates, the tech giant could run out of workers to hire in the US by 2024, and even sooner in some important logistics regions like Phoenix, Arizona, and the Inland Empire of Southern California. I broke news of the research after it was leaked to me the following year.[3] While Amazon's attrition rates were 123 percent and 159 percent in 2019 and 2020, respectively, average turnover rates in the retail industry were much lower: 58 percent and nearly 70 percent, and even lower across the broader US transportation and logistics industries, according to the Bureau of Labor Statistics, at 46 percent and 59 percent. In an internal survey of Amazon workers who left their job in 2021 for a competitor, the employees "rated Amazon significantly worse on work fitting skills or interests, demands of the work, shift length and shift schedule."

The turbulence continued a year later when Amazon announced that it had vastly overbuilt its warehouse network during the pandemic in expectation of continued record online shopping, only to see the growth of the industry plateau as shoppers began frequenting stores once again and inflation led some to cut back on discretionary spending. By late 2022, under new CEO Jassy's direction, the company had either closed down, or canceled or delayed plans for, more than sixty warehouses, totaling more than 50 million square feet of space.[4] Amazon also paused the expansion of its Amazon Fresh grocery stores and began charging Prime members extra delivery fees for Fresh grocery orders under $150. In some markets, the company now had too many workers as well, and would count on its abysmal attrition rates to help get its warehouse productivity numbers back where it liked them.

Worker organizing efforts were also not going away. At Amazon, the Amazon Labor Union victory at the fulfillment center in Staten Island was followed by another, ultimately unsuccessful union bid, at a smaller sortation center in the same New York City borough. But a few months later, workers at an Amazon warehouse in upstate New York also filed for a union election. That effort also ended in an election loss, but the Amazon Labor Union's Chris Smalls promised that his union would "continue and expand our campaign for fair treatment for all Amazon workers."[5]

The deaths of workers also led to internal outrage in 2022. One was a thirty-eight-year-old Walmart employee who had heart issues and collapsed in a store bathroom after her family said she had feared being reprimanded or penalized for leaving work despite feeling ill.[6] A subsequent shareholder proposal for a dedicated paid sick leave policy for Walmart store associates was voted down by Walmart investors. The other was an Amazon warehouse employee who collapsed and died while working on one of Amazon's busiest shopping days of the year: Prime Day. Some of his colleagues said he and others had been complaining to superiors that the facility was too hot on a day when outdoor temperatures rose above 90 degrees.[7] Amazon maintained that his work did not contribute to his death, but a federal workplace safety investigation was still outstanding. Forty-four percent of Amazon shareholders voted in favor of a shareholder proposal requesting an independent audit and report on Amazon warehouse working conditions, though a majority is needed for the proposal to pass. Assuming Jeff Bezos voted against the proposal as his board had recommended to investors, his vote and ownership stake may have been the difference between the call for the audit passing or not.

Workers at both companies continued to push for higher pay as well. In the fall of 2022, Amazon said its average entry-level pay in the US was increasing to $19 an hour, with workers starting off anywhere between $16 and $26 hourly depending on role and location. At Walmart, the average wage was around $17.50, though some higher-level roles could pay as much as $34 an hour in its warehouses and $32 in its stores. Along the way, the company cut its decades-old quarterly bonus program to supplement hourly pay bumps.

"It wasn't only the fact of the money," Cynthia Murray, the twenty-two-year Walmart store veteran and organizer, said of the bonuses, known as MyShare. "It was the fact that they felt the company appreciated the hard work that they did to put out the products to sell them in order to get that profit. For as much money as Doug [McMillon] has taken in every year, cut his money and give the workers a steady bonus."

McMillon told me that some type of cash bonus could return in the future—"Incentives are important," he agreed—but he stressed that many employees told the company that increased hourly rates were more important, and that the company will continue to increase wages, in part by improving productivity with the help of robots.

"That starting wage rate is something we've been working on, but I worry sometimes that people get too focused on just that starting wage rate," he said. "The average and the top end matter, too."

The Walmart employment system, he argued, "is designed for people to be rewarded for moving up."

*　　*　　*

Outside each company, upstarts continued to nip at their heels, too. Instacart, the grocery delivery company that partners with physical grocers and which was founded by a former Amazon engineer, received a huge boost from the pandemic and closed 2021 with nearly $2 billion in revenue. While that number was still a fraction of the titans' and mostly focused on one product category, a planned initial public offering would give the company more funds to continue its expansion beyond groceries. Gopuff, a nine-year-old company that started as a late-night munchies delivery service in college towns, also broke into the mainstream among younger demographics, with help from the pandemic. Rather than deliver from grocery stores like Instacart's core service, Gopuff stocks its own CPG inventory in barebones mini-warehouses and delivers them to customers' doors within thirty minutes. In the apparel industry, private-market investors valued China-based Shein, an online powerhouse in the fast fashion industry, at $100 million in April 2021.

Then there was Shopify. The Canadian software company got its start when its founder was frustrated by the lack of tools to easily create his online snowboard shop, so decided to make his own. He eventually began selling the software instead to other small businesses via a monthly subscription model. With more brick-and-mortar shops forced to sell online during the pandemic, Shopify's revenue skyrocketed and Wall Street pumped up its value to nearly $180 billion, around one and a half times the largest market cap that Target, the giant US retailer, ever achieved. And that was even with Shopify not yet providing comparable offerings for two of the key services that Amazon does: warehousing and shipping, and a ready-made spigot of tens of millions of customers via an online shopping marketplace.

Still, the close relationship between Shopify and its small and midsize merchants—"Arming the rebels," was a common company refrain—as well as moves it was making to begin offering merchants shipping services and tools to attract new customers, had Amazon paying attention. In April 2022, Amazon launched a feature called "Buy with Prime," which allowed sellers who use Shopify a way to give Amazon's Prime members the shipping and payment experience they would find on Amazon but on the merchant's own website. In return, Shopify began warning its merchants that Amazon's new feature violated its terms of service.[8] The beginning of a new e-commerce war seemed to be brewing.

Yet, by the last quarter of 2022, many of the upstarts that might one day threaten Amazon and Walmart found themselves on shaky ground. Shopify's stock price dropped 80 percent between October 2021 and October 2022, compared to a 30 percent decline for Amazon and less than 10 percent for Walmart. Gopuff slashed more than 10 percent of its staff and shut down dozens of warehouses as it delayed going public. Instacart cut its own valuation by nearly 40 percent, ahead of its own planned IPO.[9] No one knew exactly what their futures would hold, but the idea that one of them might truly threaten or disrupt the two respective titans of physical and online retail in the US didn't seem any more realistic than it had a few years earlier. Of course, it was possible that someone unexpected would emerge out of the blue to upend them just like Amazon had done to Walmart decades earlier. On cue, news broke in late 2022 that TikTok had plans to build out its own warehouse network to support a push into e-commerce.[10]

"With millions of loyal users globally, we believe TikTok is an ideal platform to deliver a brand-new and better e-commerce experience to our users," a company job listing said at the time.

Even if the company was right, any large fulfillment network would likely take many, many years to pull off, even if things went smoothly. The Amazon-Walmart battle still felt mostly like a two-company race.

*   *   *

I don't remember exactly when the pleadings started, but I remember the shock with which I received them. From small Amazon sellers, to big brands that were sick of the one-sidedness of doing business with Amazon, to government insiders who feared Amazon's growing power but didn't trust that regulators or lawmakers had either the will or legal grounds to curb it: When will Walmart step up its game and provide a viable alternative to the Jeff Bezos empire? Walmart, the Main Street killer. Walmart, the union-busting bully. Walmart, the e-commerce laughingstock. Now being asked to be Walmart, the savior?

Sure, during the first two decades of the twenty-first century, Amazon's rise had indeed transformed Walmart into an underdog for the first time since Sam Walton's early years as CEO. And no matter the criticism of the company's tactics, there is undoubtedly consumer benefit from the retailer's low-price history. But in a healthy economy and society, is Walmart something to root for? Is Amazon, for that matter? Rational people can make rational arguments on either side of the debate. For me, I don't think there's a one-size-fits-all answer.

But in an ideal world, the continued competition between these rivals will pressure both to evolve in ways that provide more societal good than harm—whether in the form of lower prices for cash-strapped consumers, convenience for those whose busy lives or physical limitations require it, more humane working conditions for everyday people, or, maybe, someday, positive changes to health care if we're lucky.

The problem is that an ideal world is often not the real world. Admittedly, that's a lot of hope and optimism laid before two megacorporations whose actions haven't always inspired those feelings. So outside forces—whether they be regulators, new startups, or labor groups—will still be necessary to apply pressure where the rivalry alone is not producing the best outcomes, and not only for citizens in their lives as consumers, but as workers and community members too.

Because a world where one winner sells all is a world where everyone loses.

ACKNOWLEDGMENTS

Winner Sells All never comes to be without the trust all of my sources placed in me. That is not something I take for granted, and I owe a lot to every single one of them. This history is also theirs. I hope I did it justice.

This book might not exist either without an email that arrived in my inbox on the evening of April 7, 2020, only a few weeks after the United States plunged into the Covid-19 abyss.

"I realize it's an unprecedented time, and I don't mean to put extra pressure on you, on top of everything you are dealing with. However, the world is realizing how important e-commerce is. And you happen to have a book proposal in the works about this very subject. Have you had any time to work on it?"

The sender was Ethan Bassoff, a literary agent who had first contacted me the prior summer after he read an oral history of Amazon Prime that I published. Ethan and I began working on a book proposal together about the Amazon/Walmart rivalry shortly thereafter, even before I had agreed to hire him. But when the pandemic hit, and my work and home lives were turned upside down, I took a pause. Sorry, Ethan, but that email kind of annoyed me at the time. The truth, though, is that I needed that nudge. We finished the proposal over the next two months and rushed it out to publishers. Ethan's edits and guidance then, and his counsel in the years since, were pivotal. I've been lucky to have him, and his persistence, at my side.

My editor, Hollis Heimbouch, at Harper Business took a chance on a first-time author with an ambitious idea that often felt too big to tackle. Her edits, feedback, and patience are crucial to whatever success this book ends up having. The sharp eye of Rachel Kambury, my associate editor, and her reminders about the real-world impact of these two industry giants made this book better. I'm also grateful for the behind-the-scenes work of Christina Polizoto, Jared Oriel, Beth Silfin, James Neidhardt, and the rest of the Harper Business staff who played key roles in this project and pushing it across the finish line.

At Walmart, Dan Bartlett welcomed me in despite knowing I was not drafting a hagiography. Ravi Jariwala and Erin Hulliberger made what could have been a long, difficult process easier. Erin, in particular, was a worthy sparring partner, but always a respectful one. Chris Oster and Jordan Deagle at Amazon were as helpful as you might find inside that company.

I might not have ever stumbled upon the wild worlds of retail and e-commerce if not for Kara Swisher and Walt Mossberg, who hired me in 2013 to cover Amazon at Recode's predecessor, All Things Digital. I've learned so much from both of them. I'm thankful for Samantha Oltman, my boss at Recode, who was supportive of this book even when it meant taking an extended leave from my day job. Sam also challenged me to widen the lens of my daily reporting to connect the dots between Amazon's and Walmart's actions and how they shape the lives of everyday people. I was fortunate to have worked with a long list of other stellar journalists at Recode, including Peter Kafka, Ken Li, Edmund Lee, and many others. Each of you has taught me valuable lessons and I have nothing but love for you all.

Even though we didn't know each other very well, Christina Farr was a generous sharer of healthcare-related knowledge and contacts, which made one of my favorite chapters possible. Mark Bergen, Mike Isaac, and Max Chafkin provided helpful perspectives as fellow first-time authors.

Of course, there's zero chance this book would have seen the light of day if not for the love and support of my family and close friends. Joe, Justin, and Steve are the best buds a guy could ask for. My cousin Mike's motivating texts meant more to me than he probably realized.

My bonus mom, Marguerite, welcomed me into her home for an important week of writing at a critical juncture of my book leave. Beyond that, her love and confidence in me helped buoy my spirit. My siblings, Bernard and Christie, and my brother-in-law, Jason, offered constant encouragement and helpful feedback, whether from next door or the other side of the world. Their belief in me picked me up during trying times.

I would give up this book, and much more, to be able to share just one more day with my parents, Patricia and Bernard. Wherever you both are, I can only hope I've made you proud. Your legacies are enormous.

Visits to my attic "office" from my children, Sebastian and Scarlett, provided bursts of light on what felt like dark days. I'm not sure I deserved the patience they showed me, but I will be forever grateful that they did. And, yes, Daddy will seriously consider writing a children's book next.

Where do I even start with the love of my life, Tyrene—my confidant, my biggest supporter, my inspiration, my first and last reader. I'm not sure either of us knew what we were signing up for when I agreed to a book deal in the summer of 2020. Yet you never made me feel guilty for the sacrifices this book required, even when it may have been called for. I will spend the rest of our days trying to make it up to you. I love you forever.

NOTES

Winner Sells All is not only a business book but a history book as well. And as such, one based on fact. Between early 2020 and early 2023, I conducted hundreds of hours of interviews with more than one hundred fifty people who shared key insights into how Amazon and Walmart operate and how they've viewed each other over time. The vast majority of them worked at one—or in some cases, both—of the companies at some point in the last three decades. A great number of facts in this book—from discussions at key company meetings to internal disputes between executives—came from these sources and their first-hand knowledge of events chronicled in these pages.

Some of these employees and executives were willing to speak to me on the record about their experiences and recollections. Among them were more than a dozen company leaders who held top positions at either Amazon or Walmart at the time of their company-sanctioned interviews with me. But many others would only speak to me if I granted them anonymity, for valid reasons, including not having company permission to do so or for fear of retribution for speaking with candor about two titans that do not look fondly upon those who expose closely guarded strategies or squabbles to the outside world. I don't take the use of anonymous sources lightly; I declined to include considerable information from anonymous sources that I could not corroborate independently or otherwise had reason to doubt.

I conducted almost all of my interviews either in-person, by video conference, or via phone. One exception involved Greg Foran, the former Walmart US CEO who is currently the CEO of Air New Zealand. Foran would only answer questions and offer comments by email. I don't often accept such ground rules but agreed to them in this instance because of his crucial role in the events chronicled in this book.

In some instances, I re-created dialogue based on the recollections of people who participated in or were present for the discussion in question. This does not mean that quoted participants spoke to me. That said, those mentioned in the dialogue were made aware of the information being printed. The exception is former Walmart CEO David Glass, who died in early 2020 shortly before I began reporting this book and whose conversation with Robert Davis in Chapter 1 was recreated using Davis's recollection.

I also sourced information from news reports I deemed credible, public statements at conferences, my own previous reporting covering these two behemoths, as well as speeches and interviews found on YouTube. Brad Stone's books *The Everything Store* and *Amazon Unbound* and Sam Walton's memoir *Made in America* were helpful resources.

PROLOGUE

1. https://money.cnn.com/magazines/fortune/fortune_archive/2005/04/18/8257009/index.htm.

1: WHAT IF?

1. https://www.nytimes.com/1999/04/06/business/the-media-business-wal-mart-agrees-to-settle-lawsuit-against-amazon.html.
2. https://money.cnn.com/magazines/fortune/fortune_archive/2001/06/11/304647/.
3. https://archive.fortune.com/magazines/business2/business2_archive/2003/02/01/335981/index.htm.
4. Brad Stone, *The Everything Store: Jeff Bezos and the Age of Amazon* (New York: Little, Brown, 2013).
5. https://progressivegrocer.com/walmartcom-president-step-down.
6. https://www.nytimes.com/2001/07/24/business/wal-mart-assumes-complete-control-of-its-online-store.html.
7. https://www.digitalcommerce360.com/2006/02/15/walmart-com-2005-sales-top-1-billion/.
8. Stone, *The Everything Store*.
9. https://www.computerworld.com/article/2597093/amazon-charging-different-prices-on-some-dvds.html.
10. Stone, *The Everything Store*.

11. Stone, *The Everything Store*.
12. https://www.wsj.com/articles/SB1037918101430594628.
13. https://www.cnet.com/tech/services-and-software/amazon-pricecheck-app-use-it-get-a-discount/.
14. https://www.boston.com/news/local-news/2011/12/09/amazon-price-app-is-attack-on-small-stores-snowe-says/.
15. http://latimesblogs.latimes.com/technology/2011/12/retail-group-lashes-out-after-amazon-announces-price-check-app-promotion.html.
16. https://www.wsj.com/articles/SB10001424052748704396504576204791377862836.
17. https://www.wsj.com/articles/SB10001424053111904772304576468753564916130.
18. https://www.wsj.com/articles/SB10001424052748704498804574557943780026958.
19. https://judiciary.house.gov/uploadedfiles/00151722.pdf.

2: JET FUEL

1. https://www.bloomberg.com/news/articles/2013-10-10/jeff-bezos-and-the-age-of-amazon-excerpt-from-the-everything-store-by-brad-stone?sref=qYiz2hd0.
2. https://www.vox.com/2015/1/9/11557622/five-ways-the-guy-behind-diapers-com-plans-to-challenge-amazon-again.
3. https://www.vox.com/2015/1/9/11557622/five-ways-the-guy-behind-diapers-com-plans-to-challenge-amazon-again.
4. https://www.bloomberg.com/news/features/2017-05-04/can-wal-mart-s-expensive-new-e-commerce-operation-compete-with-amazon?sref=qYiz2hd0.
5. https://www.youtube.com/watch?v=KXs0TYejsZc.
6. https://www.wsj.com/articles/wal-mart-in-talks-to-buy-web-retailer-jet-com-1470237311.
7. https://www.vox.com/2016/8/7/12395114/walmart-jet-acquisition-3-billion-price.

3: HOMETOWN BOY

1. https://www.reuters.com/article/us-walmart-fcpa/walmart-to-pay-282-million-to-settle-seven-year-global-corruption-probe-idUSKCN1TL27J.
2. https://www.harvardmagazine.com/2021/05/doug-mcmillon-s-business-school-address.
3. https://www.youtube.com/watch?v=041qYmA0d6Y.
4. https://www.harvardmagazine.com/2021/05/doug-mcmillon-s-business-school-address.
5. https://www.dignitymemorial.com/obituaries/bentonville-ar/morris-mcmillon-9918245.
6. https://www.harvardmagazine.com/2021/05/doug-mcmillon-s-business-school-address.
7. https://www.harvardmagazine.com/2021/05/doug-mcmillon-s-business-school-address.
8. https://www.youtube.com/watch?v=WnC0BhV7XDw.
9. https://fortune.com/2015/06/04/walmart-ceo-doug-mcmillon/.
10. https://fortune.com/2015/06/04/walmart-ceo-doug-mcmillon/.
11. https://fortune.com/2015/06/04/walmart-ceo-doug-mcmillon/.
12. https://inequality.org/great-divide/2016-agendas-tout-ceo-pay-reform/.
13. https://www.youtube.com/watch?v=WnC0BhV7XDw.
14. https://www.nytimes.com/2004/01/18/us/workers-assail-night-lock-ins-by-wal-mart.html.
15. https://corporate.walmart.com/twenty-first-century-leadership.
16. https://ldh.la.gov/assets/oph/Center-PHCH/Center-CH/stepi/specialstudies/2014Popwell Ratard_KatrinaDeath_PostedOnline.pdf.

17. https://www.youtube.com/watch?v=WnC0BhV7XDw.
18. https://www.nytimes.com/2013/03/09/business/man-who-helped-image-of-wal-mart-steps-down.html.
19. https://www.cnbc.com/2019/09/03/the-full-memo-from-walmarts-ceo-about-pulling-back-on-gun-sales.html.
20. https://www.nytimes.com/2009/09/20/business/20amazon.html.
21. https://hbr.org/2017/03/we-need-people-to-lean-into-the-future.
22. https://fortune.com/2015/06/04/walmart-ceo-doug-mcmillon/.
23. https://www.vox.com/2014/5/28/11627338/coming-up-new-walmart-ceo-doug-mcmillon-at-the-code-conference.

4: THE TAKEOVER

1. https://www.cnbc.com/2016/08/09/wal-mart-ceo-doug-mcmillon-on-what-he-saw-in-jetcom.html.
2. https://www.vox.com/2016/9/19/12980868/walmart-jet-marc-lore-stock-retention-incentive-bonus.
3. https://corporate.walmart.com/newsroom/2017/04/12/empowering-customers-with-more-ways-to-save-introducing-pickup-discount.
4. https://corporate.walmart.com/newsroom/innovation/20170725/how-easy-reorder-is-making-shopping-even-easier.
5. https://corporate.walmart.com/newsroom/innovation/20170922/why-the-future-could-mean-delivery-straight-into-your-fridge.
6. https://corporate.walmart.com/newsroom/business/20160919/five-big-reasons-walmart-bought-jet-com.
7. https://cdn.corporate.walmart.com/ea/31/4aa1027b4be6818f1a65ed5c293a/wmt-usq-transcript-2017-10-10.pdf.
8. https://www.cnbc.com/2018/02/20/walmart-q4-2017-earnings.html.
9. https://www.marketwatch.com/story/walmarts-jet-website-may-not-be-reaching-customers-beyond-city-limits-2018-02-21.
10. https://www.businessinsider.com/walmart-sells-out-of-black-friday-sales-on-thanksgiving-2017-11.

5: PRIME ATTACK

1. https://www.vox.com/recode/2019/5/3/18511544/amazon-prime-oral-history-jeff-bezos-one-day-shipping.
2. https://www.businessinsider.com/meet-the-average-wal-mart-shopper-2014-9.
3. https://www.vox.com/2014/3/13/11624518/amazon-prime-price-rises-to-99-and-you-know-youll-still-pay-for-it.
4. https://www.vox.com/recode/2019/5/3/18511544/amazon-prime-oral-history-jeff-bezos-one-day-shipping.
5. https://www.vox.com/recode/2019/5/3/18511544/amazon-prime-oral-history-jeff-bezos-one-day-shipping.
6. https://s2.q4cdn.com/299287126/files/doc_financials/annual/2015-Letter-to-Shareholders.pdf.
7. https://www.vox.com/recode/2019/5/3/18511544/amazon-prime-oral-history-jeff-bezos-one-day-shipping.

8.   https://www.vox.com/recode/2019/5/3/18511544/amazon-prime-oral-history-jeff-bezos
     -one-day-shipping.
9.   https://www.cbsnews.com/miami/news/walmart-closing-more-than-150-smaller-stores
     -around-u-s/.
10. https://www.vox.com/2018/4/19/17256410/amazon-prime-100-million-members-us
     -penetration-low-income-households-jeff-bezos.
11. https://corporate.walmart.com/newsroom/innovation/20170131/two-day-free-shipping
     -just-the-beginning.
12. https://www.wsj.com/articles/wal-mart-to-scrap-its-amazon-prime-rival-1485838861.

6: NOT READY FOR PRIME TIME

1.   https://www.fmi.org/our-research/supermarket-facts/grocery-store-chains-net-profit.
2.   https://www.vox.com/2017/3/30/14831602/amazon-walmart-cpg-grocery-price-war.
3.   https://www.bloomberg.com/news/articles/2021-01-07/amazon-shutters-prime-pantry
     -an-early-online-grocery-initiative.
4.   http://ebaysellingcoach.blogspot.com/2014/05/how-will-amazon-pantry-affect-grocery.html.

7: AMAZON SENDS A WAKE-UP CALL

1.   https://www.bloomberg.com/news/articles/2017-04-11/amazon-said-to-mull-bid-for
     -whole-foods-before-jana-stepped-in?sref=Wg6QzS2e.
2.   https://www.vox.com/2017/4/14/15304234/walmart-bonobos-acquisition-jet.
3.   https://www.nytimes.com/2017/06/16/business/walmart-bonobos-merger.html.
4.   https://www.vox.com/2017/6/18/15826314/amazons-whole-foods-acquisition-22
     -billion-market-value-supermarkets.
5.   https://www.cnbc.com/2017/06/16/after-its-stock-pop-amazon-will-get-whole-foods
     -essentially-for-free.html.
6.   https://corporate.walmart.com/newsroom/2017/09/06/walmart-to-open-1-000th
     -online-grocery-pickup-location.
7.   https://corporate.walmart.com/newsroom/2018/03/14/walmart-to-expand-online-grocery
     -delivery-coast-to-coast.
8.   https://archive.fortune.com/magazines/fortune/fortune_archive/2000/06/12/281941
     /index.htm.
9.   https://techcrunch.com/2014/01/28/walmart-to-go-denver-grocery-test/.
10. https://www.vox.com/2018/2/20/17030702/amazon-prime-credit-card-whole-foods-5
     -percent-back-visa-rewards.
11. https://www.businessinsider.com/whole-foods-shoppers-say-produce-quality-plunged
     -after-amazon-takeover-2017-11.

8: AMAZONIFICATION

1.   https://www.bloomberg.com/news/articles/2019-12-17/amazon-holiday-shopping-the
     -man-who-makes-it-happen.
2.   https://www.vox.com/recode/2020/6/29/21303643/amazon-coronavirus-warehouse
     -workers-protest-jeff-bezos-chris-smalls-boycott-pandemic.
3.   https://www.law.com/therecorder/2019/08/13/robotics-manager-sues-walmart-for
     -gender-discrimination-and-harassment/.

4.   https://www.businessinsider.com/how-fedex-talent-made-amazon-a-logistics-juggernaut
     -2021-11.
5.   https://www.columbian.com/news/2014/jul/24/amazon-opens-its-first-sortation-center/.

9: THE GREATEST RETAILER ON THE PLANET
1.   https://www.youtube.com/watch?v=4tg33gyESy4.
2.   https://hbr.org/2017/12/the-right-thing-to-do.
3.   https://corporate.walmart.com/media-library/document/2019-ubs-global-consumer
     -retail-conference-webcast-transcript/_proxyDocument?id=00000169-7873-d4ef-adeb
     -7b73b8e00000.
4.   https://www.vox.com/2017/12/20/16693406/walmart-personal-styling-jet-black
     -amazon-go-prime-no-checkout-store.
5.   https://www.wsj.com/articles/walmart-seeks-outside-investors-for-jetblack-115702
     12067.
6.   https://www.wsj.com/articles/walmart-builds-a-secret-weapon-to-battle-amazon-for
     -retails-future-11553181810.
7.   https://www.vox.com/2018/10/2/17924862/walmart-eloquii-acquisition-100-million
     -plus-sized-fashion.
8.   https://www.businessinsider.com/walmart-has-looked-at-acquiring-luggage-company
     -away-2018-10.
9.   https://www.vox.com/recode/2019/12/12/21012920/andy-dunn-walmart-bonobos
     -leaving-departure-digital-native-brands.

10: OLD SCHOOL VS. NEW SCHOOL
1.   https://www.vox.com/recode/2019/7/3/18716431/walmart-jet-marc-lore-modcloth-amazon
     -ecommerce-losses-online-sales.
2.   https://www.vox.com/2017/4/2/15153844/amazon-quidsi-shutdown-explanation-profits.
3.   https://www.wsj.com/articles/walmarts-secret-weapon-to-fight-off-amazon-the
     -supercenter-11576904460.
4.   https://twitter.com/CourtReagan/status/1002257682626240512.
5.   https://www.wsj.com/articles/top-walmart-exec-pays-43-79-million-for-swanky-new
     -york-penthouse-1528814182.
6.   https://www.vox.com/recode/2021/1/15/22232033/marc-lore-walmart-leaving-jet-city
     -future-capitalism.

11: RETAIL DOCTORS
1.   https://www.propublica.org/article/the-justice-department-sues-walmart-accusing-it-of
     -illegally-dispensing-opioids.
2.   https://www.propublica.org/article/walmart-was-almost-charged-criminally-over-opioids
     -trump-appointees-killed-the-indictment.
3.   https://www.cnbc.com/2017/05/16/amazon-selling-drugs-pharamaceuticals.html.
4.   https://corporate.walmart.com/newsroom/2021/06/29/walmart-revolutionizes-insulin
     -access-affordability-for-patients-with-diabetes-with-the-launch-of-the-first-and-only
     -private-brand-analog-insulin.
5.   https://www.wsj.com/articles/BL-VCDB-18882.
6.   https://news.yahoo.com/amazon-failed-disrupt-prescription-drug-084029260.html.

7. https://profusa.com/injectable-body-sensors-take-personal-chemistry-to-a-cell-phone-closer-to-reality/.

8. https://www.cnbc.com/2018/06/05/amazon-grand-challenge-moonshot-lab-google-glass-creator-babak-parviz.html.

9. https://www.youtube.com/watch?v=b3qbX6LS3Ro.

10. https://www.wsj.com/articles/why-the-amazon-jpmorgan-berkshire-venture-collapsed-health-care-was-too-big-a-problem-11610039485?mod=article_inline.

11. https://www.kff.org/coronavirus-covid-19/press-release/telehealth-accounted-for-8-of-outpatient-visits-more-than-a-year-into-covid-19-pandemic-suggesting-a-more-permanent-shift-in-how-patients-receive-care/.

12. https://www.aboutamazon.com/news/retail/amazon-care-now-available-nationwide-as-demand-continues-to-grow.

13. https://www.businessinsider.com/amazon-ceo-andy-jassy-shares-bold-vision-for-healthcare-business-2022-3.

14. https://www.youtube.com/watch?v=iNs6cDUKl7Y.

15. https://cbs12.com/news/nation-world/walmart-may-start-nationwide-initiative-potentially-changing-how-millions-get-healthcare.

16. https://www.businessinsider.com/walmart-healthcare-strategy-health-clinics-2021-2.

17. https://www.fiercehealthcare.com/hospitals/why-former-walmart-health-exec-left-for-bioiq.

18. https://www.youtube.com/watch?v=I3Tc0T_adSU.

19. https://news.bloomberglaw.com/antitrust/amazon-one-medical-receive-ftc-request-for-more-information?utm_source=rss&utm_medium=ATNW&utm_campaign=00000183-0021-da0b-a1a3-b1bde37a0001.

12: PANDEMIC POWER STRUGGLE

1. https://www.vox.com/recode/2020/2/25/21151289/new-amazon-go-grocery-store-supermarket-cashiers-whole-foods-seattle.

2. https://www.vox.com/2017/6/16/15816180/amazon-whole-foods-deal.

3. https://www.vox.com/2019/10/29/20936984/amazon-prime-grocery-delivery-fresh-fee-whole-foods-instacart.

4. https://www.vox.com/recode/2020/2/27/21154357/walmart-plus-walmart-grocery-delivery-unlimited-membership-amazon-prime.

5. https://www.vox.com/recode/2020/9/1/21409628/walmart-plus-benefits-free-grocery-delivery-amazon-prime-comparison.

6. https://www.nytimes.com/2020/04/05/technology/coronavirus-amazon-workers.html.

7. https://www.vox.com/recode/2020/6/29/21303643/amazon-coronavirus-warehouse-workers-protest-jeff-bezos-chris-smalls-boycott-pandemic.

8. https://www.vox.com/recode/2020/3/22/21190372/amazon-prime-delivery-delays-april-21-coronavirus-covid-19.

9. https://www.vox.com/recode/2020/6/29/21303643/amazon-coronavirus-warehouse-workers-protest-jeff-bezos-chris-smalls-boycott-pandemic.

10. https://www.mcall.com/news/watchdog/mc-allentown-amazon-complaints-20110917-story.html

11. https://www.nytimes.com/2021/03/16/technology/amazon-unions-virginia.html.

12. https://www.nytimes.com/2021/03/16/technology/amazon-unions-virginia.html.

13. https://www.nytimes.com/2005/02/10/business/worldbusiness/walmart-to-close-store-in-canada-with-a-union.html.

14. https://www.vox.com/recode/2020/6/29/21303643/amazon-coronavirus-warehouse -workers-protest-jeff-bezos-chris-smalls-boycott-pandemic.

15. https://www.vice.com/en/article/n7jy9w/amazon-workers-in-new-york-have-started -walking-off-the-job-this-is-a-cry-for-help.

16. https://www.vice.com/en/article/5dm8bx/leaked-amazon-memo-details-plan-to-smear -fired-warehouse-organizer-hes-not-smart-or-articulate.

17. https://www.vox.com/recode/2020/4/5/21206385/amazon-fired-warehouse-worker -christian-smalls-employee-backlash-david-zapolsky-coronavirus.

18. https://www.vox.com/recode/2020/6/29/21303643/amazon-coronavirus-warehouse -workers-protest-jeff-bezos-chris-smalls-boycott-pandemic.

19. https://www.cityandstateny.com/policy/2021/02/amid-building-boom-amazon-faces -complaints-from-warehouse-workers/175177/.

20. https://www.nytimes.com/2022/04/02/business/amazon-union-christian-smalls.html.

21. https://theintercept.com/2021/03/25/amazon-drivers-pee-bottles-union.

22. https://www.vox.com/recode/2021/3/28/22354604/amazon-twitter-bernie-sanders-jeff -bezos-union-alabama-elizabeth-warren.

23. https://www.wsj.com/articles/amazon-washington-biden-carney-antitrust-11646763777.

24. https://www.vox.com/recode/2020/6/29/21303643/amazon-coronavirus-warehouse -workers-protest-jeff-bezos-chris-smalls-boycott-pandemic.

25. https://www.cnbc.com/2021/05/17/amazon-exec-dave-clark-pushed-for-mailbox-in -alabama-union-election.html.

26. https://www.wsj.com/articles/former-amazon-worker-leading-staten-island-union -efforts-arrested-11645726397.

27. https://www.youtube.com/watch?v=ymGM9I_WWX8.

28. https://www.reuters.com/legal/government/amazon-calls-election-re-run-after-workers -voted-first-us-union-2022-04-08/.

29. https://www.vox.com/recode/2022/9/7/23340103/amazon-labor-union-ceo-andy-jassy -nlrb.

13: WALMART 2040

1. https://www.vox.com/recode/22264330/amazon-ceo-andy-jassy-jeff-bezos-aws.

2. https://www.geekwire.com/2022/amazon-sued-for-ending-free-whole-foods-delivery-as -prime-benefit/.

3. https://www.cnbc.com/2020/11/02/walmart-ends-contract-with-robotics-company -bossa-nova-report-says.html.

4. https://www.vox.com/recode/22423706/walmart-memo-retail-amazon-target-instacart.

5. https://www.businessinsider.com/amazon-prime-air-faa-regulators-investigation-drone -crashes-2022-5?r=US&IR=T.

6. https://www.vox.com/recode/2022/9/7/23333406/amazon-prime-2-day-shipping-delays -taking-long.

7. https://www.vox.com/recode/2021/2/26/22297554/amazon-race-black-diversity-inclusion.

8. https://www.vox.com/recode/2021/2/26/22297554/amazon-race-black-diversity-inclusion.

9. https://www.wsj.com/articles/a-grassroots-campaign-to-take-down-amazon-is-funded -by-amazons-biggest-rivals-11568989838.

10. https://medium.com/swlh/amazon-needs-a-competitor-and-walmart-aint-it-5997977 b77b2.

11. https://economictimes.indiatimes.com/industry/services/retail/how-greg-penner-went -all-guns-blazing-for-flipkart/articleshow/64104098.cms?from=mdr.

12. https://www.vox.com/recode/22423706/walmart-memo-retail-amazon-target-instacart.
13. https://www.businessinsider.com/walmart-pushes-employees-to-enroll-in-its-amazon-prime-rival-2022-8.

14: WINNER SELLS ALL
1. https://allthingsd.com/20110418/exclusive-wal-mart-paid-300-million-plus-for-kosmix.
2. https://www.nytimes.com/2022/07/28/business/amazon-revenue-slow-growth-rate.html.
3. https://www.vox.com/recode/23170900/leaked-amazon-memo-warehouses-hiring-shortage.
4. https://www.bloomberg.com/news/articles/2022-09-02/amazon-closes-abandons-plans-for-dozens-of-us-warehouses.
5. https://www.vox.com/recode/2022/10/18/23410675/amazon-union-vote-results-upstate-albany-new-york-alb1.
6. https://medium.com/@forrespect/my-sister-would-have-done-anything-to-keep-her-job-at-walmart-a5465e67ab53.
7. https://www.thedailybeast.com/amazon-employee-who-died-on-prime-day-rafael-reynaldo-mota-frias-was-hardworking-dad.
8. https://www.marketplacepulse.com/articles/shopify-tries-to-fight-buy-with-prime.
9. https://www.wsj.com/articles/instacart-cuts-valuation-by-nearly-40-11648223029.
10. https://www.axios.com/2022/10/11/tiktok-chases-amazon-fulfillment-centers.

INDEX

ABOUT THE AUTHOR

JASON DEL REY is a veteran business journalist who spent a decade at Recode, a leading online technology publication, reporting on Amazon, Walmart, and how technology is transforming retail, both online and in stores. He is the host of *Land of the Giants: The Rise of Amazon*, a narrative podcast series about the tech giant's rise and the impact of its relentless ambition on hundreds of millions of people across the globe. He was also the producer of Code Commerce, an event series featuring unscripted interviews with the most influential executives and entrepreneurs working at the intersection of technology and commerce. In 2019, the National Retail Federation named him one of the 25 People Shaping Retail's Future. He lives in northern New Jersey with his wife and two children.